Creating Trauma-Informed, Strengths-Based Classrooms

of related interest

The Trauma and Attachment-Aware Classroom
A Practical Guide to Supporting Children Who Have Encountered
Trauma and Adverse Childhood Experiences
Rebecca Brooks
ISBN 978 1 78592 558 0
eISBN 978 1 78592 877 2

A Treasure Box for Creating Trauma-Informed Organizations
A Ready-to-Use Resource for Trauma, Adversity, and Culturally
Informed, Infused, and Responsive Systems
Dr. Karen Treisman
ISBN 978 1 78775 312 9
eISBN 978 1 78775 313 6

The Teacher's Introduction to Attachment
Practical Essentials for Teachers, Carers and School Support Staff
Nicola Marshall
ISBN 978 1 78775 313 6
eISBN 978 0 85700 973 9

Building a Trauma-Informed Restorative School
Skills and Approaches for Improving Culture and Behavior
Joe Brummer with Margaret Thorsborne
ISBN 978 1 78775 267 2
eISBN 978 1 78775 268 9

Working with Relational Trauma in Schools
An Educator's Guide to Using Dyadic Developmental Practice
Kim S. Golding, Sian Phillips and Louise Michelle Bombèr
ISBN 978 1 78775 219 1
eISBN 978 1 78775 220 7

A Practical Introduction to Restorative Practice in Schools
Theory, Skills and Guidance
Bill Hansberry
Foreword by Margaret Thorsborne
ISBN 978 1 84905 707 3
eISBN 978 1 78450 232 4

CREATING TRAUMA-INFORMED, STRENGTHS-BASED CLASSROOMS

Teacher Strategies for Nurturing
Students' Healing, Growth, and Learning

Tom Brunzell, PhD
and Jacolyn Norrish, PhD

Jessica Kingsley Publishers
London and Philadelphia

First published in Great Britain in 2021 by Jessica Kingsley Publishers
An Hachette Company

1

Copyright © Tom Brunzell and Jacolyn Norrish 2021

A CIP catalogue record for this title is available from the
British Library and the Library of Congress

ISBN 978 1 78775 374 7
eISBN 978 1 78775 375 4

Printed and bound in Great Britain by TJ Books Ltd

Jessica Kingsley Publishers' policy is to use papers that are natural,
renewable and recyclable products and made from wood grown in
sustainable forests. The logging and manufacturing processes are expected
to conform to the environmental regulations of the country of origin.

Jessica Kingsley Publishers
Carmelite House
50 Victoria Embankment
London EC4Y 0DZ

www.jkp.com

MIX
Paper | Supporting
responsible forestry
FSC
www.fsc.org   FSC® C013056

This book is dedicated to
the students at the Berry Street School
for their courage, passion, resilience, and hope.

Contents

Acknowledgments

This book was written on the traditional lands of the Wurundjeri people of the Kulin Nation, and we acknowledge their Elders past, present, and emerging. Our hope is that together, through our collective efforts, education equity is indeed possible for all communities.

Our book builds on the courageous learning and efforts of inspirational students, teachers, leaders, allied professionals, and researchers across the fields of education, therapeutics, and wellbeing. Specifically, we must thank the following people who made this journey possible.

The strategies contained in this book have emerged from the Berry Street Education Model (BSEM; Brunzell *et al.* 2015), originally co-authored by the authors of this book along with Sarah Ralston, Leonie Abbott, Maddie Witter, Teresa Joyce, and Janelle Larkin, and created under the nurturing guidance of Sandie De Wolf, Marg Hamley, and Anne Smithies, with close consultation in its early development with Jane Barr, Sue Nilsen, Elodie Ryan, Paul Ambrose, Lynette Moore, Tricia Quibell, Susan Warming, Annette Jackson, and Richard Rose. BSEM also acknowledges the generous philanthropic support from principal supporter, Perpetual Trustees, inaugural and supporting partner, Newsboys Foundation, and major philanthropic partners: Helen Macpherson Smith Trust, Colonial Foundation, and the Tony Williams Foundation.

We thank the leadership of Berry Street, Victoria, and their ongoing support to forward our strategies around the world: Michael Perusco, Annette Jackson, Jenny McNaughton, Joanne Alford, Maddie Witter, Teresa Deshon, Amy Mazzitelli, Damian McKee, and Rebecca Robinson.

We are inspired and thankful for the past and present members of the BSEM and Berry Street's central education teams: Leonie Abbott, Michele Sampson, Brendan Bailey, Cheree Taylor, Christina Dawson, Michael Hardie, Jack Greig, Joanne Olsen, Grace Langton, Benji Gersh,

Jennifer Colechin, Orville Gardener, Stephanie Willison, Sarah Waite, Catherine McLennan, and Sally Ball.

The development of trauma-informed positive education, the conceptual underpinning of the BSEM, continues to evolve at the University of Melbourne Graduate School of Education. Thank you to Professor Lea Waters and Associate Professor Helen Stokes for your research supervision and guidance; along with Dr. Malcolm Turnbull, Associate Professor Peggy Kern, Anne Farrelly, and Ruth Forster.

We thank these leaders in our field who we are privileged to include as supporters and friends of Berry Street: thank you to Justin Robinson and the team at the Institute of Positive Education at Geelong Grammar School for their ongoing support and friendship; to Dr. Paige Williams for being a source of wisdom and inspiration; and to Dr. Jo Mitchell for being a driving force for wellbeing sciences in Australia.

We thank special friends and colleagues who played important roles in the review and development of this book: Dr. Judith Howard and Rob Sheehan.

Thank you to our team at Jessica Kingsley Publishers: Stephen Jones, James Cherry, Emily Badger, Isabel Martin, Emma Holak, and Winsey Samuels.

Jacolyn would personally like to thank some special friends and family: Thank you to Jill Griffiths for inspiring my love of writing. Thank you to Bridget Robinson and Dr. Matthew Roberts for their mentorship. A heartfelt thank you to Kymberly Seccull for all her help. Thank you to my husband, Damen, for his unwavering support and with love to my children, Isla, Eddie, and Allie. Thank you to my parents, Jenny and Trevor, my siblings Bradley, Jo, and Ryan, and their families. With gratitude to the Turnbull family.

Tom would personally like to thank valued colleagues: Thank you to the founding staff of the KIPP Infinity Charter School, Harlem, New York City. Thank you to the Class of 2013, Dave Levin, Joe Negron, Dilcia Ceron, Gerard Griffith, Maddie Witter, and Michael Vea, and to Professor Martin Seligman and Professor Angela Duckworth from the University of Pennsylvania for supporting KIPP's pioneering practice and research in positive education.

To Maddie and Mike Witter, thank you for the adventure of Australia. Maddie Witter has been my closest friend and collaborator for over 20 years, spanning two continents as part of many teams together. Her own innovative practice development has led many schools around the world to increase pedagogical capacity, and she continues to have profound influence on the ways that we understand and support vulnerable students. Michael Witter has been a trusted friend, confidant, researcher, and practice leader throughout our shared journey in his capacity as a leader at KIPP Infinity Charter School in New York City and now a valued community partner at Teach For Australia.

To conclude, I thank my first teachers—my parents Gloria and Gene—and send much love to my siblings Kristen, Jon, and Ashley. And finally, to Patrick, my husband, for our years together across communities and cultures and for the countless patient hours you have spent encouraging and waiting for one project to conclude and the next to arise; thank you for your love and support.

Authors' Note

A NOTE ABOUT PRIVACY

We value the privacy of the children and young people we work with, as well as that of their teachers, parents, and caregivers. We are also committed to providing an authentic and realistic representation of some of the difficulties children and young people face and some of the complex ways they behave in the classroom. In writing this book, we have taken careful steps to balance these two priorities.

The stories included in this book are based on real examples from our work with schools. However, identifiable characteristics, such as names, ages, and demographic details, have been changed. In some cases, we have received permission from the people involved to include a story or example. In other cases, we have created a 'constructed' story by meshing two or more experiences together and changing the details so that individual children, young people, or teachers cannot be recognized. We hope our readers understand this is a necessary step to protect the rights and privacy of the students, teachers, and families who have inspired this book.

A NOTE ON PRONOUNS

We have written this book from the perspective of our Berry Street team. You will see common references to 'our work' and 'our team.' We are grateful to our colleagues for their teamwork and collaboration and for their willingness to share their work through this book. At times, it has been helpful to share a personal story. Please note, when the word 'I' is used, it represents the voice of Dr. Tom Brunzell.

Preface

The first time I tried to become a teacher, back in 2001, I failed. I applied to become a New York City Teaching Fellow, a government-sponsored pathway to recruit new teachers from non-teaching backgrounds. Coming off a week of the flu, I was still hazy, arrogantly unprepared, and did not yet respect the professionalism required to enter the teaching profession. When asked the final interview question 'How long do you intend to work in education?', I stammered, having never truly considered the answer. 'Five years… Maybe longer?' I knew I had nervously made a naive, irretrievable mistake.

The very next week, applications were due for Teach For America (TFA), a national non-profit organization that nurtures diverse networks of education leaders with a commitment to eradicate educational inequity. As they are anchored in values of social action, impact, and community development, I knew instinctively that TFA were my people. I was hopeful I could join this dynamic and inspiring group of educators, advocates, policymakers, and community members. Thanks to my unsuccessful application to the New York City Teaching Fellows, I was armed and ready to ace the TFA interview process. I was thrilled to be accepted into TFA and spent the next months preparing for my new life as a teacher.

My first classroom was in a public school in the Bronx. I will never forget my first day of teaching, waking up at 5am to take the D-train up to Tremont and Grand Concourse in the South Bronx. The school was built within the shell of a 19th-century hospital, decorated with aged and decaying filigree, with a five-story walk up to my classroom. In my hands was a package of multicolored construction paper, some markers, and an empty lesson planning book. I nervously greeted each of my students with a handshake, as we were told to do in TFA. By 9.30am, when my fourth-graders were playing the name game, I realized I had no idea what time the lunch period was, or even where my students were supposed to go to get their trays of food. I distinctly remember leaning down and asking Luis, a nine-year-old in my class, 'Uh, what did you do last year for lunch?' He replied, 'We were with the little kids, but now we're in fourth grade, I don't know…' I remember announcing to the class, 'We are going to take a tour of our school!' After two loops marching around the campus, we finally found the lunchroom. And thus, our year began.

Luis was late to school most days. I quickly realized he was known as the toughest boy in the toughest neighborhood—a neighborhood where my fourth-graders were happy to point out where they thought the drama and deals were made on the streets. Luis was too thin, he had a wild glimmer in his eye, no friends, and was far below academic standards for his age. Luis was the student in my class who was the loudest when he could not complete the assignment, the quickest to start an argument with another student, and the first to wrangle his classmates' attention when he did not immediately get what he wanted. All too frequently, Luis and I would end the lesson yelling at each other. I would yell at him, 'Sit down and calm down!' He would yell back at me, 'Whatever!', and push all his work onto the floor.

It was 2002, and it became quickly apparent that he still ruminated continuously on the 9/11 tragedy. All the children in my first class were still focused on 9/11, in part because many of their parents worked the nightshift cleaning office buildings in downtown Manhattan and told me they watched the news footage on the evening television, replay after replay. When Luis refused to do the work I assigned, and not knowing what else to do, I allowed him to draw while he waited for me to help him. Every day, his drawings were the same: two tall rectangles and a plane crashing into them. Eventually, we decided to collect them all in a folder, and soon the folder was bursting with new versions of the same drawing.

I did home visits with Luis, going to his apartment building three blocks away from the school to connect and to work together with his caring mother. His mother welcomed me into their home and tried her best to reinforce the 'good behavior' lectures I was giving Luis. But his mother's language made me uneasy and escalated because sometimes she lectured him the same way I would. I sensed that Luis would vacillate between embarrassment and shame during those visits. It was only later that I reflected and realized his mother and I were using the same language, and neither of us was making a visible difference in improving Luis' behavior in the classroom.

I thought the only way I could create a classroom-based relationship with Luis was by matching his escalation to prove to him that I could handle the drama. I adjusted the entire class for him, and there were days when I felt I was only really teaching one student. I made every single mistake with Luis and that class of students, including bribing them to stay on task with candy—that is until one day, Luis and his friend broke into my closet to steal the candy supply. I handled this transgression in the same way I did most days: by making a big scene and aggressively and loudly lecturing them for an hour. I was out of control.

This anger propelled me—and it would last a long time. I would spend most days feeling hyped up on adrenaline until 7pm, collapse at night, and begin again the next morning at 5am. Without any coaching or supervision to help me understand classroom stressors, I began to mirror the dysregulation of my students. Most of the teachers in my school did. Walking the halls of that school, I could hear echoes of teachers raising their voices. It all made sense and was reinforced in the staffroom: If they yell at you, you yell back at them. If they were angry, you show them that you were in control by being angrier than them. This cycle was daily, hourly, sometimes by the minute. There were days when Luis came to school and pushed another student in line first thing in the morning, and I would yell at him in front of all the other students before we walked up the five flights of steps.

Teaching for me in those first years meant being buzzed up on cortisol and adrenaline. I know I was so dependent on it that in the mornings, I would double-step up the five flights to get my heart going because I could not face the kids without being hypervigilantly ready for the day. I justified my anger and aggression in a number of ways, and I had many reasons to explain to myself why I behaved in the ways I did. My naive assumption that my students came from homes filled with escalated behaviors convinced me that anger was the most effective way to communicate to them; however, my misguided logic convinced me that my anger would be more conscious and for the right social justice reasons—these kids *will* learn. It was only years later I realized I was mirroring and modeling the escalated behaviors of my students.

My students' daily efforts paid off. As TFA teachers, we were encouraged when we produced data that showed literacy and numeracy achievements rising. My students' data was promising, reaching to more than two-years' learning in just one year. It was because we were unrelentingly rigorous—and frankly, I now look back and know I created a culture of fear to dominate my students and get them back on task.

This success was hollow because I knew there had to be another way—a new way for me to craft an identity as the teacher I wanted to be.

The next career-defining opportunity came when I was asked to be a co-founder of the KIPP Infinity Charter School in West Harlem. KIPP (Knowledge is Power Program), founded by TFA alumni, is a national network of public schools seeking to systemically improve the life outcomes of educationally underserved communities. Together with a small group of devoted teachers, we set out to create a school that aimed to do nothing short of change our students' education trajectory. We were determined they would be the first in their families to go to university and find stable and enriching employment—if they climbed the mountain with the tools and strategies we hoped to provide.

My aggressive and hypervigilant behavior did not end.

As the Dean of Students, I was responsible for leading the school's student behavior and wellbeing supports. While our high expectations for classwork and homework completion lifted academic achievement gains to among the highest in all of New York City, we went in *hard* on the minutiae of student misbehavior. Our approach was based on the broken windows theory (Wilson and Kelling 1982). The theory explains that efforts to prevent small infractions (in our case, uniforms, lateness, and homework) help to create an atmosphere of high expectations and lawfulness, wherein more serious transgressions do not occur. This worked for most of our students. We saw incredible gains for our students through a high-values culture based on strong student-teacher relationships. We flourished in a culture that promoted inquiry, collaboration, discussion, stamina, reflection on data, and—above all else—urgency.

However, there were some students who did not succeed in this environment. The students who struggled the most were *my* students. As Dean, I was responsible for all our students, but those who spent the most time with me in my office, where I counseled, coached, and listened to them, required the most support. They were witnesses to violence and destabilization. They yearned for close family relationships. In the classroom, teachers observed these students' complex learning needs and daily attempts to make up years of failed classroom experiences.

Together, the KIPP Infinity team and I struggled to make sense of how to maintain high expectations for all students, yet still acknowledge that some students were too far behind in their capacities to meet these expectations. Our team tried everything: student study teams, clinical supports, home visits, greater punishments, suspensions. We even tried keeping some of these students for two hours after school so they could finish their homework. But we did not see lasting change in the students we cared about the most.

One fateful day, the co-founder of KIPP, Dave Levin, pulled me aside. 'Hey,' he said, 'I met this professor from the University of Pennsylvania. He wants to work with a New York City public school to see if their research applies to our kids, and to see how to build on the grit and other strengths they already practice and bring to school every day.' At that moment, I reached into my bag and pulled out Professor Martin Seligman's (1995) book, *The Optimistic Child*, which I was then highlighting furiously for my master's degree research. 'You mean this guy? I'm obsessed.' And I was. I was obsessed with this new idea of a whole-school approach to resilience and changing my understanding of children and their unmet needs. I was obsessed with forging a new path for our school and our students, and I had hoped the groundbreaking work of Seligman and his colleagues could inspire us to do better. I had begun to make some durable changes to my own life because of Seligman's (1990) earlier book, *Learned Optimism*.

I became the team leader for a unique project joining the KIPP New York City network schools and the Riverdale Country School, and I commenced working directly with Seligman and his colleague, Professor Angela Duckworth. Duckworth's research was of great interest to us. She looked beyond the role of talent, ability, and natural intelligence in students' academic performance to explore the importance of effort, grit, perseverance, and passion (Duckworth *et al.* 2007; Duckworth and Seligman 2005). Together, we designed ways to integrate the new science of character strengths into the school culture and curriculum; we considered how to build on our students' courage and grit to meet life's challenges; and we taught our students the mindsets of highly resilient people. We were privileged to participate in Duckworth and colleagues' (2013) research designed to increase students' self-regulation and goal-setting. We did not have a name for it then, but what we were doing was implementing a positive education approach throughout our entire systemic school network.

And then, a few years later, came a second fateful and life-changing opportunity. My colleagues and good friends, Maddie and Mike Witter, and I were invited to Victoria, Australia, for a speaking and learning tour. There I met the good folks of Berry Street, one of Australia's largest child welfare organizations, working with children and their families by providing safe homes, healing childhood trauma, helping children learn, building stronger families, and advocating for childhood. Berry Street has a multicampus independent school for students who have been excluded from mainstream education, some of them in out-of-home care. After that first visit, Berry Street created a position for me on the school leadership team and sponsored me and my partner to relocate to Melbourne. My remit: to bolster the practice and quality of Berry Street's education programs across the state of Victoria.

Berry Street, and the adventure of Australia, became my unexpected new home. It was at Berry Street that I first learned the term *trauma-informed practice*, which we define as understanding and addressing the impact of trauma on students and on learning. Berry Street gave me time and encouragement to create a new model of practice pedagogy for teachers—and the opportunity to unify ideas I had been developing for more than a decade. I was led by these questions: How can schools meet the needs of their most vulnerable students, and at the same time maintain a culture of consistently high expectations? How can we assist students in meeting their own needs for academic success? How can we assist teachers to create a strengths-based classroom which acknowledges the need for differentiation for students who are working far below academic standards?

In my search for knowledge and mentorship, I began meeting with experts from the University of Melbourne Graduate School of Education. First, I met Associate Professor Helen Stokes and, soon after that, Professor Lea Waters. Relevant to this work, both Helen and Lea center their research on educational approaches to wellbeing, school leadership, and effective implementation of teacher practice. Over many years, I have been fortunate to benefit from their wisdom through the supervision of my doctorate and ongoing co-authorship of our research together. It is important to recognize that they became collaborative architects of the conceptual model of trauma-informed positive education, and Helen's team continues to evaluate the longitudinal outcomes of Berry Street's efforts across Australia.

Finally, I met Dr. Jacolyn Norrish, a psychologist and researcher with expertise in both positive education and family mental health. When we first met, Jacolyn shared with me that it was an exciting time for positive psychology in Australia. Academics and practitioners who were passionate about the science of wellbeing and human thriving were working hard to establish a new field within the unique contexts of Australian communities. There were newly emerging professional networks, conferences, and university courses devoted to the study of human strengths and optimal functioning. Jacolyn's own doctorate research investigated school-based applications of positive psychology.

I was energized and inspired when Jacolyn told me about her involvement in the Institute of Positive Education, an initiative of Geelong Grammar School aimed at nurturing the growth of positive education and improving student wellbeing through providing training, research, and development. A few years after our initial meeting, Jacolyn authored *Positive Education: The Geelong Grammar School Journey*, a book sharing Geelong Grammar School's stories and learning about how to support flourishing across a whole-school community (Norrish 2015).

The day we met in Melbourne, Jacolyn and I had our first of many robust conversations. We spoke about our shared belief in the unparalleled opportunity of transforming schools to stand as places of resilience, growth, learning, and wellbeing. We also discussed the complexities and challenges of applying strengths-based approaches in communities with many unmet needs. It was clear to me that we shared a belief in the importance of applying evidence-based wellbeing strategies in ways that did not ignore or minimize the systemic disadvantage many children and young people face.

Jacolyn and I strongly contend that teachers will benefit from the integration of the sciences of trauma-informed learning and wellbeing psychology into their classroom strategies. We are especially grateful for the opportunities to work with multicultural schools. We acknowledge the traditional custodians of the Aboriginal lands on which we have worked, and we acknowledge their Elders, past, present, and emerging. We value and support schools with multicultural students, including those newly arrived through refugee communities and schools in which many language groups are represented. In working with these schools, we have learned much about the importance of integrating an understanding of culture and community into efforts to nurture wellbeing and build academic rigor.

This book recognizes the resilient efforts of students like Luis. They come to school to learn. And they are often taught by teachers who want the best for their students and who know that, to be effective teachers, they have so much to learn themselves. This book represents the translation from research to practice for more than 40,000 teachers who have participated in the Berry Street Education Model (Brunzell *et al.* 2015). The strategies in this book stand on the shoulders of hardworking teachers who are searching for new ways of teaching and learning that acknowledge the full developmental spectrum of our humanity. In this book and beyond, we continuously thank this growing network of teachers for their innovation and contribution of critically important developments to our field.

The teachers we have worked with are our community. We want to open our doors to you too. Join us as we pursue our lifelong aim to give all our young people access to the transformational power of education.

Dr. Tom Brunzell

CHAPTER 1

Introducing Trauma-Informed, Strengths-Based Classrooms

In this chapter, you will learn about:

- simple, complex, and developmental trauma
- the healing power of the classroom
- the value of trauma-informed, strengths-based classrooms.

Emily was a new teacher, fresh from a university teacher pre-service training course. She had earned a teaching position in a school located in a rapidly growing outer suburb and was allocated to a Grade 5 class for students who had developed a reputation for resisting their teachers. Emily started her first days of teaching filled with determination and optimism. However, she quickly found her university training to be insufficient when confronted with the substantial challenges she was experiencing in the classroom. Every day, Emily would face students who openly defied her, or gave up and walked out of class without permission. She was dealing continually with students who created social drama with their peers. Emily felt a sense of despair and hopelessness at some of the circumstances her students were living with. She often felt inadequate when confronted with the barriers to learning her students faced.

Emily was assigned a mentor, an extremely experienced senior teacher who had been at the school for a long time. Emily's mentor, determined to help 'toughen up' the softly spoken Emily, shared strategies that felt uncomfortably authoritarian to her. All the advice Emily received from her mentor focused on the importance of maintaining firm boundaries through strict consequences. However, when Emily doled out all the consequences by 11am, and her students still showed signs of dysregulation, she intuitively knew she needed more strategies than simply threatening consequences.

The week before we first met her, Emily's mentor had made a comment: 'I am not sure if you're tough enough to stand up to these kids. You need to think about what it takes to be strong enough in front of these students.' The mentor implied, not so subtly, that Emily might be better suited to working with students who didn't have as many learning needs. Needless to say, Emily's confidence plummeted, her self-esteem was low, and she was beginning to question her lifelong dream of becoming a teacher and working towards social equity for students.

Emily found our team at Berry Street through her own hunt for teacher strategies. She enrolled in our training course with her principal's support. Emily was hooked from the moment she began learning about our strategies for building trauma-informed, strengths-based classrooms. Emily learned about the impact of trauma on young people's brains, emotions, behaviors, and learning capacities. Emily developed an interest in mindfulness and began to share mindfulness strategies with students in her classroom. She worked hard to implement classroom routines and rhythms that created a sense of safety and connectedness for her students. To start with, Emily's students resisted the changes she was trying to implement. She persisted, and her new practice began to take hold.

Now, Emily still experiences stressors and frustrations on many days; however, she strives for and celebrates the small wins that happen in her classroom every day. A small win in Emily's eyes may be a student grasping a complex skill for the first time, a student remaining on task for their goal of five minutes, or a student proactively regulating their emotions before they get to their usual point of blowing up. Emily's students know that, while she might not have the answers to address their escalated and strong behaviors, she will always treat them with respect and empathy. Her classroom is a place of humor and playfulness—and equally, of academic rigor and stories of learning success.

Previously, Emily felt overwhelmed by the difficulties and barriers to education her students experienced. Now she also sees genuine capabilities in all of them. Now she has a well-developed toolkit for helping her students to de-escalate when they are in a state of distress or feeling overwhelmed. Every day, Emily integrates tools that build her students' stamina for focusing on learning tasks, and she watches as her students' learning thrives as a result.

Emily can explicitly name unique character strengths for each of her students, and, most importantly, her students know she sees the best in them. She has a deep understanding of how a student's history of unstable relationships may lead to unpredictable social behaviors, and she has strategies that help her connect with her students. As opposed to feeling deflated and overwhelmed by a lack of future opportunities her students may face, Emily now has great optimism for their futures. When we last spoke, Emily was thrilled to share with us her latest opportunity of mentoring a new graduate teacher. Needless to say, she is no longer doubting her decision to become a teacher—or her passion for working with students impacted by adversity.

PURPOSE OF THIS BOOK

What keeps us motivated is that beautiful moment when we are working with a teacher—perhaps a teacher who has struggled with feelings of stress and self-doubt—and the light bulb goes on for them. We love it when a teacher realizes there are so many more things they can do to increase their students' motivation, engagement, and willingness in the classroom. We live for those golden moments when teachers realize they had it within themselves all along; they just needed some support.

Our aim in writing this book is to share what we have learned and make a difference on a wider scale. Our team devotes its time to understanding the theory and research on how to work with students presenting unmet learning needs in the classroom. We have translated what we have learned into practical strategies for creating supportive learning environments for all students, including those who come from the most complex backgrounds. We want the ideas and strategies we have spent years creating and refining to help teachers create classroom environments where children and young people can heal and grow.

Our evidence-based strategies were developed to support students with complex unmet needs, and research has shown that these strategies are helpful for all students (Farrelly, Stokes, and Forster 2019;

Stokes, Kern *et al.* 2019; Stokes and Turnbull 2016; Stokes, Turnbull *et al.* 2019). We are deeply committed to the education of children who may sit at the boundary of the school community. We want to make a difference for students with even the most confronting or overwhelming histories of academic and behavioral difficulties. Through sharing our ideas, strategies, and successes, we aspire to make classrooms a source of stability, safety, and regulation for students who come from destabilized communities. Box 1.1 outlines the core values of social action underpinning our work.

BOX 1.1: Our values of social action

- Strong relationships matter. Every student must feel they have an advocate in their school.

- Teachers can make a difference. Teachers must be supported to love what they do.

- Teachers require strategies that can be embedded and integrated into the rhythms of the school—our ideas are purposefully designed so they do not create additional work or stress for teachers.

- Even students with significant behavior concerns have the right to enriching educational opportunities.

- Students who present in escalated ways are often the ones teachers find it most difficult to connect with—they are the students who most need our help and support.

- Culturally responsive pedagogy means teaching that empowers students to understand the impacts of systemic racism and systemic inequity through an emancipatory mindset.

THIS BOOK IS FOR YOU

This book is for teachers, and for allied education professionals who assist in the classroom, including education support staff, learning specialists, cultural advisors, and school leaders. In this book, when we use the words 'teacher' or 'educator,' we include school leaders and staff holding allied educational roles within the school community.

We know that educators experience many competing demands for their time and attention. This book aspires to provide ready access to concise, relevant, useful overviews of the latest developments in theory and research. We want educators who read this book to feel they have a better understanding of how trauma impacts students; we want them to make better sense of sometimes confusing or unpredictable behaviors students may exhibit daily. We want teachers to finish this book feeling they have tools and strategies they can implement in their classrooms, *immediately*. We intend to provide variety and flexibility so that teachers can pick ideas that may suit their unique classroom contexts. We are motivated by our vision of supporting teachers to feel more confident in working with the children who challenge them the most.

WHAT IS TRAUMA?

Before we provide an overview of our approach, it is useful to explore some types of trauma that may impact children and young people. In an ideal world, all children grow up in safe and secure environments, nurtured by strong relationships with adult caregivers. In that world, children and young people confidently explore the world and seek independence, knowing their families love them and maintain safe and stable homes for them to return to. In this ideal world, children show up to school ready to learn, with their emotional, psychological, and physical needs met in the context of supportive relationships with dependable adults. Sadly, we know, this ideal world is far from reality.

We define trauma as an overwhelming experience that undermines a person's belief that the world is good and safe (Berry Street Victoria 2013). The phrase 'overwhelming experience' is purposefully broad and encompassing. We know there is a range of experiences that may profoundly impact how a child or young person sees the world. Traumatic experiences may range from surviving an accident or dangerous event, experiencing community poverty and instability, or suffering ongoing abuse, violence, or neglect.

It is useful to further differentiate between simple, complex, and developmental trauma (Australian Childhood Foundation 2010). Simple trauma can occur after a highly stressful experience, such as an accident, medical procedure, fire, or other natural disaster. Experiencing an incredibly stressful event is especially detrimental if the child receives little emotional or psychological support from trusted adults that helps them process and integrate their experiences (Gunnar 1998; van der Kolk 2005). However, with one-time events, families are not often stigmatized, and they are encouraged to seek community support.

Complex trauma, sometimes called relational trauma, involves multiple or ongoing incidents. It can involve threats to personal safety, violence, or violation of a young person's rights (Australian Childhood Foundation 2010). Examples include witnessing ongoing family violence, surviving emotional, physical, or sexual abuse, or experiencing physical or emotional neglect. Complex trauma is often associated with intense feelings such as shame and disconnection from others and the community.

Developmental trauma refers to times when the impact of early adversity is so significant that it affects a child's emotional, social, physical, or neurological development (van der Kolk 2005). Developmental trauma occurs early in life. It includes experiences such as abuse, neglect, and separation from attachment figures. Similarly, it is important to be aware that high levels of maternal stress while babies are in utero has a lasting impact on children's emotional, cognitive, and language development (Talge, Neal, and Glover 2007). As a result of exposure to early stress and trauma, children may develop a range of unhealthy coping strategies. In addition, they may not develop key capacities for living, such as the ability to regulate emotions, manage impulses, and perform executive functions (van der Kolk 2005). Box 1.2 provides links to excellent resources on stress and trauma.

BOX 1.2: Resources on stress and trauma

The National Child Traumatic Stress Network (USA) provides a comprehensive overview of trauma types, including community violence, refugee trauma, traumatic grief, intimate partner violence, and the trauma of medical events: www.nctsn.org/what-is-child-trauma/trauma-types.

The Center on the Developing Child at Harvard University has a range of resources on understanding child development, including valuable information on the impact of toxic stress on child brain development: https://developingchild.harvard.edu.

THE IMPACT OF TRAUMA

Compounding these concerns, many children we work with have been exposed to a range of stressful and distressing experiences such as the impacts of intergenerational poverty, racism, having a parent with a physical or mental illness, parental separation, or instability in their caregiving and housing. We are also mindful of the impact of intergenerational trauma: the enduring impact of trauma passed from one generation to the next (Atkinson, Nelson, and Atkinson 2010).

A common misconception may be that trauma happens only in low socio-economic communities. Evidence shows this is not so. The National Child Traumatic Stress Network (2020) estimates that up to two-thirds of children are exposed to a traumatic event before the age of 16 years old. There may be a temptation to think of trauma as something that happens in other communities, and not in one's own school or neighborhood. The reality is that almost all teachers have worked with students exposed to distressing and stressful experiences. Many forms of traumatic events, and interpersonal violence in particular, often occur in private or secretive circumstances: they may not be visible to others. Therefore, teachers who work with children may not have comprehensive knowledge of what is going on for them at home.

Experiencing trauma can greatly impact a young person. Children who experience neglect, conflict, violence, or instability often struggle with self-confidence and self-esteem. It is common for them to feel worthless or vulnerable. Children who have experienced trauma can find it difficult to form strong, positive attachments (Pearce 2016). As we discuss in Chapter 2, Understanding the Effects of Childhood Stress and Trauma in the Classroom, trauma has an impact on a neurobiological level. When a child or young person experiences trauma, it can impact brain structures and functioning (Bremner 2006; van der Kolk 2014). Through making sense of how some experiences, such as neglect, violence, abuse, grief, loss, and instability, may impact on children and young people, we believe we can begin meeting their developmental needs in ways that support them to heal, grow, and learn.

THE HEALING POWER OF THE CLASSROOM

Children and young people who attend school with a range of complex concerns often require professional help for their distress and difficulties. Neither our team nor this book asserts that a teacher should aim to be a student's therapist or counselor. Teachers are not explicitly trained to explore the complex personal histories of their students—and the classroom environment is by no means the appropriate place to do so. However, we are also aware that many families that desperately require professional help lack the resources to obtain it from a qualified health professional such as a psychiatrist, psychologist, or social worker. For them, the healing nature of the classroom and school community is of primary importance.

Our work is based on understanding that classroom and school environments have enormous therapeutic capacity for vulnerable young people. It is clear to us that when children come from unstable homes, their school may be the most stable and consistent place in their lives. It is important not to underestimate the benefits students derive from a predictable school routine that creates a sense of safety and belonging. It is also important not to underestimate the value for students of being exposed to adults—their teachers and other staff members—who model appropriate relationships and who treat them with respect and kindness.

To meet students' unmet developmental needs, we advocate strongly for the value of integrating therapeutic principles into the classroom. We contend the classroom can be positioned as a powerful place of intervention for post-traumatic healing. Our experience continually shows us that when teachers are empowered to respond actively to the impact of trauma on learning, and to design their classrooms with attention to wellbeing principles, the benefits for students are long-lasting and far-reaching.

💡 **KEY IDEA:** For all students, the classroom has the potential to be a place in which they feel safe, secure, welcomed, and accepted. This has tremendous healing power.

THE CYCLE OF TRAUMA

Experiencing trauma, stress, and adversity has a profound and lasting impact on students' learning. We know from research evidence that students from vulnerable communities are more likely to miss school, have lower rates of school completion, and are at risk of economic and job instability after they finish their education (Bunting *et al.* 2018; Fry *et al.* 2018). Many students we have worked with experience a range of barriers to their learning, and are at risk of disengaging from their education and giving up.

Here are just a few examples of the issues and challenges we see regularly:

- Jem has had a number of different caregivers over the past three years since her father left her in the care of her aunt. No one has detected Jem's eye-sight problems, and when she tries to read the words are blurry. She does not understand why reading is so difficult for her when everyone around her seems to progress quickly. Jem feels highly distressed whenever she is asked to read in front of her peers. Her teachers believe she does not want to read anymore. They respond by questioning her motivation and telling her to try harder.

- Liam's mum has a painful back injury and can no longer drive him to school. It is possible for him to catch public transport to make it on time; however, it takes him several hours per day. He finds it easier just to skip school most days. His mum is understandably preoccupied. She understands the importance of education, but she does not have the resources to get him to school on her own. His teachers believe he is too lazy to get to school.

- Kim lives in a home impacted by family violence. She is in an almost constant state of fight or flight. Her brain is so busy scanning the environment for sources of threat that her ability to focus on learning material is severely compromised. Her teachers now believe she must have a hyperactivity or oppositional condition that requires diagnosis.

- There is not enough food to go around in Brady's house. He comes to school hungry. His hunger is a huge barrier to his motivation and engagement. It also makes him prone to escalated outbursts. His teachers have come to label him as 'too aggressive'.

You will notice from these examples that there are complex barriers to the students' learning. You may have noted that the teachers' initial observations do not provide proactive pathways of support. In situations such as these we often encounter a worrisome cycle. Learning involves taking risks in front of one's peers, and this can be highly stressful for students when they feel unsure about their competencies and abilities. When students experience barriers to their learning, such as those described above, it undermines their confidence, especially when they see their peers succeeding.

On the surface, this appears to look like lower effort, motivation, and willingness in the classroom. It seems as though the student disengages from the task rather than face the discomfort of learning difficulty. Lower effort and willingness exacerbate the student's poor academic outcomes, reinforcing their belief that they are 'dumb' or 'don't have what it takes.' As a result, the student spends a lot of school time off task, or does not attend school at all. This contributes to the worrisome cycle: the student's low confidence and effort contribute to poor learning outcomes, which in turn decreases their self-efficacy and motivation even further. And the cycle continues.

Unfortunately, this cycle of increasing disengagement can be reinforced by messages at home or at school that a student has limited academic potential. Teachers may attribute the student's lack of academic progress to factors within their control (like low effort, low motivation, or off-task behavior), without considering underlying factors that may contribute to the student's limited capacity to maintain attention and on-task behavior in the classroom.

The cycle may also be reinforced by family or community values and beliefs that education is not as important as getting real-world work experience as early as possible. For example, we have come across families in which most members drop out of school as soon as possible to work within the community. We met one student whose four older brothers all left school by the age of 14 or 15. It took us a long time to shift this student's attitude and set a goal together to finish secondary school. It also took this student a long time to come to believe it was perfectly acceptable for him to *want* to do his best at school, and go on to tertiary studies. That belief was challenged by considerable family pressure to pursue work without a degree. We have learned from our practice that wanting to achieve at school sometimes puts young people at risk of being ostracized by their families. Understandably, this is a huge barrier to their learning in the classroom.

What is also very clear to us is that, for some students, education can be the most powerful pathway towards a better future. Often we see teachers overwhelmed and disheartened when they focus on the challenges a student has outside the school environment. However, it is imperative that teachers do not underestimate the difference school can make. We believe when students have enough moments of connection at school, they keep returning day after day. When students stay in school and achieve the best possible academic outcomes, we widen their future possibilities dramatically.

💡 **KEY IDEA:** For students who experience difficulties and disadvantage, supporting them to achieve the best academic outcomes possible is one of the most important pathways to widening their future possibilities.

READY TO FOCUS

We have seen, time and time again, that when a child's attention is focused on survival, there is little left over for learning. Take a student who is almost always on the edge of a state of fight-flight-freeze, or a child who is constantly scanning the environment for signs of threat; these students are not ready to engage with learning content in a meaningful manner. Children who have experienced trauma may have difficulties with executive functioning, memory, concentration, and language delays (Kavanaugh *et al.* 2017; Spratt *et al.* 2012). Such students are often off task.

We need to respond to students' unmet developmental needs before asking them to engage in complex cognitive tasks required for learning. To learn, reason, integrate information, and make decisions, students need to be in a relatively calm state, not a highly stressed state. We cannot expect students to engage in their learning when their focus is on survival. We cannot become frustrated with students for being off task when they actually do not have the capacity to maintain their attention in the classroom. We have to appreciate that many students struggle to maintain their attention and be on task because their distressing and stressful experiences have left them ill-equipped to do so.

An underpinning tenet of our work is that, before students have successful schooling experiences, they need to be supported to come into a state where they are *ready to learn*. A child who is ready to learn is not in a state of dysregulation and internal chaos. Their heart is not racing at an elevated rate. When a child is ready to learn, they can concentrate, reason, and remember. They have access to the parts of their brain that help them integrate new information and connect different ideas together. They are tracking the teacher or focusing on the learning task, not scanning the classroom for threats.

INTRODUCING TRAUMA-INFORMED CLASSROOMS

A trauma-informed classroom is one in which an understanding of how trauma and stress affect students is integrated into all aspects of teaching and learning. In a trauma-informed classroom, the teacher makes sense of a student's behavior and capacities through the lens of how trauma impacts learning. All aspects of the school day—its rhythms, rituals, practices, and the physical environment—are informed by an evidence-based understanding of stress and trauma.

Trauma-informed approaches to education have two primary goals, each guiding our work with vulnerable students:

1. To heal their dysregulated stress response and build their self-regulatory capacities.

2. To support students to form enduring and healing attachments.

Let's discuss both goals.

HEALING DYSREGULATED STRESS RESPONSES

All teachers know students whose stress response goes from zero to 100 at seemingly small events. When supporting students to be ready to learn we need to understand that trauma greatly impacts a young person's ability to regulate their stress response and arousal systems. We see this dysregulation when a child is *hyper-aroused*, or in a state of heightened emotions, escalation, or distress (Siegel 2020). A student in a hyper-aroused state can be difficult to calm or contain. We also see dysregulation when a child is in a state of *hypo-arousal*, or in a state of detachment, disconnection, or dissociation. Students in a state of hypo-arousal do not have the physical resources ready to engage with learning.

Throughout this book, we introduce you to the importance of somatosensory regulation, including rhythmic, repetitive, patterned activities. We focus on strategies that help students to moderate their heart rates, soothe their stress-response systems, and regulate their level of arousal. We will discuss the importance of regulatory activities such as creating rhythmic breaks in the classrooms through desktop drumming, mindful breathing, visualizations, yoga, and music-based activities. We will also share the importance of supporting students to develop healthy strategies for regulating their own emotional states, such as labeling difficult feelings and learning strategies for de-escalating heightened emotions.

💡 **KEY IDEA:** A trauma-informed classroom explicitly integrates strategies that help students to regulate their state of arousal, and to soothe their dysregulated stress-response system.

SUPPORT STUDENTS' ATTACHMENTS

Our second focus for creating trauma-informed classrooms is to increase students' relational capacity and attachments. (We elaborate on relationships and attachment in later chapters.) An attachment is a deep and enduring bond to another person (Ainsworth 1964; Bowlby 1969). Infants and children rely on secure, warm, and consistent caregiving from adults in their lives to form secure attachments (Hoffman *et al.* 2017). When early caregiving is warm and nurturing, children come to see themselves as lovable, others as trustworthy, and the world as a safe and exciting place (Powell *et al.* 2016).

Sadly, some children do not experience safe and trusting relationships with early caregivers. When children are exposed to conditional or inconsistent relationships, there can be impacts on their patterns of relating to others (Pearce 2016). Some students have a greatly distorted sense of what is appropriate in relationships; others may continually have anger and violence modeled to them. Many students arrive to the classroom with significant interpersonal challenges and difficulties in trusting and relating to others. A priority in trauma-informed education is supporting students through consistent and caring student-teacher relationships. When teachers nurture strong relationships with students, they help to address the impact of disrupted attachments.

We recommend that teachers strive to create a sense of emotional and relational safety in their classrooms and develop relationships based on empathy and warmth. We believe teachers have the capacity to serve as frontline trauma healers for their vulnerable students. Teachers have the opportunity to be an adult in a child's life who consistently shows them warmth, respect, and empathy—and this has profound healing power. We also contend all students put the best effort into their learning when they believe the teacher genuinely cares about them, and when they like and respect their teacher.

💡 **KEY IDEA:** A trauma-informed classroom is one in which the teacher seeks to develop nurturing and healing relationships with students built on consistency, warmth, and respect.

WHAT DO WE MEAN BY STRENGTHS-BASED?

You will notice that the two approaches to creating trauma-informed classrooms discussed so far—first, supporting students' self-regulatory capacities, and second, increasing students' relational capacity and attachments—emphasize healing. Indeed, our experience is that most approaches to working with students focus on repairing emotional and physical dysregulation and building nurturing attachments through developing strong student-teacher relationships. We want to take this one step further. We advocate strongly that this healing approach can be further enhanced by integrating a strengths-based perspective. We contend that students need explicit opportunities to identify their character strengths, build their psychological resources, and aspire to growth and wellbeing.

INTRODUCING POSITIVE PSYCHOLOGY

We propose that positive psychology has a valuable contribution to make in supporting learning and wellbeing in classrooms. Positive psychology is a field of practice and study that focuses on wellbeing, human strengths, and optimal functioning (Gable and Haidt 2005; Seligman and Csikszentmihalyi 2000). The related field of positive education focuses on integrating evidence-based wellbeing concepts into schools to build student, school, and community flourishing (Norrish 2015). Through drawing on advances in positive psychology and positive education movements, teachers can create classroom environments that foster and nurture wellbeing.

Professor Lea Waters and Associate Professor Helen Stokes of the University of Melbourne have provided significant innovation in research and guidance on developing trauma-informed positive education (Brunzell, Stokes, and Waters 2016a). Here we also draw on the work of Professor Corey Keyes (2002) and his two-factor model of mental health. Keyes contends that mental illness and mental health are not opposite ends of the same continuum, but separate (though related) constructs. Take, for example, a young student who shows symptoms of attentional dysregulation and complex behaviors, but who also demonstrates remarkable kindness, resilience, and post-traumatic growth. We cannot understand this student without paying explicit attention to both his difficulties *and* his unique strengths and psychological resources. To best equip him for the future, we need to identify and build his character strengths, and draw out and nurture his emotional and relational resources. Box 1.3 invites you to reflect on the struggles and strengths of a student in your life.

🔆 **KEY IDEA:** Trauma-informed approaches can be greatly enhanced by deliberately focusing on identifying and cultivating students' strengths and psychological resources.

BOX 1.3: Teacher reflection and discussion questions

- Think about a student in your life who has demonstrated complex behavior in the classroom. What difficulties or developmental struggles does this student face?

- What positive strengths and resources does this student have to build on for future success?

OUR DEVELOPMENTAL APPROACH

We have drawn all this learning together to create a developmentally informed approach. It provides the basis for the chapters that follow. The book is structured on the five domains of Body, Relationship, Stamina, Engagement, and Character.

- *Body* helps teachers and students to develop strategies for de-escalating strong emotional and physiological responses to stress.

- *Relationship* helps to nurture strong student-teacher relationships, and ground students in a sense of safety and belonging.

- *Stamina* supports students to maintain focus and attention in the classroom through learning skills and strategies in areas such as emotional intelligence, resilience, and growth mindsets.

- *Engagement* provides pathways to cultivating students' interest, curiosity, and flow, and focuses strongly on building positive emotions in the classroom.

- *Character* helps students to identify, develop, and grow their strengths and psychological resources.

A FOCUS ON STRATEGIES

In the early stages of our work with schools around Australia, we met continually with educators working closely with students who struggled with their own behavior and learning. We asked them what they needed to best support the students in their care—and then we listened. Teachers asked for concrete strategies to help their students to re-engage with their learning, and to become more regulated and connected in the classroom. We listened as teachers said they were not interested in complex theories without practical applications. Nor were they interested in extensive one-size-fits-all curriculums they could not adapt to their unique needs. The teachers we heard from were desperate for practical, yet flexible, strategies they could implement in their classrooms, today.

The observations of these teachers grounded our vision. Working with experts in the fields of both trauma and wellbeing, we designed practical strategies for creating trauma-informed, strengths-based classrooms. We focused on concrete ways and practical tools teachers can use to create classroom practices, rhythms, and rituals that support both healing and wellbeing. We strongly believe teachers find great benefit in tailoring our strategies to their unique classroom needs and contexts. The feedback we have received attests to that belief. It is our pleasure to share with you in this book a range of these strategies and ideas.

To sum up, our approach to trauma-informed, strengths-based education uses practical, evidence-based strategies to help students:

- build self-regulatory capacities

- develop strong student-teacher relationships

- nurture growth, identify strengths, and build psychological resources.

AN INVITATION

We all know students who show up to school and test the teacher's resolve within the first hour of the day. We all know students who can derail an entire lesson with one comment. Throughout this book, we invite you to look at these students from a fresh perspective. Before feeling frustrated at their behavior or hopeless at their situation, we ask you to learn about the impact trauma, instability, and stress may have had on these young people's behavior, relationships, and learning capacities. We ask you to think of students you have struggled to like and see them in a new light. We invite you to focus on the small wins.

As you work your way through this book, we ask you to remind yourself continually of the potential you have to make a lasting, life-changing impact on the students in your care. We remind you of the power of education to change the trajectory of a student's future. We invite you to choose strategies and techniques that may help your students to build their self-regulatory capacities, soothe their elevated heart rates, and de-escalate their stress response systems. We ask you to commit to being an adult who models appropriate, caring, warm relationships with students who have complex unmet needs. We ask you to intentionally notice, celebrate, and nurture the strengths and psychological resources your students have. We will support you in creating classrooms that foster a sense of predictability, safety, and consistency for students who may lack these things at home.

We love it when, instead of feeling overwhelmed, teachers find that working with students becomes the most rewarding aspect of their roles. We have worked with countless teachers, like Emily at the beginning of this chapter, who thrive when they have a well-developed toolkit for working with students who sit on the edges of the classroom community. We have seen teachers have deep 'aha' moments as they change their entire view of a student to one of deep empathy, understanding, and warmth. We have loved the moments when teachers get in touch with us to share their small wins—and not so small wins—with students who may have years of academic and behavioral difficulties behind them. Time and time again, we have seen teachers move from feeling confused and disillusioned to a state of purpose and confidence. We hope this book is a similarly positive step for you.

CHAPTER 2

Understanding the Effects of Childhood Stress and Trauma in the Classroom

In this chapter, you will learn about:

- the effects of stress and trauma in the classroom

- the impact of the fight-flight-freeze response on students' ability to learn

- reconceptualizing student behavior through the lens of their unmet needs.

We would like to introduce you to three students we have come across in our work with schools: Kain, Rhiana, and Cassie. Kain, aged seven, was always on task in the classroom. He followed all the rules and kept his possessions immaculately arranged in his pigeonhole. It was easy to miss that at the slightest evidence of conflict or chaos, Kain's eyes became wide and he scrunched up his hands. He spoke rapidly and, at times, appeared to be on the edge of tears. Whenever he made even the smallest mistake, he would apologize repeatedly. He was polite and interacted well with others, but if you looked closely, you could see he did not grow close to his teachers, and he did not seem to have any lasting friendships.

Rhiana, aged 11, was popular and charismatic; the student everyone wanted to sit near. When she was on task, she was an engaged, curious, and motivated student. However, when she was asked to do something that did not appeal to her, she could escalate quickly, sometimes yelling or swearing at her teachers. At other times, Rhiana appeared to be unfocused and distracted, as if her mind was somewhere else. Rhiana could read books two grades higher than expected of students of her age, and when she focused on her work she completed the learning activities with ease. As her reading level was so high, she often told her teachers that being at school was a waste of her time, and she frequently missed classes or did not attend school at all. She also used reading to avoid other classroom assignments. Eventually, her teacher realized it was easier just to let her read the chapters in books than persist with encouraging her to complete her numeracy lessons.

Cassie, aged 15, presented the most oppositional behavior her teacher had ever witnessed. She was rarely on task, frequently verbally abusive to staff and students, and could get violent when she did not get what she wanted. She had a long history of bullying other students physically and online, and she had been excluded from several schools. Often, Cassie could be seen pacing the hallways with the assistant principal and wellbeing staff trailing behind her. While it could be hard to see past Cassie's challenges and difficulties, her teacher had noticed she showed incredible kindness and empathy to animals, and acted with tenderness when engaging with younger children in the school community.

UNDERSTANDING STRESS AND TRAUMA

As we think about these three students, we see they are displaying different complex behaviors that impact both their learning and the classroom environment. In this chapter, we introduce some core aspects of stress and trauma, with the aim of helping teachers better understand the complex behaviors of students like Kain, Rhiana, and Cassie. Our objective is to help teachers develop insight into the many different ways trauma and adversity can contribute to students acting in unpredictable and dysregulated ways in the classroom.

As we begin to take an overview of core concepts relevant to stress and trauma, we want to be clear: this chapter does not aspire to turn teachers into clinicians or therapists. Professionals who work clinically with young people with trauma histories require specialized skills and training. Nor does this chapter claim to be a comprehensive overview of the vast range of concepts relevant to childhood adversity—that is well beyond the scope of this book. However, we do aim to help teachers reconceptualize their students' behaviors by viewing them through a trauma-informed lens. We also want to help teachers develop a respectful, informed language for discussing the unmet needs of children. We believe when teachers have a well-developed understanding of stress and trauma, they can respond to students like Kain, Rhiana, and Cassie in ways that support their growth and learning.

SURVIVAL STRATEGIES

As we seek to understand some of the complex behaviors students exhibit in the classroom, it can be helpful to think of these as survival strategies. In the absence of safe and secure relationships and environments, children develop all sorts of ways of regulating their distress or emotional states (Bombèr 2007). We see teachers have 'aha' moments when they begin to understand complex behaviors as strategies children develop to survive and feel safe. We remember that behaviors which might be considered unacceptable could be a confused child's efforts to attempt to gain power in a situation perceived as threatening. Here are some examples:

- A student who has experienced relationship instability becomes highly independent and appears not to need anyone.

- A student who experiences violence at home is hypervigilant in their environment, constantly scanning for threats, leaving fewer cognitive resources for learning.

- A child who has received little care or attention acts in extreme ways so that adults notice them and attend to their unmet need for connection.

- A student who is repeatedly told they are stupid and worthless protects their identity and self-worth by not putting any effort into their work.

- A student who has no sense of control or safety at home controls their environment by exerting their will and causing chaos at school.

- A student who lives in an unpredictable home is highly compliant and behaves perfectly to avoid attention.

💡 **KEY IDEA:** Students who have experienced trauma have often developed coping or survival strategies that may appear as disruptive behavior or challenging interpersonal styles.

ADVERSE CHILDHOOD EXPERIENCES

As we seek to understand the experiences of students in the classroom, we turn first to a revolutionary research collaboration, led by researchers Professors Robert Anda and Vincent Felitti, that has greatly informed the field of childhood trauma (Anda *et al.* 2006; Felitti *et al.* 1998). Anda and Felitti were among the first people to investigate what they referred to as adverse childhood experiences (ACEs) and their impact on health and wellbeing throughout the lifespan. The initial ACE study was conducted in the 1990s in San Diego, California, and comprised a sample of 17,337 adults who attended a large health care service for a medical examination that also included a health and psychosocial history (Anda *et al.* 2006; Felitti *et al.* 1998). Two weeks after their examination, the adults who attended the health service received a questionnaire by mail. The questionnaire investigated their first 18 years of life and focused on ten ACEs: three forms of abuse (physical, emotional, and sexual); five categories of challenging family experiences (substance use in the home, mental illness in the home, parental separation and divorce, witnessing domestic violence, and parental incarceration); and two forms of neglect (emotional and physical).

We summarize the results of these studies into three key findings. First, early adverse experiences are *prevalent*. Findings were that 67 percent of adults who took part in the study described experiencing at least one ACE, and 11 percent described experiencing at least five. The second key point is that ACEs often *co-occur*. If a person experienced one ACE, there was an 87 percent chance they experienced at least one other category of ACE, and a 50 percent chance they experienced three or more. The third key finding is that ACEs can have a *lasting impact* on health and wellbeing across the lifespan. Anda and Felitti found that people who experienced early adversity reported lower educational and occupational outcomes, poorer physical and mental health, and reduced life expectancy, compared to those who did not experience childhood adversity (Anda *et al.* 2006; Felitti *et al.* 1998).

Since Anda and Felitti's early studies, investigation of ACEs has grown significantly. A recent systemic review and meta-analysis identified 37 ACE studies, exploring 23 outcomes, with a total of 253,719 participants (Hughes *et al.* 2017). While the majority of studies were conducted in the USA and the UK, there was one study from each of Canada, China, New Zealand, the Philippines, Saudi Arabia, and Sri Lanka, and one article that included data from eight Eastern European countries. We have summarized the results from ACE research in Box 2.1. It is noteworthy that the more categories of childhood adversity a person experiences, the higher their risk of physical and mental health issues.

🔆 **KEY IDEA:** Research into ACEs has led to an understanding that trauma is prevalent and that it can have a devastating and lasting impact on a person's life.

BOX 2.1: Summary of ACE outcomes

People who have experienced ACEs are at risk of a range of worrying outcomes, including:

- mental health problems, such as depression, anxiety, and post-traumatic stress disorder

- death by suicide

- health-risky behaviors, such as smoking, substance use, alcohol use, unsafe sexual practices, and physical inactivity

- chronic health conditions, such as lung cancer, diabetes, heart disease, auto-immune disorders, and sexually transmitted diseases

- relationship difficulties and becoming the victim of domestic and family violence as an adult

---

- engaging in violent behavior towards self and others

- dropping out of education, or being suspended or expelled from school

- fewer educational and employment opportunities, and reduced income

- increased risk of early death.

(Anda *et al.* 2006; Hughes *et al.* 2017)

UNDERSTANDING STRESS

As we consider the lasting impact of early adversity across the lifespan, we become increasingly committed to creating trauma-informed, strengths-based classrooms that help address the consequences of childhood stress and trauma. As we seek to understand stress in the classroom, we consider that humans have evolved to have a highly sophisticated system for responding to dangers, primarily driven by the autonomic nervous system (van der Kolk 2003, 2014). The autonomic nervous system has two branches: the sympathetic nervous system, and the parasympathetic nervous system. A critical role of the sympathetic nervous system is the fight-flight response. When facing danger, people experience a rush of stress hormones that mobilizes their bodies to either fight the threat or flee from it. The fight-flight response leads to a range of physiological changes: heart rate increases, breathing rate increases, and non-essential functions, like digestion, slow down. Fight-flight is a crucial survival response designed to be short in duration while the person responds to the threat.

The parasympathetic nervous system maintains the body at rest. It is often referred to as the rest and digest system. When the parasympathetic nervous system is activated, breathing and heart rate slows, and gastrointestinal (digestive) activity increases. While the parasympathetic nervous system serves to maintain the body at rest, via the freeze response, it also plays a role in responding to danger (Roelofs 2017; van der Kolk 2003). In some dangerous situations, fight or flight is not possible, and the most effective defensive reaction is to freeze and stay as still as possible. During a freeze response, breathing slows down, heart rate reduces, physical movements are minimized, and there is numbness against pain. Together, these stress pathways are known as the fight-flight-freeze response.

💡 **KEY IDEA:** The fight-flight-freeze response is a highly developed survival system that helps keep people safe in times of threat.

STRESS AT SCHOOL

An understanding of the stress response helps to make sense of complex behaviors children may enact in the classroom. For example, we ask you to consider the following behaviors through the lens of fight-flight-freeze:

- A teacher asks a student a complicated question and the student responds by cursing back at the teacher (fight response).

- A child is struggling with a computation problem, thinks they cannot do it, and so scrunches up and throws their work away (fight response).

- A young student cannot successfully complete a reading task and so hides under a pile of cushions in the corner of the room (flight response).

- A teacher asks a student to stand at the front of the classroom and present their work to their peers. The student immediately walks out of the classroom (flight response).

- A teacher asks a student to deliver an oral presentation. The student appears to be frozen in their chair (freeze response).

- The class is exploring an emotional topic and a student looks out the window, appearing distracted and detached from the moment (freeze response).

While all students feel stressed at times, fight-flight-freeze responses may be more regular and intense for children who have experienced trauma (van der Kolk 2014). Sights, sounds, smells, or sensations that remind people of their traumatic experiences can lead to intense fear and overwhelming physical sensations, or can cause painful emotions or memories to resurface. For some students, simple events that occur throughout the day—the slamming of a door, a change in routine, an unfamiliar person entering the room, a conflict with a peer—may become incredibly stressful and overwhelming. When a teacher raises their voice to emphasize a point to a student, the student can interpret the teacher's escalation in a number of ways—many of them unhelpful if the student has a history of aggression or violence within the family. As we respond to these students with increased patience, empathy, and understanding, we help to soothe their dysregulated stress response systems. In Boxes 2.2 and 2.3, we encourage you to look deeper at stress in the classroom, to consider how it impacts both students and you.

BOX 2.2: Teacher reflection and discussion questions

- Do some of your students become more easily stressed than others?

- What are some fight behaviors you have observed in your classroom?

- What are some flight behaviors you have observed in your classroom?

- What are some freeze behaviors you have observed in your classroom?

BOX 2.3: Insight into times you feel stressed

We asked some teachers in our community to share situations in which they felt their fight-flight-freeze response becoming activated, and they provided us with the following examples:

- When I feel like I am losing control of the class.

- When a student treats another student in an unfair way.

- When I ask the class to do something and some students ignore me.

- When I have to speak at an assembly.

- When staff members talk over each other in meetings.

Sadly, some teachers shared that they felt queasy and had difficulty sleeping on Sunday nights, as they began thinking about the week ahead. Developing a greater understanding of situations that activate our own fight-flight-freeze responses empowers us to take positive steps towards self-care and self-regulation. With this in mind, here are some reflection questions that may help you gain greater insight into your own stress reactions:

- What are some situations in which you feel stressed in the classroom?

- What are some situations in which you feel stressed outside the classroom?

- What physical symptoms may indicate that your stress response is becoming activated?

- What strategies can you use to calm down your activated stress response?

- What self-care activities can you use to maintain a state of wellbeing over time?

ENDURING STRESS

While we understand that some stress is normal and healthy, the stress response is designed to be a short-term response to a threat, not a permanent state of being. Dr. Craig Hassed (2002) uses the analogy of the stress response being like the accelerator of the car: it plays a crucial role in mobilizing action, but it is not designed to be used continually without also using the brake. We suspect most people can relate to a time when their stress system was wound tight, with a huge range of biological, emotional, relational, and psychological consequences.

Although experiencing chronic stress can be harmful to everyone, children are particularly at risk. As children are at such a vulnerable and formative stage of their development, exposure to chronic stress can have a highly detrimental impact on the development of their brain architecture (National Scientific Council on the Developing Child 2014; Shonkoff and Garner 2012). This is even more likely in the absence of supportive attachment figures who can help to buffer the impact of adverse experiences (Gunnar 1998).

Children who have experienced trauma or disrupted attachments can develop highly dysregulated stress response systems. Just like an accelerator which is constantly on, children may have their stress response firing all the time. Indeed, children who have experienced stress and trauma may have a resting heart rate that far exceeds the normal range (van der Kolk 2005). Similarly, high levels of two significant stress hormones, cortisol and adrenaline, can impact the development of neural networks and can lead to difficulties in regulating emotions and behaviors (National Scientific Council on the Developing Child 2014).

We often see the impact of dysregulated stress responses in classrooms. For example, one student struggles to sit still, is continuously fidgeting, and always up and down from their chair. The student speaks rapidly, their eyes are darting around the room, and their breathing is fast and shallow. Another student finds it difficult to connect with other students and appears to be in a daze. They speak slowly and rarely seem to be listening to the teacher. We understand that both these children may be showing signs of enduring stress. We develop empathy for these students when we understand that they require substantial support and the use of strategies that help to regulate their stress response systems.

-Ọ- **KEY IDEA:** Stress is a normal part of life; however, chronic or enduring stress without respite can be highly detrimental, particularly for children.

THE WINDOW OF TOLERANCE

Window of tolerance theory is another useful framework that we find teachers greatly value as they seek to understand how stress and trauma impact their classroom (Ogden, Minton, and Pain 2006; Siegel 2020). According to this theory, there is a window of arousal states that are optimal for brain processing and functioning. Figure 2.1 visually depicts this theory. When a student is within their window of tolerance, they may experience a range of feelings, thoughts, and sensations; however, they can self-regulate their responses and tolerate their internal experiences. At times, the student will be pushed outside their window of tolerance to a state of dysregulation. Above the window of tolerance is a state of sympathetic hyper-arousal—that is, a fight-flight response. A student above their window of tolerance may appear chaotic, anxious, or aggressive. In contrast, below the window of tolerance is a state of parasympathetic hypo-arousal. A child in this state may appear unfocused, exhausted, flat, withdrawn, or hard to motivate. Students may oscillate between the two extremes, showing signs of activation and aggression, and then signs of withdrawal and disconnection.

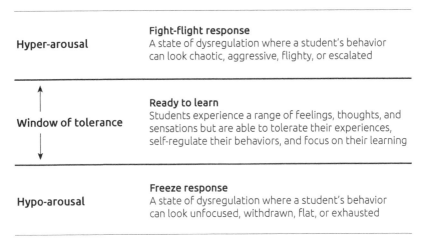

Figure 2.1: Window of tolerance in the classroom (adapted from Ogden, Minton, and Pain 2006, and Siegel 2020)

Young people who have experienced nurturing, stable environments, and secure relationships, often have a *wide* window of tolerance (Siegel 2020). Such students have had ample, frequent, and nurturing co-regulatory experiences that have enhanced their capacities for self-regulation. Consequently, they can tolerate a range of experiences without being pushed into a disruptive or dysregulated state. However, a child who has experienced insecure attachments in their life, and has contended with the impacts of trauma, chronic fear, and stress, may have a *narrow* window of tolerance. Simple classroom stressors, such as finding a learning task difficult, the classroom being overstimulating, or the teacher raising their voice, can push the student into a state of hyper- or hypo-arousal.

Window of tolerance theory is a useful framework for many reasons.

First, it contributes to our development of a respectful language for discussing children's behaviors and experiences. Imagine a school community wherein teachers speak about students being outside their window of tolerance, rather than using negative or critical language to describe students' behavioral dysregulation (e.g. 'This child is selfish and only wants to do what they want to do!'). It also helps us with our observations of students—we can notice when students are struggling at the bounds of their windows of tolerance, and detect patterns in the moments that lead to hyper- and hypo-arousal.

Window of tolerance theory provides an invaluable metaphor for what we are aspiring to with our trauma-informed, strengths-based approach. When students are outside their window of tolerance, we can attend to their unmet needs and help them to return to a more comfortable and ready to learn state. Chapters 4 and 5 offer numerous strategies that support students' self-regulatory capacities. Over time, we aspire to widen students' windows of tolerance so that they can encounter a range of experiences without being pushed into hyper- or hypo-arousal.

💡 **KEY IDEA:** Supporting students to widen their window of tolerance enhances their capacity to cope with a range of experiences, without being pushed into a state of dysregulation.

THE DEVELOPING BRAIN

When we attend to signs of stress in the classroom, and support students during times when they are outside their windows of tolerance, we shift how we respond to students in ways that can enhance their healing and learning. Next, we turn our attention to theories of brain development that can help further our understanding of children's unmet needs. We start by acknowledging that the brain is an incredibly complex system. Describing the brain in simplistic ways does not do justice to its complexity. While we are mindful of this limitation, we do think it is valuable to integrate some neurodevelopmental concepts that may help teachers understand some complex behaviors that students can exhibit.

A core premise of a neurodevelopmental approach is that different parts of the brain develop at different rates, starting from conception (MacLean 1990; Siegel 2020). According to this theory, the brainstem is one of the first parts of the brain to develop in the womb. The brainstem connects the brain with the spinal cord; it takes in information from the body and helps to regulate core bodily functions. Following this, the limbic area is organized predominantly in the first six years of life, although it continues to evolve throughout the lifespan (van der Kolk 2014). The limbic area lies deep within each hemisphere of the brain. Along with the brainstem, it plays a role in processing emotions and regulating behaviors. The brainstem and the limbic system activate a fight-flight-freeze response when there is danger—we refer to these parts of the brain together as the 'survival brain.'

The thinking part of the brain is the cortex. It is the most complex and sophisticated area of the brain. The majority of cortical development occurs before a person is 25 years of age, although neural networks continue to form throughout life (Siegel 2020). The cortical brain is made up of lobes (frontal, parietal, occipital, and temporal). The pre-frontal cortex is the area of the brain located at the front of the head (the forehead region), and is involved in complex information processing. The pre-frontal cortex is highly active when a person is using their working memory and engaging in other tasks that require storing and manipulating information. We can generalize by saying that when someone is making intentional choices, they are accessing their pre-frontal cortex.

NEURODEVELOPMENT AND LEARNING

Understanding a neurodevelopmental approach can help teachers make sense of student behavior in the classroom. Learning requires a student to be functioning at a cortical level. When students feel safe and are using their thinking brain, they can integrate information, problem-solve, access their working memory, and maintain on-task behaviors. However, if students begin to feel unsafe (physically *or* emotionally), the brainstem and limbic systems become active and mobilize the fight-flight-freeze response. In such situations, the cortical (thinking) part of the brain goes offline to allow the limbic and brainstem (emotional or survival) systems to facilitate physiological and behavioral responses to threats (Siegel 2020; Siegel and Payne Bryson 2012).

Let's consider situations where a student is successfully completing a higher-order math problem, is engaged in a rigorous conversation about a learning topic, or is hard at work on an imaginative piece of writing. These tasks require highly active, cortical functioning. If something occurs that evokes a stress response, the student's behavior may change both quickly and substantially. For example, the student may get up out of their seat and run out of the classroom, pushing a chair over on their way out. We may respond to this student as if their behavior appeared defiant and destructive by choice. However, it is more helpful if we understand that the student is functioning in survival mode—they are experiencing a stress response and need our help and support to return to a thinking state.

We gain further insight into how we can support students when we consider that children who have experienced chronic stress, environmental instability, and relational inconsistency may have underdeveloped brain architecture. The brain develops in a use-dependent manner (van der Kolk 2014). If a child often feels stressed and unsafe—and rarely feels safe or secure—their brainstem and limbic systems become highly attuned, *only* noticing stressors in the environment. In comparison, the neural networks of the cortical brain structures required for sustained attention, impulse control, memory, reasoning, and problem-solving may be less developed.

Students with an underdeveloped capacity to regulate their own stress response may find many behaviors required at school—such as sustaining attention, remaining on task, controlling their impulses—incredibly difficult. We see profound growth for students when teachers begin to understand that in many situations, students' off-task behavior is neither their fault nor a deliberate choice, but the result of underdeveloped neural networks. When we respond to students with patience and understanding, over time, we support their cortical development and build their capacity for self-regulation and sustained learning.

> :bulb: **KEY IDEA:** Children and young people who have experienced chronic stress and adversity may spend much of the time in their 'survival brain' as opposed to their 'thinking brain.'

UNPREDICTABILITY = RISK

As we seek to further understand the impact of stress and trauma in the classroom, our BSEM Senior Trainer, Jennifer Colechin, shared a helpful idea with our team: the concept of *unpredictability = risk* (Brunzell *et al.* 2015). The simple premise is that young people perceive the unpredictable as risky and threatening. For example, novel situations—such as new environments, a disruption in routine, or times when their teacher is away—are themselves the reasons that students escalate in their environment.

In times of uncertainty, students can often display emotional dysregulation and increased fight-flight-freeze behaviors. Students may also revert to predictable behaviors that make the world feel less risky and less uncertain to them. While these behaviors may look confusing from the outside, they often follow a predictable pattern. We should also remember that changes and adversity outside school can lead to increased stress behaviors at school. We have provided an example to illustrate this concept in Box 2.4.

BOX 2.4: An example of unpredictability = risk

A common example of unpredictability = risk is when the classroom teacher is away and a substitute teacher takes the class. Not only has the schedule changed because a new educator is trying to adapt to pre-existing classroom routines, but there is a different adult in the room. When a substitute teacher takes the class, all students may become a little more escalated or more vigilant.

However, students with a wide window of tolerance are often able to tolerate these changes, remain in a thinking state, and adapt to the changes. Students who have experienced trauma may struggle to remain within their window of tolerance and may exhibit considerable behavioral or emotional dysregulation. When we consider unpredictability = risk, we can see that students are not deliberately trying to make the substitute teacher's life difficult. Students may be struggling with significant internal dysregulation in a situation that does not feel safe and predictable to them.

The concept of unpredictability = risk applies to all of us, including teachers and students. For example, a student who has experienced violence, neglect, or abuse from adult caregivers may find it unfamiliar and risky to be treated with care and consistency from their teachers. Similarly, a student who is frequently excluded from the classroom may find it confusing and confronting to experience a genuine sense of belonging and connectedness to their classroom community. This idea helps teachers understand that sometimes students will deliberately push away pro-social behavior to preserve their own sense of identity and self-concept. Knowing this can help teachers to develop insight, patience, and understanding when students act in resistant ways.

We would also like to share that we often have the idea of unpredictability = risk challenged in our work with schools. One teacher provided the example of a student who had stolen cars and engaged in other highly risky, adrenaline-inducing behaviors. The teacher believed this student was *addicted* to unpredictability, not scared of it. However, from our point of view, chaos and risky situations are what the student is used to. They feel predictably 'themselves' when they have an activated fight-flight response and their body is flooded with adrenaline and cortisol. In contrast, we suspect that calm environments may feel unfamiliar and threatening. The student may need substantial co-regulatory support to help them engage in quiet learning activities in a meaningful and sustained manner.

UNMET NEEDS

When students display behavior that appears on the surface to be defiant or angry, teachers can often respond as if the students were intentionally making a choice to be disrespectful. Teachers who are not yet trauma-informed often personalize these student behaviors: 'Why is this student taking it out on me? I am not the enemy!' We see profound moments of growth for teachers when they understand students have significant unmet needs that compromise their capacity to sustain on-task behaviors. (We invite you to reflect on students' unmet needs in Box 2.5.) Every off-task behavior is telling us something: one or more of a student's needs is not being met. In fact, the student is trying to meet their unmet needs, but it looks maladaptive when the student is unable to learn.

We invite you to consider an example that may help illustrate this concept. Consider a student who appears frustrated when they have difficulty completing a numeracy problem, disengages from the task, and swears at their teacher when the teacher tries to help. We could react to this student as if they are a constant source of stress and frustration. Alternatively, we could respond as if the student was having difficulty regulating their physical and emotional unmet needs in a moment when their self-esteem and identity are challenged in front of their peers. We could remind ourselves of how hard it must be for the student to persist when they have a deep belief that they are stupid and that any efforts to complete the work will be useless. This empathetic and understanding mindset has enormous implications for how we respond to the student in the moment, as well as the goals we have for the student over time.

In particular, we focus on understanding students and their behaviors through the lens of five needs, which sometimes they meet in healthy ways, and other times strive to meet in unhealthy ways:

- *Physical needs:* regulating one's physiological state.

- *Emotional needs:* relating to ourselves and others in healthy ways.

- *Cognitive needs:* learning and higher-order thinking.

- *Energetic needs:* managing oneself non-verbally.

- *Spiritual needs:* connecting with something greater than oneself.

BOX 2.5: Students' unmet needs in the classroom

We invite you to reflect on the experience of a student in your life who may have acted in complex ways in the classroom:

- What unmet needs may this student have had?

- What was the impact on the student's learning?

- What was the impact on the student's capacity to form enduring relationships?

- What challenges or obstacles got in the way of meeting this student's unmet needs?

- How could the school community have better supported this student's wellbeing?

REVISITING KAIN, RHIANA, AND CASSIE

Now that we have looked at a range of concepts relevant to stress and trauma in the classroom, let us revisit the three students we introduced at the beginning of the chapter who were demonstrating varying, complex behaviors. When we understand students like Kain, Rhiana, and Cassie from within a trauma-informed context, we can start to make sense of what we are observing and what they need from adults in their lives to support their healing and growth.

Kain is often hypervigilant. He may have developed survival mechanisms, such as being quiet and unassertive, to ensure he does not cause any additional stress or chaos. As our understanding of stress and trauma grows, we become more attuned to the signs he may be experiencing enduring stress, such as his wide eyes and clenched hands. In particular, we are mindful of Kain's unmet emotional needs, and the fact that he appears to have few enduring bonds with staff or students. This becomes our priority as we seek to ground him in a sense of safety and belonging at school.

For Rhiana, we consider she appears to have a narrow window of tolerance. She frequently appears to display both hyper-aroused (escalated, loud) and hypo-aroused (distant, distracted) behaviors. We understand that Rhiana has significant academic and social strengths, but that she needs to be supported to use them in positive, respectful ways. A priority strategy for Rhiana is to teach her about noticing escalation in her own body when encountering uncertainty in the classroom, and to have pre-agreed ways to communicate, de-escalate, and self-regulate with the help of her teacher.

Our view of Cassie changes completely when we view her behaviors through a trauma-informed lens. We are mindful that Cassie likely has a narrow window of tolerance, and we see significant dysregulation of her stress response system, including extreme fight-flight reactions. Cassie needs frequent, healing, self-regulatory, and nurturing co-regulatory experiences (as we cover in later chapters) to help address her underdeveloped neural capacities and soothe her dysregulated stress response system.

As we revisit the experiences of these three students, we would like to make one more important point. Teachers have a moral and professional responsibility to uphold the safety and wellbeing of the children in their care. As teachers learn about trauma, they can become highly skilled at detecting the warning signs associated with adversity. They can grow increasingly concerned about the safety of children and young people within their communities. We want to be clear that this book's focus is whole-classroom strategies for growth and healing: it is not intended as a resource for identifying students who are at risk of harm. If you have concerns about a student's welfare, we urge you to speak immediately to members of your school's leadership and wellbeing teams who will seek outside clinical help and proactively ensure the student's safety.

SUMMARY AND CONCLUSIONS

We would like to direct your attention to Box 2.6 where we provide an overview of terms that are instrumental in developing our understanding of children. We believe having a well-developed language for conceptualizing and describing student behaviors is central to responding to these students in respectful and nurturing ways. In Chapter 3, we explore more about how shifting our language plays a key role in understanding and responding to students with a range of unmet needs.

We conclude this chapter with a few points on how we understand children. It is easy to feel deflated when we think about students who have experienced relational instability, chronic stress, and early adversity. Bearing witness to some of the hardships children go through can be confronting. Learning about the profound and enduring impact of trauma can lead teachers to feel helpless and hopeless. Within each classroom there may be stories of heartbreaking sadness. Yet it is important to remember that there are equally stories of courage, survival, resilience, and persistence. We certainly do not want to minimize the adversity some students go through. However, we do not want our empathy to stop us recognizing students' incredible strengths and unique qualities. In moments when we feel deflated or hopeless, we remind ourselves to have hope for students' futures; we hold ourselves accountable for doing everything we can to nurture their academic growth.

So, while we remain aware of students' unmet needs and challenges, we are constantly looking for and celebrating their strengths, successes, and accomplishments. We see Kain's compassionate concern for the wellbeing of others. We look constantly for examples of Rhiana's emotional intelligence and her well-developed ability to read what other people are experiencing. We gain great insight into Cassie's unmet relational needs when we observe she is kind and compassionate in situations where the recipients of her attention (children and animals) are unthreatening. We commit to helping her build on these strengths and form enduring bonds with her peers and teachers. While we remain committed to healing the impact of trauma and adversity, we also see our students for the capable, resilient, intricate people they are. We look for strengths, especially when students cannot see them for themselves.

BOX 2.6: Creating a trauma-informed, strengths-based language

Here are some useful terms for developing a respectful, trauma-informed, strengths-based language in the school and classroom.

Self-regulation: the capacity to manage our emotions, behaviors, and physiological states.

Dysregulation: a state of emotional, behavioral, physical, or psychological chaos and unpredictability.

Co-regulation: supporting a student's regulation and capacity to self-soothe through maintaining a calm, supportive presence.

Hyper-arousal: a fight-flight state, which is evident when students appear aggressive, distracted, flighty, or anxious.

Hypo-arousal: a freeze state, which is evident when students appear numb, distracted, unmotivated, or withdrawn.

Hypervigilance: a protective mechanism through which a student is highly sensitive to threats and is constantly scanning the environment for danger.

SELF-REFLECTION CHECKLIST

After completing this chapter, please check you can do the following:

✓ Appreciate the impact of trauma in the classroom.

- ✓ Recognize signs of fight-flight (hyper-arousal) and freeze (hypo-arousal) in students.

- ✓ Observe moments when students are above, within, or below their window of tolerance.

- ✓ Identify moments when students function from their 'thinking brain' and their 'survival brain.'

- ✓ Identify how students' unmet needs may impact their learning, behavior, and relationships at school.

- ✓ Look for students' strengths and pay attention to their well-developed resources, capacities, and achievements.

CHAPTER 3

A Developmentally Informed Approach to Learning

In this chapter, you will learn about:

- the importance of proactive, pre-emptive approaches to creating trauma-informed, strengths-based classrooms

- the developmental domains of Body, Relationship, Stamina, Engagement, and Character

- valued pathways for creating whole-school change, including developing a shared language and prioritizing consistent behavioral expectations.

Jalen, a Grade 3 student aged eight, had significant difficulties regulating his behaviors and remaining on task in the classroom. We first learned about Jalen when his principal called us in desperation, asking our team to come and help their school manage what she described as his defiant and disruptive behavior. We agreed to help, and as a first step we allocated two hours to observing Jalen and his class. The school leadership team first briefed us on Jalen's school history and his struggles over the last two years. They said he would quickly escalate when he did not get his way and that escalations were happening four to five times each day. The principal said to us, 'At this point with Jalen, we have to manage the *big* things, not the small ones.'

On the day of our visit, the principal showed us to a busy classroom, introduced us to the teacher, quietly pointed out Jalen, and left us to observe. At this stage, Jalen was doing well. He was engaging respectfully with others and seemed interested in the learning activities. Things started to go downhill at the morning snack break when the teacher asked the class to go to their bags and get their food. The students found their snacks, sat down at their tables, and started to eat their apples and muffins. Jalen unwrapped his snack, clearly did not like his sandwich, and threw it on the ground. Everyone—the teachers and other students—appeared to ignore this. Next, Jalen climbed up on top of the table and sat with his legs crossed. Again, there was no response or reaction from anyone.

We went over to the teacher and asked, 'Is anyone going to remind Jalen to sit down in his chair?' The teacher responded, 'Oh no, at this point with Jalen, we manage the big, not the small. This isn't a big thing—he does this every day.' Next, Jalen leaned over another child and took the other child's muffin. Again, we looked at the teacher— Jalen was taking another student's food! The teacher shook her head, 'No. Still small. He will escalate too quickly if we make a big deal of this.'

After snack time, the teacher asked the students to sit down for their numeracy lesson. At this point, Jalen poked a student in the back. Receiving no reaction, he moved to the next student and poked them in the back. Still no response. We had seen enough. Jalen had violated the sanctity of the classroom—he had used the furniture in the wrong way, taken other children's food, and touched students inappropriately during a lesson. What is more, the teacher made no acknowledgment of his behavior. We went back to the principal's office to debrief.

On our return, the principal greeted us with a curious look and asked, 'You were meant to be observing for two hours; why are you back after only 40 minutes?' We explained what we had witnessed and inquired as to why the teacher did not respond when Jalen was taking other children's food and poking them in the back. We received the same response: 'With Jalen, we manage the big.' The principal explained that Jalen's behaviors could be so extreme that staff had agreed to let minor transgressions pass and focus on times when Jalen was out of control.

It was not long before we witnessed one of Jalen's 'big' moments. He had left class without permission, broken into the school bike shed, and taken another student's bike. As we arrived at the scene, he was riding the bike over the school yard during recess. Students were screaming, pointing, and avoiding him. The eyes of the principal, the leadership team, and the teachers turned to us. Someone near us exclaimed, 'This is definitely a big thing! You are the experts; what are we meant to do here?' We turned and said, 'Go and safely get him off that bike!'

With a considerable amount of effort, someone managed to get Jalen off the bike and returned him to his classroom. By this time, all the staff involved looked stressed and exhausted. We went to a meeting room to debrief the events. The staff explained to us that, most days, there was an incident where Jalen acted in ways that went well beyond the expectations of a positive and respectful school community. It was clear this was causing a great deal of distress and disruption to the teachers, the leadership team, and other students. It was also deeply unsettling to parents and carers who became upset when their own children were affected. The staff hoped to create a plan for responding to times when Jalen was completely out of control. They wanted our help.

We had a lot of empathy and compassion for the challenges the school community was facing. However, we also had to be clear about our role and approach. We were not there to tell them how to respond to events like Jalen taking a bike and riding it across the school yard. We were there to help them focus on moments when Jalen was showing early signs of dysregulation. Through proactively responding when Jalen first showed disruptive behaviors, we aimed to address his unmet needs in ways that helped him to move forward positively. We need to support students to regulate their emotions and behaviors long before they reach the stage of escalating the whole school. We aspire to create classroom and school communities that both meet students' unmet needs and teach students proactive ways to seek support long before they steal a bike and ride it around the school.

A PROACTIVE AND PRE-EMPTIVE APPROACH

We believe strongly that when their unmet developmental needs are addressed, students have the best intentions to learn and can be supported to self-regulate and engage in the classroom. The words we use to describe our work are *proactive* and *pre-emptive*. Our approach is proactive because it involves setting up strategies, routines, and environments that give students the very best chance of succeeding at school. Our work is pre-emptive because we detect when students show early signs of escalation, dysregulation, or distress—it is at that moment we want teachers to focus on facilitating students to reach out for support, before meltdowns occur.

We want to support teachers to adopt consistent practices:

- Build classroom communities that are places of safety, belonging, and positive emotions.

- Help students to strengthen their capacities for self-regulation, rather than reacting to their behavior.

- Teach students about their own physical signs of escalation and about proactive help-seeking.

- Structure the school day to maximize students' potential for engagement and connection.

- Pre-empt difficulties before they happen and set students up with every possible opportunity for learning success.

TRAUMA-INFORMED, STRENGTHS-BASED CLASSROOMS

This chapter explains our approach in more detail. It highlights essential concepts for teacher practice. To give you a refresher from Chapter 1, we build trauma-informed, strengths-based classrooms with three core aims:

- Build the self-regulatory capacities of the body and emotions.

- Support students to build their relational capacity and experience a sense of relatedness and belonging at school.

- Integrate wellbeing principles that nurture growth, identify strengths, and build students' psychological resources.

There are five domains in our work: Body, Relationship, Stamina, Engagement, and Character. We will introduce each domain in turn.

INTRODUCING *BODY*

Body is a suite of mindsets, strategies, and interventions that focus on helping students to develop their self-regulatory capacities. We have deliberately named the first domain Body because we urge teachers to first think: 'Something is not right here—what's going on to dysregulate my student's body?' This way of thinking is quite counter to teachers' usual response. Often, teachers we have worked with witness dysregulation and think, 'This student is making a poor choice. I probably need to explain the choices once again.' But often these 'choices conversations' end up being unhelpful lectures that do not help regulate the student's body.

The Body domain contains a range of skills and strategies aimed at developing students' capacity for physiological and emotional regulation. Students learn about the fight-flight-freeze response and are taught to identify signs of the stress within themselves and others. Educators commonly call this social-emotional learning. For us, these skills and strategies have a tangible and immediate application: they are essential to trauma-informed practice. In the Body domain, students are provided with strategies to first understand and then take care of themselves in the classroom. In this way, we equip students with concrete tools for recognizing times in the day when they are escalated or dysregulated, and we support them to use strategies for returning to a ready-to-learn state. Sensory activities are woven throughout the day to provide calm and de-escalating messages to students' central nervous systems. Body also has a strong focus on mindfulness as a pathway to helping a student become present in the moment, centered in their body, and ready to learn.

🔆 **KEY IDEA:** The Body domain focuses on building students' capacity for de-escalation, soothing their activated stress responses, and helping them to become present, centered, and ready to learn.

INTRODUCING *RELATIONSHIP*

Underpinned by foundational work in attachment theory (Ainsworth 1968; Bowlby 1969), the Relationship domain supports teachers to form strong, nurturing relationships that help students to heal, grow, and learn. This domain is based on the extensive evidence base that consistently shows student-teacher relationships are critically important for student engagement and learning (Cornelius-White 2007). In Relationship, we support teachers to communicate acceptance and connect meaningfully with students; we know students do their best work for teachers they like and who they genuinely believe like them.

Nurturing strong relationships and creating a sense of belonging and safety at school is imperative for all students. This takes on special importance when we consider the needs of students affected by trauma. We have seen, time and time again, how healing it is for a child or young person to have at least one enduring relationship with a trusted adult. However, we also know that students who have a history of volatile relationships and disrupted attachments often find it difficult to form durable, trusting bonds. Educating teachers on the complex relational behaviors that vulnerable students may enact empowers them to persist in developing relationships with students who may act in dysregulated and unpredictable ways.

> :💡: **KEY IDEA:** We aim to support students to form meaningful, durable bonds with teachers, and to experience a sense of belonging and relatedness at school.

INTRODUCING *STAMINA*

In most schools we have worked with, there are students who find it difficult to remain on task for more than one or two minutes at a time. Understandably, this has a huge impact—when a student spends a lot of time off task it both limits their own progress and disrupts other students' productive learning time. In the Stamina domain, we focus on creating academic rigor for students by supporting them to overcome barriers to their learning, and building their capacity to sustain attention and engagement. We want to create opportunities where *all* students can see the results of their efforts in terms of their academic growth.

A foundation of our approach to Stamina is understanding that learning can be an uncomfortable process. To learn requires a student to go beyond the security and comfort of what they already know and take risks. This risk-taking often occurs in front of their peers, and students can feel exposed or judged, especially if they believe they are not as capable as other students in the class. In Stamina, we equip students with skills and strategies that enable them to persist during moments of learning discomfort. Through nurturing students' growth mindsets, resilience, and emotional intelligence, we expand their capacity to stay focused, even when unhelpful self-talk or uncomfortable emotions threaten to disrupt them from their learning.

> 💡 **KEY IDEA:** All children—particularly those who have experienced chronic stress and trauma—need to be supported to sustain effort in the classroom, and to demonstrate perseverance and resilience in their learning.

INTRODUCING *ENGAGEMENT*

It is easy to identify students who are engaged in a lesson or activity—they appear interested, curious, and motivated. When students are engaged, their body language communicates their desire to learn more; they actively ask questions that extend a topic or create depth to a discussion. These students are so engaged in their learning that they have to be told to stop and transition to the next activity. It is equally easy to identify disengaged students. They appear bored, uninterested, or distracted. Without an element of deep engagement to keep them hooked on the learning activity, disengaged students are at risk of behaving in ways that limit their own learning and disrupt others.

The Engagement domain focuses on concrete pathways for cultivating students' interest and curiosity in the classroom. A cornerstone of the Engagement domain is Csikszentmihalyi's (1990) flow theory, which is the state of deep immersion and peak experience that results when people are engaged in inherently meaningful challenges. It is also within Engagement that we see the power in the classroom of positive emotions, play, humor, and fun. Positive emotions enhance engagement and creativity (Fredrickson 1998; Lyubomirsky, King, and Diener 2005) and can be used effectively to diffuse conflict and nurture connectedness. Through intentionally weaving in moments of positive emotions throughout the day, teachers create atmospheres conducive to growth, engagement, and learning in the classroom.

> 💡 **KEY IDEA:** Engagement focuses on pathways to cultivating students' interest, curiosity, flow, and positive emotions in the classroom.

INTRODUCING *CHARACTER*

Building students' character strengths and psychological resources is crucial in trauma-informed, strengths-based classrooms. We know that some students, particularly those with a history of emotional and behavioral difficulties, may have had few opportunities to explore their strengths, or even understand they have strengths inside themselves. Some students may be so used to speaking about their deficits and difficulties that conversations about their positive qualities may be completely unfamiliar territory for them. For all students, particularly those who have experienced instability, there is great value in creating conversations about what they value and what they do well.

In our work in Character, we draw on Peterson and Seligman's (2004) VIA classification of 24 strengths, which are listed in Box 3.1.

BOX 3.1: The 24 VIA character strengths

Appreciation of beauty and excellence		Bravery
Creativity	Curiosity	Enthusiasm (zest)
Fairness	Forgiveness	Gratitude
Honesty	Hope	Humor
Kindness	Leadership	Love
Love of learning	Modesty and humility	Open-mindedness
Persistence	Perspective and wisdom	
Prudence	Self-regulation (self-control)	
Social intelligence	Spirituality	Teamwork

The 24 character strengths in the VIA are based on a study of personality traits valued across times and cultures (Dahlsgaard, Peterson, and Seligman 2005). The VIA is an evidence-based pathway to building wellbeing. It fits well within classrooms and provides a rich vocabulary for helping students to articulate, grow, and draw on their unique strengths. The Character domain also has a special focus on the strengths of gratitude and hope, as these strengths have well-established benefits for both academic learning and wellbeing (Marques, Lopez, and Pais-Ribeiro 2011; Park, Peterson, and Seligman 2004; Snyder 2002; Snyder *et al.* 1997). We elaborate on the VIA framework of strengths in Chapter 8, Character.

TRAUMA-INFORMED, STRENGTHS-BASED APPROACH

This developmental approach has two purposes:

1. To build *all* students' capacity for academic, social, emotional, and psychological growth.

2. To increase self-regulation, engagement, and academic outcomes for the most at-risk students.

In two important ways, a trauma-informed, strengths-based approach supports students who may have unmet developmental needs. First, the whole class is exposed to therapeutically-informed principles that address their regulatory and relational needs, as well as identify and grow their unique strengths and psychological resources. Second, as the level of behavioral and emotional regulation of the whole class increases, teachers have more time to notice and respond to students whose unmet needs may be less obvious within busy classrooms. Our aim is that teachers spend less time dealing with disruptions and drama. This clears space for assembling stronger academic instruction foundations. It also frees time for facilitating opportunities to identify and support the needs of students who require additional support.

A whole-school approach includes several areas for attention:

- Focus on educating and upskilling teachers and other staff members.

- Practices, rhythms, and routines that benefit all classes across a school.

- Values for fostering wellbeing and collective healing which anchor the whole school.

- Promotion of inclusion and collaboration within the wider school community with parents, carers, and families.

LEVELS OF INTERVENTION

We must be clear about what this book aspires to do and what it does not. Children and young people with complex needs require multiple levels of support. In the language of educational interventions, it is useful to think of students with complex emotional, psychological, learning, or behavioral difficulties as needing multi-tiered systems of support (Victoria State Government Department of Education and Training 2020):

Tier 1: Universal interventions aimed at all students, focused on promoting wellbeing and social and emotional learning skills in the classroom.

Tier 2: Targeted interventions that support the needs of at-risk students, also suitable for use in classroom contexts.

Tier 3: Specialist interventions focusing on the complex needs of at-risk students, delivered by qualified health and educational professionals.

We conceptualize this book as aligned with Tier 1 and Tier 2 levels of interventions. Our trauma-informed, strengths-based strategies are designed for teachers to apply in the classroom. Furthermore, the strategies are suitable for all students in the school community, although they were certainly developed with the most vulnerable students in mind. This book does not focus on Tier 3 level interventions such as those appropriate for use with students with complex needs in therapeutic settings. This specialized level of intervention is essential for supporting students who enact complex behaviors, but we want to be clear it is not a core focus of this book.

EMBEDDING THE STRATEGIES

We hope teachers use this trauma-informed, strengths-based approach as a lens through which to reflect on their own practice, and to teach *with* and *through* it. Our vision is for our principles and strategies to be embedded in all levels of school. Here, we would like to introduce you to some fundamental principles that create a foundation for positive and healing school communities. We think of these principles as vehicles through which trauma-informed, strengths-based strategies gain momentum in a school community, creating pathways towards whole-school change.

Principles underpinning the approach include the following:

- Creating a shared language is an invaluable step towards building trauma-informed, strengths-based communities.

- Consistency is the highest aim of behavioral management.

- Rhythm, repetition, and routines are essential in helping students become ready to focus and learn.

- It is vital to invest in teacher observation and feedback.

CREATING A SHARED LANGUAGE

A few months after we finished working with one school, we were invited back to see how things were progressing. During our visit, we had the opportunity to attend a meeting of educators who discussed how to support a student previously excluded from two other schools due to behavioral difficulties. A teacher commented, 'We have seen some amazing progress in terms of his stamina; however, we need to continue to work on his self-regulation towards the end of the day when he shows signs of escalation and hyper-arousal and tends to try to meet his needs in unhelpful ways.' The other teachers nodded in agreement, and the group worked together to brainstorm strategies they could use to work on this objective. Our team members looked at each other, silently sharing one common response: brilliant.

When we come back to a school, we have a pressing question at the forefront of our minds: is the language of trauma-informed, strengths-based communities embedded into the fabric of the school? If we overhear staff and students using terms from across the approach, we know the community has progressed down the path of whole-school change. If we do not hear the language used explicitly and often, we suspect our strategies may have gained momentum only in isolated pockets of the school.

We advocate that a trauma-informed, strengths-based language is used with staff, students, parents, carers, and members of the wider community. Building this language occurs on many levels. Teachers intentionally introduce students to the language through curriculum links, activities, and strategies. Strategically placed visuals and images can create classroom environments that reinforce core concepts. Staff take part in professional development activities that create depth to their understanding and provide opportunities to reflect on how different concepts may fit within the culture of their school.

We would also like to note that the language can be adapted and expanded for each unique school community. Some schools use the phrase 'ready to learn.' Others feel the term 'ready to focus' is a better fit for their goals and needs. Some schools use the language of 'growth mindset' and 'fixed mindset' (Dweck 2008). Other schools prefer terms such as 'green-light thinking' and 'red-light thinking.' We have seen words from cultural and language groups integrated to create a sense of ownership and agency in different communities. The specific terms used are much less important than having a shared language that is meaningful to a school community.

> :bulb: **KEY IDEA:** The greatest change occurs when schools invest in building a language for trauma-informed, strengths-based communities across the whole school. Helping staff and students to develop a shared language takes time, but the results are worth it.

CONSISTENT AND FIRM EXPECTATIONS

A point we cannot stress strongly enough is the importance of consistency, especially when it comes to behavioral management. It is highly distressing for students if one day they are allowed to swear with no consequences and then the next day they are punished. Or if one student is allowed to come in late and then another student does so and is publicly admonished. It is also important to aim for consistency between teaching staff. Say, for example, one teacher is relaxed about time and keeps his students after the lesson ends to finish their tasks. The students then move to another class where the teacher is strict about punctuality and gives detention to those students who come in late. This shifting ground can be destabilizing for students.

Here we come back to the idea we introduced in Chapter 2: *unpredictability = risk*. Providing consistent and transparent expectations creates a sense of safety, as students know what is required to be a positive and respectful member of the school community.

When expectations continually shift, students need to devote a substantial amount of their attentional and cognitive resources to monitoring their ever-changing environments for threats and risks. For students who have experienced stress and instability—who are often already hypervigilant and greatly sensitive to their environments—unpredictability can compromise their sense of safety, and detract from their capacity to remain in a ready to learn state.

Just as our expectations for our students need to be consistent, they need to be *firm*. Dave Levin, co-founder of the USA-based Knowledge is Power Program (KIPP), has taught us that every action you ignore you have just given permission to. Revisiting the broken windows theory (Wilson and Kelling 1982) introduced in the Preface, we contend that supporting students when they first show signs of behavioral dysregulation prevents more serious problem behaviors from occurring and creates a culture of respect.

It is also important to keep in mind that many students who have experienced instability and disrupted attachments have a deeply unfulfilled need for a sense of personal power and control. We discuss this in more depth in Chapter 5, Relationship. A relational power strategy we often see is students testing boundaries, seeing how far they can push their teachers. When boundaries and expectations are relaxed, changeable, or even non-existent, the teacher and the student can become trapped in cycles of power maneuvers. In contrast, when students consistently meet firm but fair expectations, testing the teacher's resolve and pushing boundaries quickly becomes fruitless and boring. The students develop respect for the teacher, feel a sense of safety and predictability, and settle into focusing on their learning. We explore high expectations in more detail in Box 3.2.

> ☀ **KEY IDEA:** It is vital that all students know what is expected of them, and that educators are transparent and consistent about the natural consequences of behavioral and relational ruptures. This negates the need for disruptive power maneuvers and provides students with a sense of safety and containment.

BOX 3.2: The importance of high expectations

By holding firm expectations for students, we clearly communicate a belief in their potential to succeed. Take a situation where a teacher sets a homework task for the class but tells one student they do not have to complete the work. By relaxing the standards for one student, the teacher may be trying to create a connection or demonstrate an understanding of the student's difficulties. However, the student may misinterpret the situation as the teacher not believing they are capable of doing the work, or even that the teacher does not care about their education.

In comparison, when a teacher holds students to firm but fair standards, students sense there is an adult in their lives who cares about them enough to expect the best from them. Keeping students accountable communicates that the teacher genuinely believes they are capable of academic progress. Likewise, ensuring that students adhere to behavioral and relational standards sends a message that the teacher believes in their capacity to be respectful and contributing class members. We must remind ourselves here that many of our students have unmet developmental learning needs that require pedagogical scaffolding and differentiation to ensure they can succeed. This takes valuable teacher time and attention—time and attention that is well spent! Taken together, this combination of warmth yet consistency provides students with a sense of control and safety they crave and desperately need.

RHYTHM AND REPETITION

Another core theme that underpins our approach is the importance of rhythm and repetition for student wellbeing and healing. Integrating rhythms into the school day, week, and year is a powerful healing intervention for students who may experience the world as an unpredictable and chaotic place. Rhythms and repetition help students to build confidence that positive events will occur, and improve their flexibility when unexpected events are encountered.

As we will discuss in Chapter 4, Body, we advocate using repetition and rhythm at a micro-level through the use of patterned, repetitive activities. Rhythmic interventions—such as throwing and catching balls, drumming on desks, body percussion, yoga, dance, walking on treadmills, and music—provide essential opportunities for students to self-regulate. Furthermore, these activities help build an invaluable sense of structure and consistency into the school day. Patterned activities can also be applied in a responsive manner when teachers recognize early signs of dysregulation or escalation in their students.

We also recommend that teachers create a sense of rhythm and structure at the macro-level by setting up consistent routines for classroom processes. For example, a numeracy lesson may begin with a problem of the day, progress to introducing a new skill, move on to drills and exercises, and end with a collaborative opportunity to explore a real-life scenario. Students come to expect the routine. They come to understand there are parts of each lesson when they will feel confident, and parts when they will feel stretched and challenged. Classroom routines are valuable in guiding students through transitions and for involving students in the clean-up and co-maintenance of learning spaces. In Box 3.3, we provide an overview of brain breaks, which are invaluable in creating a sense of rhythm and ritual in the school day.

The importance of rhythms and routines extends to the value of creating predictable rhythms for the school week and the school year. Having a natural rhythm through the week, reflected in intentional scheduling of student assemblies, meetings, and therapeutic activities, provides students with a sense of confidence and familiarity. On a wider level, integrating rhythmic principles into the school calendar—including seasonal activities, yearly festivals, celebrations, and holidays—helps build a sense of shared community and creates valuable opportunities to build students' capacity for anticipating and savoring positive events.

:\dot{Q}: **KEY IDEA:** Students rely on the school's daily, weekly, and yearly rhythms to provide them with a much-needed sense of stability and security.

BOX 3.3: Introducing brain breaks

Brain breaks are short-burst opportunities for students to self-regulate and develop a sense of ritual and rhythm. They are designed to last between two and five minutes. They can be interwoven into the school day at any point to support student willingness, engagement, and regulation.

Some examples are:

- silent ball (passing a ball from student to student using non-verbal cues)
- clapping call-and-response games
- mindful breathing
- physical stretching
- visualizations
- viewing a humorous picture or clip.

Brain breaks can be used at planned points throughout the school day, such as the start of a lesson or a transition time. Alternatively, brain breaks are invaluable in responding to students' psychological or emotional states. For example, if the class is at a point of high activation, a mindfulness brain break may help students become ready to focus. If students are losing momentum, a positive emotions activity or some aerobic exercise may increase their energy levels and engagement.

TEACHER OBSERVATION AND FEEDBACK

We see the most significant outcomes in terms of student academic, social, and emotional learning when schools have well-developed systems for teacher observation and feedback. In some schools we have worked with, a member of the leadership team observes each teacher delivering a lesson every week. This provides a wealth of opportunity for teacher growth and learning. We have also met with a number of schools where teachers have not been observed for years. In our opinion, this is a huge missed opportunity for teachers to enhance their practice and learn ways to support their students.

For school leaders reading this, it is imperative you know what is going on in your classrooms. We know of instances where teachers use derogatory language, shame individual students, and use aggressive behavior. Equally worrisome, we have met teachers who were struggling deeply in private, too scared to share their concerns, and in desperate need of support they were not getting. We hope these situations do not occur in your school. We strongly contend that if such things are happening, you need to know about them and take swift action to support all involved.

In addition to these extreme circumstances, we strongly advocate using observation and feedback processes with all teachers—from new graduates to highly experienced teachers with years or decades in the profession. We empathize that many people find observation of their classroom practice daunting and anxiety-provoking. At the same time, our experience is that it actually builds teachers' confidence and enjoyment over time. When approached in a benevolent and supportive way with a specific focus on evidence of student learning, teacher observation and feedback become positive and constructive pathways towards professional growth. We have included examples of respectful and constructive teacher feedback in Box 3.4.

In addition to supporting teachers' professional learning, the observation and feedback process is invaluable when considering the needs of students: it means there is another set of eyes in the classroom on a regular basis. This is incredibly helpful in identifying students who may have unmet social, emotional, or academic needs and who may be less evident in the context of busy classroom life. Furthermore, teacher observation and feedback are invaluable if a teacher finds it difficult to work with a particular student or group of students. Everyone benefits when teachers share their concerns with trusted peers, and when colleagues work together to brainstorm strategies for meeting students' unmet needs.

BOX 3.4: Examples of constructive teacher feedback

These examples indicate how to phrase constructive, respectful teacher feedback. You will notice some feedback identifies what is going well in the lesson. You will also notice other points of feedback speak honestly about areas for growth and improvement.

I loved how you introduced the lesson aims, and it was fantastic how you reminded students to think about strengths when developing the characters for their stories. Specifically, you mentioned four

---

different strengths when redirecting four different students. I did notice that Ben was kicking another student's chair. It is important to proactively address that sort of behavior. That tells everyone you have seen it and you are on to it. Let's come up with some ways we can address those moments so that we support Ben without shaming him.

As the lesson progressed, I became aware that Amelia was spending a lot of time fiddling with her pencils and little time actually writing. Is this something you have noticed? Do you have any insights into what is going on for her at the moment?

The lesson started really well, but I observed the students' stamina started to wane about halfway through. When you begin to see those signs of student dysregulation surfacing, it is a good idea to stop the class and do a brain break for a few moments. What are your thoughts? Is this something you have tried in the past?

REVISITING JALEN

Now that we have introduced core concepts of our trauma-informed, strengths-based approach, let's revisit Jalen who we introduced at the beginning of the chapter. Jalen was showing severe signs of behavioral, emotional, and physiological dysregulation. As we inquired more about Jalen's life, we learned that his mother and father were separating. Just when Jalen thought he had his head around his home life, his world shifted and he had to get used to a new normal. We also learned that Jalen had been exposed to violence and substance use from a young age, and that on many days he fended for himself. Jalen did not see the world as a place of safety, predictability, and love—his world was one in which he needed to be in a constant state of watchfulness and self-preservation.

When we put ourselves in Jalen's shoes, we began to understand that when he felt threatened, stressed, or vulnerable, he would go to great lengths to regain a sense of control and personal power. When Jalen looked down at his own unpleasant snack and compared it to the lovingly made muffins and carefully cut up fruit of other kids, it evoked strong and uncomfortable emotions for him. We began to see that at times when Jalen experienced those distressing internal experiences, and without the tools to self-soothe, he would often fall back on power maneuvers. These were the times when he sat on the table or poked other kids.

Jalen's strategy for survival was to push for control, to show everyone he could do exactly what he wanted, whenever he wanted. By pushing everyone until he found a boundary that would hold, Jalen was trying to create the sense of safety he craved so desperately. One day it was taking a bike and riding it around the school; the next, it was breaking into a teacher's locker and taking a phone.

Our goal for Jalen's teacher was to focus intentionally on proactive strategies that Jalen could use to communicate privately with his teachers. He needed and was developmentally ready to notice his own escalation and then have ways to seek support. Jalen did not benefit when minor off-task behaviors that disrupted the sanctity of the classroom were ignored. He needed an adult in his life to say, 'I believe in you enough to tell you not to put your feet up on the table while I am teaching; whether or not it is clear to you right now, you can do better than this.' Dealing with Jalen's early behavioral transgressions was a key opportunity to help him address his unmet needs for body and emotional regulation, and relational repair. Our interpretation was that Jalen had a deep—and unfulfilled—need for an adult caregiver to be warm but firm with him. From our experience, the students presenting the most dysregulated behaviors are the ones who thrive in the most caring yet firm environments.

We have to remember that having an adult take charge in a kind yet firm way was completely new territory for Jalen. He was not used to adults treating him as a worthwhile and capable young person. He was used to anger and power struggles. It is likely Jalen had habituated to punishment—being in trouble was his normal. In a maladaptive way it felt safe, familiar, and predictable for him. Having a durable relationship with an adult who he felt genuinely cared about him, and believed in his ability to learn and make friends, was completely unfamiliar and most likely uncomfortable for him.

As we worked with the school we told the teachers that initially they could expect Jalen to show continued signs of resistance. And indeed, as teachers worked together to hold Jalen to more consistent expectations, he enacted all sorts of behaviors to regain his sense of personal power. However, when Jalen was showing those first signs of dysregulation, the teachers started to ask themselves, 'What unmet needs is he trying to meet right now?' This shifted their perspective from frustration and helplessness to compassion and understanding.

Over time, and with our support, teachers worked together to meet Jalen's unmet needs for regulation and attachment, as well as spend time with him identifying and growing his strengths. His teacher created a morning ritual where Jalen helped with a task. This drew out his strength of leadership. It allowed him to experience a moment of success and belonging early every morning, providing a strong foundation for constructive interpersonal interactions throughout the school day. Jalen benefited greatly from brain breaks, especially ones of high physical intensity, that allowed him those essential moments to decompress and de-escalate.

Jalen's teacher created a subtle system for him to communicate his need for support via trading sticky notes, placed on the top right corner of his desk. This prearranged communication strategy meant Jalen could let his teacher know he was starting to struggle, without attracting the attention of the whole class. As soon as the teacher saw Jalen reach for a sticky note, she would take a deep breath and center herself, ready to support him. Humor was also invaluable in pre-empting behavioral difficulties. His teacher often intervened early with a funny but respectful comment that defused the situation and opened up a pathway for Jalen to step back from the edge of escalated behavior while preserving his own self-concept.

Those small wins—when Jalen expanded his capacity to deal with painful internal experiences without acting in ways that tested the teacher's resolve—slowly and surely came more often. Over time, the difference in Jalen was visible and significant. As his capacity for behavioral and emotional self-regulation increased, the staff began to see a hardworking, caring kid with an astute sense of humor. His teacher's patience and effort changed the trajectory of a young person's life, and it had a profound, positive effect on the entire school community. We strongly believe this message of hope applies to other young people who have severe behavioral and relational challenges.

A LONG-TERM INVESTMENT

When we speak to educators about our approach, their concerns often come down to time constraints. We frequently have conversations where team members feel they do not have time to address students' complex unmet needs. Similarly, staff may not believe they have time or resources to invest in teacher observation and feedback processes. We approach the time conundrum by posing questions. Who has the staff and resources to deal with the huge fall-out when a student has smashed the windows in the bathroom? Who has time to respond to parents who are distressed that their child has had their lunch taken, five days in a row? We ask educators to estimate exactly how much time they currently spend reacting to problems. We ask them to consider investing in our proactive and pre-emptive strategies that, over time, reduce the time spent responding to behavioral problems. Most of the time they quickly see our point.

We also want to reiterate that when a student is in a moment of struggle with emotional or behavioral dysregulation, there are many immediate things a teacher can do to defuse the situation. The teacher may let the student get what they want, react in an overly harsh and punitive manner, or criticize or shame the student. A common one we see is placating an off-task or disruptive student with screen time so the rest of the class can continue with their work.

Without a well-developed toolkit for dealing with difficult moments, teachers fall back on unhelpful approaches: they defuse a situation in the short term but do nothing to build students' capacities or psychological resources over time. Through equipping teachers with a range of effective strategies, we empower them to respond at the moment of dysregulation, while being continually mindful of the students' future growth and development. Therefore, as we aspire to meet students' unmet needs, we ask these questions:

- Where are we now? (How can I support the student at this moment?)

- What unmet needs is this child trying to meet?

- Where do we want to go? (What are my student's needs for growth? How do I want their capacities and resources to develop?)

There are no quick fixes for addressing deeply entrenched behavioral concerns. We know things may get worse before they get better. Students may push hard against new boundaries before they accept that the teacher has the strength and patience to maintain their consistent expectations. Staff may rail against new systems and processes when they have years of experience of doing things a certain way. Parents or members of the community may claim to understand that a consistent behavioral management approach is best for the school community—but loudly and persistently advocate exceptions be made for their children.

We cannot promise you an easy journey towards building trauma-informed, strengths-based classrooms. It takes time to create a shared, respectful, compassionate language for regulation and wellbeing. It is an investment to implement rhythms and routines that build school and classroom environments that minimize challenges in the first place. When a student has experienced disordered or disrupted attachments, their capacity to connect with others needs to be built, layer by layer. Regressions and relapses are expected. Likewise, students' stamina for learning may increase one minute at a time, with setbacks on many days. We cannot promise it will always be easy. But take a long-term view of meeting your students' unmet needs and we believe, strongly, the journey is worth it.

SELF-REFLECTION CHECKLIST

After completing this chapter, please check you can do the following:

- ✓ Consider how your own students are traveling in the domains of Body, Relationship, Stamina, Engagement, and Character.

- ✓ Prioritize building a shared language as a pathway towards a whole-school approach of creating trauma-informed, strengths-based communities.

- ✓ Advocate for the importance of a consistent and firm approach to behavioral management so off-task and disruptive behaviors are responded to in a predictable, consistent, and transparent manner.

- ✓ Appreciate the importance of rhythm and rituals in creating safety and predictability for students.

- ✓ Prioritize teacher observation and feedback as a valued pathway towards whole-school change.

CHAPTER 4

Body

In this chapter, you will learn about:

- supporting students to meet the unmet regulatory needs of the body

- strategies for helping students to become present, centered, and ready to learn

- the importance of co-regulation and self-regulation for students' wellbeing and academic learning.

Dev and his older sister had been in out-of-home care since he was five years old. Now 12 and in Grade 6, Dev hated school, was more than three years behind in his learning, and seemed convinced that putting in any effort was pointless. His teacher, Mr. Freeman, was deeply concerned about Dev and viewed him as a lonely and isolated kid. Mr. Freeman saw that Dev had few enduring relationships with adult figures, and was determined to act as a source of kindness, warmth, and understanding for him. Mr. Freeman believed that if he could form a strong connection with Dev, by working together, Dev could make progress in his academic learning.

Mr. Freeman tried to connect with Dev over a range of topics—music, gaming, sports, cars, and hobbies. Despite Mr. Freeman's best efforts, Dev always appeared reserved. When Mr. Freeman sat down to chat with him, Dev appeared anxious and distracted. On the rare occasions when Dev did open up, the flow of conversation did not always make sense, and he would oscillate between speaking rapidly and not speaking at all. Dev rarely misbehaved in class; however, he often had a vague or absent expression on his face and appeared to be staring off into space. A devoted and caring teacher, Mr. Freeman persisted despite feeling he was not making any progress. After months of effort, Mr. Freeman wondered what more could be done to support Dev. What could he do next?

INTRODUCING *BODY*

We often meet teachers like Mr. Freeman. They are highly motivated to develop a nurturing relationship with a vulnerable student. Sometimes this has positive outcomes and the student and teacher form an enduring and trusting bond. Other times, students who need a warm and reliable adult in their lives can be difficult to connect with in the classroom. We need to remember that when students' fight-flight-freeze responses are activated they are not looking to make friends. They are physically primed to survive: to run, escape, flee, avoid, or attack. In those moments, they have one goal: preserve themselves and their self-concept, no matter how fragile it is. Sadly, students can experience so much dysregulation of their bodily systems that they are not ready to connect with others, let alone focus on their learning. We create meaningful change and healing for students through addressing the dysregulation of their bodies in the context of safe and nurturing relationships.

There are two key reasons that Body plays such a central role in our work. First, students who have experienced stress and trauma often have significant unmet needs in their own bodies. We know that some young people with a history of trauma and instability live in a chronic state of stress, anxiety, and panic. Vulnerable students often have an altered baseline of stress, greatly affecting their capacity to focus on their learning (van der Kolk 2014). Furthermore, research suggests that many students do not have—and desperately need—strategies for regulating their levels of stress and dysregulation throughout the school day (Brunzell, Stokes, and Waters 2016b). Time and time again, we witness students who struggle throughout the school day because their own bodies are unable to do what their minds tell them to do: to sit still, listen, and complete the learning tasks.

The second reason Body is integral to our approach is that it has the potential to benefit *all* members of the school community.

The fight-flight-freeze response is a universal human experience that serves to protects us all from threat and harm (Siegel 2020). All students—and all adults too—have moments of hyper- and hypo-arousal, times of dysregulation, and situations that make them feel stressed, overwhelmed, anxious, or distressed. The evidence-informed strategies we outline in this chapter support all students to be in a state in which they are ready to focus and learn.

Understanding *bottom-up regulation* and *top-down regulation* is central to our work in Body. Bottom-up approaches refer to strategies that address the body and the body's own ability to healthily manage daily stressors. Conversely, top-down approaches refer to successful strategies where a student uses their well-connected brain to make informed thinking decisions. The question of making choices is a helpful example. Often, teachers want to explain the consequences of making good choices to students (a top-down approach). However, we know students who are highly dysregulated in their own bodies often make the best choices they can at the time, often to their own detriment because they do not have access to a well-connected thinking brain. These students can be supported through bottom-up approaches that help them regulate their stress levels and re-access their thinking brains. As students' stress levels decrease, and they return to a ready-to-learn state, they are more equipped to reflect on the possible outcomes of their choices. We revisit some of the ways in which stress and trauma impact the body in Box 4.1.

:Ö: **KEY IDEA:** The strategies in the Body domain help students regulate their stress response and meet the body's unmet needs. This is beneficial for all students.

BOX 4.1: Stress, trauma, and the body

Before turning to classroom strategies, let's review ways that stress impacts the body.

- Children exposed to ongoing stressful experiences often develop a highly active and dysregulated stress response system.

- Instability and insecure relationships impact the baseline of the body's regulatory functions. This is associated with elevated heart rate, higher states of arousal, and significant bodily dysregulation.

- Young people who have experienced trauma may have their bodies constantly flooded with adrenaline, cortisol, and other stress hormones.

- Chronic stress influences the body's ability to regulate basic bodily functions such as blood pressure and temperature.

- Dysregulation in the body can outwardly take many forms, including anxiety, distraction, withdrawal, dissociation, or disconnection.

(Child Welfare Information Gateway 2015; Ogden, Minton, and Pain 2006; Siegel 2020; van der Kolk 2014)

BOTTOM-UP REGULATION

In Chapter 2, Understanding the Effects of Childhood Stress and Trauma in the Classroom, we noted that key parts of children's brains develop over time: the brainstem first, then the limbic system, then the cortical sections of the brain (MacLean 1990; Siegel 2020). The most primitive parts of the brain—the brainstem and limbic systems—are crucial to safety and survival. When a child is in a dangerous or threatening situation, the brainstem and limbic systems are activated, and the child experiences a fight-flight-freeze response. However, when the environment is no longer dangerous, the child's stress response often remains elevated, and the child lives in survival mode. If a child is in survival mode, everyday events and interactions can activate a survival-orientated reaction and lead to significant physical dysregulation. Furthermore, a child experiencing a fight-flight-freeze response cannot access the thinking (cortical) parts of their brain required for effective learning.

Bottom-up regulatory approaches directly address the fight-flight-freeze response, soothe escalated systems governed by the brainstem, and help regulate the body's arousal systems (Ogden, Minton, and

Pain 2006; van der Kolk 2014). Rhythmic and repetitive activities—for example, music-based activities such as percussion or drumming—are inherently calming. We often recommend *somatosensory* activities—that is, activities through which the body has the opportunity to coordinate and integrate sensory input from a variety of sources (Hiebert *et al.* 2013). Playing basketball is a somatosensory activity because the body must coordinate a number of sensory cues: touching the texture of the ball, hearing the rhythmic bounce on the court, seeing the positions of other players, smelling the specific environment one is playing in. Similarly, highly tactile activities, such as playing with sensory tools, squishy objects, or kinetic sand, send soothing messages to the brain. Box 4.2 highlights a range of bottom-up regulatory strategies.

To rewire their brains, students need repeated experiences in which they feel a sense of calm and safety. Over time, frequently providing soothing and regulating experiences for students helps reset their dysregulated stress response systems and meets the unmet needs of their bodies. For this reason, strategies integrated throughout our trauma-informed, strengths-based approach aim at providing bottom-up regulatory experiences for students.

💡 **KEY IDEA:** We address students' unmet needs of the body through bottom-up regulatory strategies that calm and soothe their brainstem and limbic systems.

BOX 4.2: Bottom-up regulatory strategies

This is a selection of bottom-up regulatory strategies that provide soothing somatosensory experiences:

- Rhythmic movement-based activities such as ball games, dancing, walking, running, and therapeutic martial arts.

- Playing songs or playlists where the beat hovers at around 60–80 beats per minute, similar to a resting heart rate.

- Brain breaks with a repetitive pattern, such as drumming and body percussion.

- Calming somatosensory activities such as playing with playdoh, kinetic sand, or materials of different textures.

- Using somatosensory integration supports such as fidget tools and writing supports.

- Using therapeutic tools and rhythmic furniture such as treadmills, stationary bikes, rocking chairs, swings, and hammocks.

- Regular classroom visits from therapy dogs.

TOP-DOWN REGULATION

Compared to bottom-up regulatory approaches, top-down regulation requires more developed cognitive functions that use cortical areas of the brain—that is, the thinking brain (Ogden, Pain, and Fisher 2006). The cortical parts of the brain involved in higher-order thinking organize throughout childhood, adolescence, and into adulthood. Through top-down regulatory strategies, we build students' insight and self-reflection into what is going on in the moment, empowering them with healthy strategies for meeting their own needs. When a child experiences strong emotions or the fight-flight-freeze response, we may encourage them to pause, take a breath, and make a deliberate choice as to what to do next. This is materially different to enacting their first, automatic response. When we encourage students to problem-solve a situation or to brainstorm ways of moving forward, we support their top-down regulatory capacities. Box 4.3 offers examples of ways we use top-down regulation with students.

BOX 4.3: Top-down regulation strategies

This is a selection of top-down regulation strategies that require use of the thinking brain.

- Encouraging students to identify and label their emotions. Through this focus they develop a comprehensive vocabulary for communicating their feelings and internal sensations.

- Providing students with psychoeducation (that is, learning about how their own brain works) on the fight-flight-freeze response. This enables them to identify times when they are beginning to become stressed and proactively use strategies for calming their stress response.

- Encouraging students to make explicit connections between what they are experiencing in the body (such as feeling hot, heart racing, sweaty hands) and the emotion they may be feeling (such as anger).

- Helping students to build problem-solving, restorative practices, and conflict resolution skills. These skills empower them to think through healthy responses to different stressors and scenarios.

- Encouraging students to select a character strength that can help them respond effectively to a challenging situation.

Box 4.4 provides an example of how bottom-up and top-down regulatory strategies, used together, can support a student in a state of escalation.

BOX 4.4: An example of bottom-up and top-down regulation working together

We find the bottom-up and top-down distinction particularly valuable as adults often jump straight to top-down regulation strategies when the student is just not ready. This is what happens if a teacher expects a student to explain their actions or apologize for their behaviors when the student is still in a distressed state. Some students need substantial groundwork in bottom-up regulation before they are ready to gain insights into their actions or communicate effectively with others.

Let's take a situation where a student has a misunderstanding with another student and is showing clear signs of escalation—

that is, a fight stress response is active. Drawing on both bottom-up and top-down regulation, the assistant principal accompanies the student out of the classroom, and the two walk together to the school yard. To start with, the adult sets a surprisingly fast pace as they begin to walk laps of the school yard, side-by-side, in relative silence. The adult is intentionally using bottom-up regulation to support the student's unmet needs. Side-by-side positioning is supportive, not confrontational. Their steps provide a natural rhythm that helps regulate the student's heart rate. The physical exertion of walking naturally reduces the student's level of arousal.

They walk together without talking for as long as the student needs. Once the adult can sense the student's arousal level dropping, the adult can begin to support top-down regulation, gently encouraging the student to talk about what happened. The adult uses a prompt like 'Wow, you were really escalated back there. Where did you start feeling that stress in your body?' Talking about the experience with an adult helps the student to develop insight into their physical sensations, emotions, behaviors, and interactions. The adult may encourage the student to problem-solve or brainstorm strategies to make amends, or prevent such conflicts in the future. These are top-down regulatory strategies. They require access to the cortical (thinking) parts of the brain responsible for sophisticated information processing.

Given the investment in bottom-up regulation, the student is more receptive to discussing the events in an open manner without becoming defensive. By the time the student and the adult return to the classroom, the student is much calmer and equipped with a plan for making amends with their peer. In addition, the student has had the opportunity to practice top-down regulation skills, such as developing insight into their own actions, and considering the perspectives and needs of others.

DE-ESCALATION

Now that we have explored the importance of bottom-up and top-down regulation, we would like to turn to the first of our Body domain focus areas: de-escalation. To understand de-escalation, we invite you to picture a student who is in a highly stressed, heightened, agitated, dysregulated, or hypervigilant state. Or think of a class of students on a Friday afternoon when the weather is terrible. The students have been stuck inside all day and are bouncing off the walls. Alternatively, imagine a teacher who has dealt with a stressful situation all morning and who is unable to rest in the staffroom at lunch. You may even think of a time when you felt anxious, hyperactive, or dysregulated. You may have felt your heart racing, found it hard to sit still, or had difficulty with concentration and focus. These are examples of escalated states.

The opposite of an escalated state is a state of de-escalation. De-escalation is defined as the verbal and non-verbal skills we use to center ourselves when we feel heightened. We know that all students and teachers can ground themselves and lower their level of arousal if they have many opportunities every day to practice de-escalation skills. We also know that de-escalating classrooms are routine rich and predictable. We recommend whole-classroom strategies for creating environments that promote de-escalation, such as those listed in Box 4.5.

BOX 4.5: Tips for classroom environments that promote de-escalation

- Create physical spaces that promote a sense of calm through choice of color, lighting, spatial layout, and furnishings.

- Avoid excessive visual and auditory stimulation.

- If possible, remove fluorescent lights and create soft, calming lighting.

- Create a designated home space for each young person, such as an allocated desk, where they feel a sense of ownership, safety, and belonging.

- Have a sensory station that includes baskets of fidget tools (e.g. kinetic sand, coloring sheets, playdoh, craft supplies, and other calming, soothing objects) as well as

---

a timer for students to self-regulate and return back to learning.

- Create a de-escalation, wellbeing, or calming corner with soothing colors, materials, and objects.

- Establish a clear morning routine that provides students with structure and safety as they transition to school.

- Consider a morning check-in when students identify their emotional state and level of arousal.

- Intentionally use humor to de-escalate situations. Have a collection of clips, pictures, or cartoons ready to use when students show signs of stress or conflict.

STRESS AND DE-ESCALATION

We support students' capacities in de-escalation by educating them on the fight-flight (sympathetic) and relaxation (parasympathetic) stress response systems. In particular, it is invaluable to help students develop insight into how *they* respond to stress. Underpinning our work on stress is an understanding that, while all people feel stressed sometimes, what makes each person feel stressed is different. Our relationship with dogs offers a simple illustration. One person may love dogs and find them de-escalating and calming. For someone else, even the thought of being around a dog may lead to feelings of anxiety and panic. As discussed in earlier chapters, it is also important to remember that not all stress is harmful—stress plays a role in a healthy life, and we all experience daily moments of stress when we learn new things. However, too much stress, or experiencing stress for extended periods, can have a range of negative consequences. With this in mind, it is useful for students to identify their own triggers for stress, as well as strategies that help them de-escalate. Box 4.6 assembles stress reflection questions students can respond to.

BOX 4.6: Student stress reflection questions

- What stresses you out? Tests, social media, homework, fights with friends or family members?

- What do you first notice within your body when you are becoming stressed?

- What do you physically feel or notice in your body when you are stressed?

- What helps you calm down and de-escalate when you are stressed?

- What are some healthy ways you deal with stress?

- What are some unhealthy ways you deal with stress?

To develop their awareness of stress, we encourage groups of young people to work together, brainstorming the stressors most relevant to being a student. Students frequently come up with suggestions of stress-inducing scenarios such as disagreements on the playground, homework, tests, speaking in front of others, social misunderstandings, online messaging, and times when they find learning difficult. Discussing the different situations that make them feel stressed helps normalize stress. Everyone feels stress sometimes. It is a healthy part of life. To this end, we also find that teachers who effectively introduce these concepts to students send a powerful message that they acknowledge and support them in times of stress. It is also valuable to make students aware that sometimes stress or anxiety responses can occur without an obvious cause, but even if we don't know what is causing stress or anxiety, our de-escalation strategies can still work for us.

STRESS AND THE BODY

Another valuable de-escalation strategy is building students' awareness of where they feel stress in their bodies. We have had excellent outcomes from providing students with pictures of the human body and asking them to draw the different ways they feel stressed. Students invariably come up with a range of insightful ways to depict the stress response, such as feeling queasy in the stomach, having sweaty hands, breathing rapidly, and feeling their hearts beating at a fast pace. Students also regularly identify that, over the longer term, stress may lead to headaches, muscle soreness, or difficulties sleeping. Students can use a different color to depict the relaxation (parasympathetic) response, such as a slowing heart rate and increased digestive activity.

A valuable way to further students' understanding, and to normalize that everyone feels stressed sometimes, is to provide small groups of students with large pieces of paper and invite them to work together in visually depicting the stress response. As students' awareness builds, they can attend better to the early warning signs that they are becoming stressed. They can then take action to de-escalate before they reach a state of distress or dysregulation.

Exploring heart rate as an indicator of stress further extends students' learning. When a student is in an escalated state, their heart rate is faster and potentially variable. When they are in a calmer state, their heart rate is slower and has a more regular pattern. Even a young child can learn to feel their heart rate by placing their fingers on their wrist (radial pulse) or the side of their throat (carotid pulse). Students can use biofeedback tools such as heart rate monitors to obtain data on their heart rate. They can integrate their data into mathematics or science units as they observe, record, track, and graph their heart rates throughout the day. Similarly, students can explore the effectiveness of different de-escalation strategies (such as deep breathing exercises) by taking their heart rates before and after the activity and noting any difference. These simple activities for bodily awareness also help to build students' capacities in interoception, which is discussed in Box 4.7.

💡 **KEY IDEA:** Building students' insight into how and where stress is experienced in the body provides a valuable foundation for de-escalation.

BOX 4.7: Interoception

We are fascinated by the study of interoception: the ability to sense the internal state of the body and awareness of when the body is shifting and changing (Goodall 2016; Mahler 2017). Interoception comprises two main forms of perception. Proprioception includes signals from the musculoskeletal system and the skin. Visceroception includes signals from internal organs.

Interoception helps us know when we are hungry, thirsty, or tired, when we feel pain or stress, and when we need to go to the toilet. Some people have good awareness of their body's internal state. They can pay attention to their bodily cues and act on them in a timely manner. Many students with complex needs—including students on the autism spectrum, students affected by trauma, and students with some mental or physical health conditions—may have underdeveloped interoception capacities (Goodall 2016; Mahler 2017).

As we continue to build students' bodily awareness, we are helping them to develop their interoceptive capacities. In particular, it is valuable to encourage students to attend to the early warning signs that they are becoming stressed, such as noting their palms are feeling sweaty or their heart is starting to beat faster. Becoming more aware of these early warning signs helps students proactively identify and meet their needs before they reach a highly stressed state. With this goal in mind, we constantly encourage students to reflect on their internal states. How do they notice their bodies changing? What are their early warning signs that they are becoming frustrated? What are their warning signs that they are becoming stressed? What do they notice in their bodies when they feel this way?

MINDFULNESS

Mindfulness is the next overarching concept in the Body domain that we would like to introduce and explore. Mindfulness is defined as paying attention in the moment in a purposeful and non-judgmental manner (Kabat-Zinn 1990). A core aspect of mindfulness is acceptance—rather than judge, repress, or deny our current thoughts, experiences, or sensations, we observe and allow them (Hassed and Chambers 2014). Mindfulness is invaluable in bringing students' attention to the present moment. Over time, it builds their capacity for self-regulation.

Mindfulness can take the form of meditation practices, such as focusing attention on breathing, drawing awareness to different senses, or mindfully attending to different body movements. Mindfulness meditation may also involve paying attention to external stimuli such as music, sounds, or a visual image. Mindfulness can be applied to all aspects of daily living—a student may be present and mindful when they are playing in the playground, doing a learning exercise, or listening to a friend (Langer 2000).

Substantial research links mindfulness with a range of positive benefits, including improved wellbeing, enhanced stress regulation, and superior academic outcomes (Waters *et al.* 2015; Zenner, Herrnleben-Kurz, and Walach 2014). Research has found school-based mindfulness programs improve psychological functioning, and reduce trauma symptoms and distress in vulnerable young people (Sibinga *et al.* 2016). Mindfulness may mitigate the impact of toxic stress on young people by increasing coping and resilience, and by providing respite from adverse physical effects of chronic stress states (Bethell *et al.* 2016; Ortiz and Sibinga 2017).

While the research on mindfulness in schools is encouraging, we want to be transparent. We have worked with teachers who have tried mindfulness exercises numerous times in their classrooms and had limited success. Teachers may feel that students do not take the activity seriously, or find it boring or frustrating. This can be disappointing for teachers who often have the best of intentions but feel they are not making any progress.

The resistance to mindfulness some students demonstrate makes sense to us when we think about the idea of *unpredictability = risk*. For some students, it is usual to feel stressed and dysregulated. In contrast, feeling de-escalated and well regulated may be completely unfamiliar, and therefore risky for them. Furthermore, it is useful to remember that the aim of mindfulness is not to feel calm but to notice and accept what is happening in the present moment, whatever that might be. It is understandable that some students find it highly unsettling and difficult to sit with their current experience, which may be fear, anxiety, anger, sadness, guilt, or shame.

We encourage teachers to persist and aspire to find mindfulness activities that work with their students. We have found that some students respond well to listening to nature sounds, like clips of running water and waterfalls, or listening to soothing and relaxing music. For younger students, mindfulness coloring activities or practicing simple yoga positions can be useful ways of interweaving mindfulness into the classroom.

We would like to emphasize that mindfulness should not be practiced in a prescriptive way, such as forcing students to lie down or close their eyes if they do not want to do so. Also, one of our biggest learnings is that many students find *silence* uncomfortable. We recommend that any mindfulness or de-escalation practice should provide auditory anchors—music, counted breaths, or guided instructions—that help to ground students in the present moment. A range of mindfulness brain breaks we have found useful with students is provided in Box 4.8, along with a range of helpful mindfulness resources in Box 4.9.

💡 **KEY IDEA:** Mindfulness involves noticing and accepting what is going on in the moment. Thoughtfully weaving mindfulness through the school day helps students to de-escalate their stress response and gently bring their attention to the present moment.

BOX 4.8: Mindfulness brain breaks

- Play a short clip of nature sounds or soothing music as students return from lunch.

- Have students stand up wherever they are and mindfully lean to one side, lean to the other side, lean forward, and lean back.

- Encourage students to tap into their senses by identifying three things they can see, three things they can hear, and three things they can feel.

- Invite students to notice what they can feel as they complete three different hand movements, such as three claps, three clicks, and three shakes.

- Invite students to anchor their feet to the ground and imagine they have roots that go deep into the ground. Next, have them wiggle their toes, bend their legs at the knees, and bounce up and down several times. Encourage them to attend to the different sensations each movement produces.

BOX 4.9: Mindfulness resources

Here are some of our favorite mindfulness resources.

Cosmic Kids (Yoga for the Classroom): www.cosmickids.com

Etty-Leal, J. (2010) *Meditation Capsules: A Mindfulness Program for Children.* Melbourne, Australia: Meditation Capsules.

Hassed, C. and Chambers, R. (2014) *Mindful Learning: Reduce Stress and Improve Brain Performance for Effective Learning.* Wollombi, Australia: Exisle Publishing.

Jennings, P.A. (2015) *Mindfulness for Teachers: Simple Skills for Peace and Productivity in the Classroom.* New York, NY: W.W. Norton.

Siegel, D. and Payne Bryson, T. (2012) *The Whole-Brain Child: 12 Revolutionary Strategies to Nurture Your Child's Developing Mind.* New York, NY: Bantam Books.

Smiling Mind: www.smilingmind.com.au

PRESENT, CENTERED, AND READY TO LEARN

Closely related to helping students learn mindfulness is a specific form of mindfulness we now call being present, centered, and ready to learn. At any moment, a teacher may look at their class and ask what percentage of students are focused on the learning task. Invariably, some students are thinking about their unfinished homework, some are ruminating about a conflict with a friend, and others are thinking about what is happening on the weekend.

Further compromising their capacity to be present in the moment, students who have experienced trauma or chronic stress may be hypervigilant, scanning their environment for threats (Teicher *et al.* 2002). Many students who have experienced stress and adversity also experience symptoms of dissociation, where, as a protective mechanism, the brain disconnects from thoughts, feelings, and sensations in the moment (Ogden, Minton, and Pain 2006; Orygen 2018; van der Kolk *et al.* 1996). In reality, the percentage of students at any time point who are on task and anchored in the moment may be quite low. Our focus is on helping students to become present, centered, and ready to learn:

- *Present:* bringing attention and awareness into the present moment and anchoring it there.

- *Centered:* to take care of one's physical, emotional, thinking, and spiritual needs.

- *Ready to learn:* an optimal state of arousal and engagement conducive to learning.

Box 4.10 offers reflection questions that can help teachers grasp this aspect of mindfulness from personal and professional perspectives.

BOX 4.10: Teacher reflection and discussion questions

- Where is your center?

- When are you at your most present and centered?

- When are you at your most distracted and uncentered?

- How does it feel to teach when you are in a present and centered state?

- How does it feel to teach when you are not in a present and centered state?

LEARNING TO BREATHE

We can support students to be present, centered, and ready to learn through providing them with opportunities for deep breathing. When the fight-flight-freeze response is activated, breathing is shallow, rapid, and superficial (Penman 2016). We can all easily recall a student who is panicked and trying to tell us about a drama they witnessed on the playground: they struggle to breathe, cannot finish their sentences, and are not breathing in enough oxygen. When students' breathing is shallow, their shoulders move up and down as the majority of air is drawn into the top of their lungs. In contrast, when students are breathing deeply, their diaphragms are engaged, and they draw air into all parts of their lungs. When students are breathing deeply, their lower abdomens and stomachs move. Deep breathing is an effective way of de-escalating stress and activating the relaxation (parasympathetic) response (Zaccaro *et al.* 2018).

We teach students that learning to breathe has powerful benefits in both the short and long term. In the short term, focusing attention on the breath is a simple and effective strategy for bringing attention to the present moment. If a student finds they are feeling anxious, stressed, or distressed, they can use deep breathing techniques to calm their activated stress response and help themselves de-escalate. In the longer term, regularly practicing deep breathing helps reset the body's baseline stress level. As students learn to breathe deeply, they can decrease the percentage of time they are in survival mode and increase the percentage of time they are present, centered, and ready to learn. There are many breathing strategies you can use with students, including those listed in Box 4.11.

BOX 4.11: Deep breathing strategies

- Allocate three minutes for deep breathing at three different times in the school day.

- Encourage students to breathe in through their noses and out through their mouths.

- Direct students to inhale, drawing the air down into their belly.

- Invite students to breathe in to the count of five, and breathe out to the count of seven.

- Encourage students to concentrate on how it feels as the air goes into their nose and travels down, expanding their lungs.

- Have students perform shallow breaths and deep breaths. Discuss the difference between the two for how the body moves and feels.

- Have students place a hand on their stomach or chests (or both) and feel their hands move as the air moves in and out of their bodies.

- Keep a snow globe in the classroom. Shake up the snow globe to represent a state of high activation and dysregulation. Have students practice slow breathing while the contents of the snow globe settle to the bottom, representing a calm state.

- Have students practice deep breathing as they blow bubbles.

- Invite students to lie down and place a small object or soft toy on their stomachs. The object will move up and down as students practice deep breaths.

SELF-REGULATION

As we build on our foundation of de-escalation, interweaving mindfulness into the classroom, and supporting students to be present, centered, and ready to learn, we turn to our next focus area in Body, *self-regulation*. Self-regulation is defined as the ability to alter one's behavior and influence one's thoughts, feelings, actions, impulses, and other responses (Baumeister, Leith *et al.* 1998). When we think about self-regulation, we like to start by thinking about babies and young children. During the first few years of life, babies and young children lack well-developed capacities to regulate their feelings and internal states—they often rely on attuned and responsive adults to do so for them. When a baby or young child experiences an emotion such as sadness or fear, an adult soothes them with a cuddle and some comforting sounds or words. In this way, the adult helps the baby or young child to make sense of what they are feeling, and to feel better.

A core task of child development is to take increasing responsibility for regulating your own emotions, behaviors, and internal states. Children with well-developed capacities in self-regulation can notice those subtle internal cues that tell them they are becoming escalated, stressed, hungry, thirsty, tired, or lonely. They can then take steps to meet their needs in healthy ways. When children exercise their self-regulation muscles, they can control their impulses, make effective decisions, problem-solve, and delay gratification in pursuit of valued goals. An important feature of self-regulation is that it strengthens with use—the more frequently young people have opportunities to exercise their capacity for self-regulation, the more they develop this essential life tool (Baumeister, Bratslavsky *et al.* 1998; Baumeister and Tierney 2012).

Sadly, in the absence of comforting interactions and secure attachments, many young people do not have formative nurturing experiences that pave the way for building their self-regulatory capacities (Pearce 2016; van der Kolk 2014). Students who struggle with self-regulation can enact behaviors that look impulsive, dysregulated, and unpredictable. Without well-developed capacities to notice when they are becoming escalated and take action, they often turn to survival strategies for meeting their unmet needs. It is understandable that children and young people who have experienced trauma and chronic stress—who are frequently in survival mode, with their brainstem and limbic systems highly activated—face challenges with self-regulation. Here we discuss approaches to supporting students' capacities for self-regulation, starting with co-regulation.

:ᄋ̣̇: **KEY IDEA:** A core objective of the Body domain is building students' self-regulatory capacities.

CO-REGULATION

Understanding co-regulation is essential to working with students from a trauma-informed, strengths-based perspective. To understand co-regulation, we again invite you to think about an adult rocking, cuddling, and soothing a crying baby. This is the epitome of co-regulation—we like to think of this as the adult aspiring to share some of their own calm with the baby. It is certainly inappropriate for a teacher to pick up and rock a distressed student, but we know there are many things an adult can do that either add additional stress to the situation or help the student to self-regulate.

In our experience, many teachers use co-regulation all the time without realizing it is a strategy. We see co-regulation in action when a teacher helps calm a distressed student by crouching down low, side-by-side and shoulder to shoulder with the child, and speaking softly to them. We see this when a teacher remains calm during an interaction with a student presenting dysregulated behavior. When the teacher is calm, the student receives verbal and non-verbal cues that the situation is safe, which helps soothe the student's activated stress-response system

(Porges 2004, 2015). Staying with a student in distress until they feel better both supports them in that moment and communicates a sense of genuine acceptance and support: 'You are distressed, but it is okay. I am here for you.'

To build on what you already naturally do to co-regulate students, we invite you to go one step further and be intentional and deliberate in using co-regulation as a strategy. This involves reflecting on what you do well to co-regulate your students, areas for growth, and strategies you may learn from observing other teachers. We have included tips for co-regulation in Box 4.12, and some insights into interpersonal neurobiology in Box 4.13. In Box 4.14, we provide an example of a teacher using co-regulation as a strategy with a student during a classroom lesson.

BOX 4.12: Tips for co-regulation

Maintaining a calm and soothing presence is co-regulation in practice. There are numerous options for maximizing your capacity for co-regulation:

- Position yourself to the side of the student rather than facing the student (students can find face-to-face positioning highly confrontational in potentially difficult conversations).

- Crouch down low next to the student to minimize your size and get on their level.

- Consider the tone and rate of your voice. It can help to speak softly and at a predictable rate and rhythm.

- Keep your eyes lowered—some students may find eye contact threatening in one-to-one conversations, so sometimes this can help.

- Model deep breathing as you sit with a student. If appropriate, gently invite the student to take some deep breaths with you.

BOX 4.13: Interpersonal neurobiology

We are interested in the growing field of interpersonal neurobiology and the study of mirror neurons (Siegel 2020; Siegel and Payne Bryson 2012). In essence, there is now understanding that humans' emotions and physiological states are contagious—the feelings and bodily sensations of one person influence the people around them. Mirror neurons are a highly specialized group of neurons that 'mirror' the actions and affective states of others (Siegel 2020). When we see a person stand up, neurons fire in our own brain that are related to similar movements. Similarly, when someone else is distressed or calm, our own brains respond to mirror the affective experience (Rizzolatti and Craighero 2004). The science of interpersonal neurobiology helps explain why co-regulation is such an effective strategy: a teacher remaining calm and de-escalated will have a contagious effect on a dysregulated student.

Here are some other examples of interpersonal neurobiology in action that you may be familiar with:

- A teacher interacts with a student in distress and starts to feel distressed and dysregulated themselves.

- A teacher is flustered or distressed, and the whole class becomes agitated and escalated.

- A teacher walks into the staffroom after an angry interaction with a student, and their peers start to pick up their frustration.

- A teacher works with students who have experienced trauma and experiences vicarious trauma symptoms such as difficulty sleeping, headaches, and stomach issues.

- A present and centered teacher has a calming effect on a whole class of students.

- A present and centered teacher serves as a safe haven for a student who is having a rough time at home.

BOX 4.14: Co-regulation in action

A class of students is working on an independent writing task. The teacher notices a student, Ruby, slam her pen down in clear frustration—her body language indicates she is over it and has given up. The teacher briefly experiences a temptation to ignore Ruby, but she knows that if she ignores her now, she will need to respond to a much bigger situation later on—Ruby is someone who can go from zero to 100 very quickly. Right now, the teacher knows she needs to be an avatar of co-regulation. The teacher's stress response starts to fire. It is hard work to regulate feelings of frustration and respond effectively to the situation at hand.

The teacher knows she has the ability, in that moment, either to amplify Ruby's stress response or to help her to settle back into a ready-to-learn state. The number one thing the teacher keeps in mind is not to embarrass Ruby in front of her peers. The teacher knows that if Ruby feels embarrassed she will lose all reasoning ability. Her focus will shift to defending her reputation and protecting her identity.

The teacher immediately goes down on one knee to a position lower than Ruby, and therefore unthreatening. For one brief moment, the teacher looks up at Ruby to symbolically give her the power. Then the teacher stops looking at Ruby as she finds this confronting. With gaze and attention focused on Ruby's work, the teacher says, 'Wow, Ruby, I see you have written your name, thank you very much. You have done a great heading, and you have written three clear sentences in your best handwriting. Well done. Listen, I am not going to ask you to finish the whole thing today. We don't have enough time for that anyway. However, I would love to see four more sentences.'

At this moment, the teacher is just looking for a nod or look of recognition from Ruby, before walking away. The teacher does not stand over Ruby watching what she is doing, nor explore reasons that might explain why Ruby is finding the activity difficult. Similarly, Ruby's teacher does not give her a lecture about off-task behavior, or make a scene her peers would notice. The teacher is allowing Ruby to realize it is not a big deal. She can shake it out. As the teacher moves around the room she subtly tracks Ruby; if the teacher sees that Ruby needs more support the teacher will go back and repeat the process.

We invite you to reflect on your approach to co-regulation:

- Thinking about your teaching practice, what steps do you use to co-regulate students?

- What co-regulation strategies do you do well?

- Are there some situations in which you struggle with co-regulation?

- Can you think of a time you have added stress to an interaction with a student?

- What are some ways you would like to use co-regulation as a strategy with your students?

- Thinking of teachers in your school who are co-regulation avatars, what do they do well to co-regulate students?

DECISION FATIGUE AND EGO DEPLETION

Perhaps you are familiar with times when you try to make healthy food choices; you resist a cupcake at your morning staffroom break, and say 'no!' to some chips at lunch. By the end of the day you have used up your self-regulation reserves and end up eating half a block of milk chocolate. This is a common example of the idea that a person's regulatory capacities—in this instance, their capacity to resist the unhealthy treat—are not stable but change constantly. The ever-changing nature of self-regulatory capacities makes sense if we consider the theories of decision fatigue and ego depletion:

- *Decision fatigue:* as a person makes numerous decisions, the quality of their decision-making deteriorates (Vohs *et al.* 2008).

- *Ego depletion:* a person's self-regulatory capacities draw from a limited pool of cognitive resources that deplete over time (Baumeister, Bratslavsky *et al.* 1998).

Students are continually facing decisions. Who do I talk to first thing after drop-off? Where do I play at recess? What book should I choose for independent reading? The myriad of decisions students face each day draws on their cognitive resources and can lead to them struggling to maintain a state of self-regulation. It is also useful to consider that students' capacity to make effective decisions and regulate their behaviors is compromised when their biological needs, such as food and sleep, are not met (Gailliot and Baumeister 2007; Williams and Sciberras 2016). Similarly, stress and different emotional states impact students' self-regulatory capacities (Baumeister, Zell, and Tice 2007).

We see the impact of decision fatigue and ego depletion in the classroom when, after being on task all lesson, students become fidgety and dysregulated towards the end. We see the changing nature of self-regulation when a student who was beautifully regulated in the morning then has a meltdown in the afternoon. As we understand the changing nature of self-regulation, we can support students to meet their needs before they reach a point of dysregulation. Simple tasks, such as waiting while another person is speaking, taking turns, and practicing listening attentively, are all invaluable in helping students to build their self-regulatory muscles. It is also beneficial to pay attention to students' unmet physical needs that may compromise their self-regulation. It helps to ensure that they have regular opportunities to eat healthy food and drink water. We help students to refuel their capacity for self-regulation by implementing brain breaks, and, in particular, giving students frequent opportunities to move. The example in Box 4.15 illustrates the impact of decision fatigue and ego depletion in action.

💡 **KEY IDEA:** We protect students from decision fatigue and ego depletion through building their self-regulation muscles, attending to their physical needs, and interweaving brain breaks throughout the school day.

BOX 4.15: An example of decision fatigue

Jeremy wakes up in the morning and does not want to go to school, so the effort to motivate himself to get ready has already depleted some of his self-regulation reserve. It takes him five minutes to find his school uniform, which is dirty and crumpled. He is acutely aware he has not done his homework, and his mind is racing trying to think of an excuse that will keep him out of trouble. His brother hits him in the arm when they get in the car. To start with, Jeremy ignores his brother, but then he retaliates and they both get in trouble for fighting.

Jeremy comes in through the school gate. He has to decide where to stand and who to stand with. Should he go and find his friends, or wait by himself? Then Jeremy walks into his classroom, and it is chaos. There are no assigned seats in this class, so he has to decide where to sit. Jeremy has to decide whether or not to read his book as the teacher instructs, although he does not want to as reading is stressful for him. He experiences a strong temptation to walk out. Instead, he goes to the corner and throws a book. All these micro-moments have depleted Jeremy's capacity to control his behavior and maintain a state of self-regulation. It is game over by 9.44am. At 9.45am the teacher and Jeremy are in a screaming match.

There is little the teacher can do to make Jeremy's morning at home less stressful. However, there is so much the teacher can do to support him in the classroom. The teacher finds it effective to start the day with a mindfulness brain break that allows Jeremy a chance to transition to the class in a positive way and recharge his self-regulation muscles. The teacher provides Jeremy—and the whole class—with regular opportunities to move. This gives them a break from the substantial amount of self-regulation it takes for students to sit still. The Ready to Learn Scale (see below) is also useful. It helps Jeremy build insights into his own state of regulation/dysregulation. It helps him take increasing responsibility for identifying when he is feeling dysregulated and act to meet his unmet needs.

READY TO LEARN SCALE

When we speak with teachers about tools and strategies that have the greatest impact on their classrooms, many mention the Ready to Learn Scale, a tool that allows students to self-assess their current state and communicate this to their teachers in a simple manner. In the example provided in Figure 4.1, the scale starts with a sad face and progresses to a happy face that represents a state of being present, centered, and ready to learn. The images used in the scale can be tailored for each classroom community. We have seen countless creative examples of images used to represent different states of learning readiness, including thermometers, light bulbs, plants, and colors. We have even seen a class create a scale using WiFi signals—a low WiFi signal represented feeling not at all ready to learn, and a strong WiFi signal represented a high state of learning readiness.

1	2	3	4	5
I am not ready to learn yet	I am getting ready to learn	I am okay to learn	I am good to learn	I am pumped and ready to learn!

Figure 4.1: Ready to Learn Scale (emoji images by https://openmoji.org. License: CC BY-SA 4.0)

When students arrive at the classroom in the morning, they place their names on the scale to represent how they are feeling in terms of their learning readiness. This process can be repeated throughout the day: students are encouraged to check in about how they are feeling and adjust the location of their names on the scale if necessary. The scale gives the teacher a quick indication of how the student is doing. For students, the simple act of communicating their unmet needs is soothing in itself.

This process also provides an invaluable opportunity for unconditional positive regard. Students know that wherever they place their name on the scale, even if they communicate that they are not at all ready to learn, the teacher will accept their answer in a non-judgmental and non-punitive manner. The teacher will then support them to meet their unmet needs and to cultivate a state of being present, centered, and ready to learn. (We dwell more on unconditional positive regard in Chapter 5, Relationship.)

☀ **KEY IDEA:** The Ready to Learn Scale is a simple classroom tool that helps students attend to and communicate how they are feeling.

READY TO LEARN PLANS

A Ready to Learn Plan, depicted in Figure 4.2, is a prearranged agreement between a student and teacher. These are used at times when students feel stressed or dysregulated. (Depending on school and cultural contexts, these plans are sometimes called Focus Plans, Safety Plans, or Resilience Plans.) Ready to Learn Plans go through a range of questions, including what situations make students feel stressed, what they first notice when they are becoming stressed, how they feel and behave in these situations, and what helps them to center themselves. Once the Ready to Learn Plan is created, the student can opt to activate it at moments when they feel stressed or overwhelmed. Likewise, if the teacher observes a student becoming escalated or dysregulated, the teacher can ask the student if they would like to use a strategy from their Ready to Learn Plan that will help them self-regulate.

Ready to Learn Plan

This Ready to Learn Plan will assist me to become present, centered, and ready to learn.

Name:

Sometimes at school, I get escalated or frustrated when this happens:
(Example: When someone in my group is too loud and I cannot learn.)

When I get escalated or frustrated, my behavior can look like:
(Example: I want to tell them to be quiet and to move away from me.)

The physical response in my own body is:
(Example: I can feel my heart rate increase and I take shorter breaths.)

Some things that I can do to help myself de-escalate are:

☐ Take a deep breath or do mindful breathing
☐ Ask for a two-minute or five-minute time out
☐ Spend time in the sensory station
☐ Go for a short walk
☐ Ask to talk to a friend or teacher

What else works for both you and your teacher?

Our class will review and improve our Ready to Learn Plan on this date:

Figure 4.2: Ready to Learn Plan

As we introduce this tool, we would like to draw your attention to the relational aspects of the Ready to Learn Plans where the teacher and the student have pre-selected strategies the student can proactively choose to use when feeling escalated or dysregulated. We remember that a student presenting dysregulated behaviors may be having a fight-flight-freeze response; therefore, efforts a teacher makes to connect with the student may be met with anger, retreat, or disconnection. Prearranged strategies can bypass students' defensive responses and help to communicate respect and safety. It is also beneficial for teachers to have go-to strategies they can use immediately when a student's emotions or behaviors appear dysregulated. The case study in Box 4.16 demonstrates the use of these tools for body regulation with a student called Leo, aged ten.

☀️ **KEY IDEA:** A Ready to Learn Plan is a prearranged agreement between teachers and students that provides clear and actionable ways of supporting students when they are feeling dysregulated.

BOX 4.16: Case study: Leo

Leo came in one morning and placed his name so far off the Ready to Learn Scale it was on the other side of the wall. This gave his teacher a quick indication it had been a stressful morning at home. Sadly, this was often the case. The teacher did not draw attention to Leo but quickly adjusted plans for the morning, starting the day with some physical movement and exercise—strategies the teacher knew from experience Leo enjoyed and which helped to meet his unmet needs.

After the class completed a quick circuit of the playground, they moved on to a learning task. The teacher made sure to give Leo some individual feedback and support as she moved around the class. When the class was engaged in the task the teacher had a quick word with Leo, quietly saying it sounded as if it was a tough morning and to signal if he needed to activate his Ready to Learn Plan at any stage. By recess Leo had independently moved his name from the wall to the very corner of the Ready to Learn Scale. The rest of the day was far from perfect, but the teacher went home at the end of the day feeling good about the effort Leo had put in and positive about her work with him.

We asked the teacher to reflect on what may have happened without using the Ready to Learn Scale. The teacher shared that Leo would likely have resorted to unhealthy ways of communicating his pain and distress: slamming books, swearing, yelling, and acting out. The teacher admitted they probably would have responded in frustration by yelling and sending Leo out of the classroom. Leo would have gone from an escalated home to an escalated classroom, derailing in his path the learning of the whole class and the teacher's mood.

Through working with us, the teacher came to see that Leo had an unmet need to communicate his distress to someone. Leo needed his difficulties to be seen and heard; he needed to feel as if someone cared. In the beginning, he did not have the insight, capacity, or emotional literacy to come to school and say, 'Look, things are tough at home. I am feeling unsettled and distressed. I will probably need some extra support and kindness today.' The Ready to Learn Scale provided a shortcut to communicating his unmet needs to his teacher. This created the opportunity for the teacher to respond in a proactive and pre-emptive manner at times when Leo needed help to meet his bodily and relational needs.

TEACHERS' SELF-REGULATION

So many of the fantastic teachers we have worked with are highly skilled in the art of self-regulation. However, there will always be moments that test any teacher's resolve and activate their stress response. We do not have to tell you teaching can be stressful—and we certainly do not have to tell you working with students presenting highly dysregulated behaviors can be exhausting. We know teachers experience a range of stressors outside the classroom that understandably have a considerable impact on how they feel throughout the school day. Here we come to one of the most important messages of our book: it is essential for teachers to prioritize their wellbeing if they are to have the stamina and self-regulatory capacities to support their students throughout the school day.

To maintain your capacity for self-regulation, it is valuable to know your early warning signs for stress and have prepared steps that work for you in de-escalating yourself in activating moments. It is also essential to invest in your baseline level of wellbeing throughout the week. It is invaluable to make time for activities such as exercise, mindfulness, hobbies, and relaxation strategies that decrease your overall level of stress and arousal. Protecting your capacity for self-regulation involves identifying when you may be feeling overwhelmed and asking for help when you need it. We also encourage you to consider your level of decision fatigue. Box 4.17 offers tips for actively managing decision fatigue.

BOX 4.17: Decision fatigue self-reflection

Are you prone to decision fatigue and ego depletion? Perhaps you can relate to starting the day in a present and centered state and ending it feeling dysregulated and exhausted. Which of the following strategies work for you to minimize your decision fatigue?

- Devote time to planning and preparation so you have a clear set of steps to follow throughout the school day.

- Make simple morning decisions such as what to have for lunch and which outfit to wear the night before to minimize your cognitive load in the morning.

- Ensure that you prioritize eating regularly, and proactively manage your energy throughout the day.

- Wherever possible, make important decisions early in the day.

- Use lists to plan and prioritize important tasks.

- Use break times to rest and replenish, and not to do additional activities that deplete your cognitive resources.

- Understand that using social media or scrolling the internet may feel like a relaxation strategy at the time, but it may use precious cognitive resources.

THE TRIAGE CONVERSATION

The heart of our approach is creating trauma-informed, strengths-based classrooms that maximize students' opportunities for success in both behavior and learning. However, we know there will always be moments that test students' self-regulatory capacities, and they will act in ways inconsistent with expectations of the classroom community. Here, we would like to introduce a crucial aspect of our work—the triage conversation.

We define the triage conversation as the private, respectful conversation that occurs between a teacher and a student to address the student's state of physiological, emotional, or behavioral dysregulation. The conversation does not set out to chastise or punish the student. The focus is to create opportunities for the student to move forward in a positive manner. Importantly, we never view the triage conversation as a 'forced apology'; rather, we are trying to build students' insight and self-reflection. It can take years of repeated, compassionate work together to bring some students to a point where they are comfortable and receptive to honest, growth-orientated triage conversations. We certainly encourage using restorative practices and restorative conversations (McCluskey *et al.* 2008) in triage conversations.

We provide triage conversation examples throughout this book to illustrate how our trauma-informed, strengths-based language can open up pathways to mutual respect and growth. Here are some examples of triage conversations that integrate language from the Body domain:

'We have had a difficult situation today. Let's talk about it. I noticed that your behavior escalated very quickly, but I did not see what happened. Can you tell me about it?'

'You have shown so much self-regulation this morning, but something must have happened a little while ago. Can you tell me what that was? When did you first notice your body becoming stressed and dysregulated?'

'You have had such a present morning. You were present for your friends, and you were present for your work. However, when you came back from recess, you seemed distracted and unfocused. Something must have happened; can we talk about it?'

'Gosh, it looked as if things escalated quickly out there on the playground. Before we talk about your choices, can you take me back there? What part of your body did you first notice changing? What part of your body did you first notice clenching up? What started to shift for you?'

REVISITING DEV

Let us revisit Dev, who we introduced at the beginning of this chapter. When we learned the trauma background to Dev's story, we felt so much empathy for him and great sadness at what he had experienced. At five years old, Dev was witness to family violence. In the following years, Dev and his sister moved between extended family members, some of whom believed in punishing children for perceived misbehavior, with severe physical consequences. After a few years, he was removed from the family and placed in foster homes, but he never stayed anywhere for long.

As we looked at Dev through the lens of the unmet needs of the body, it became clear to us he was almost constantly in a state of survival mode. Dev had an altered baseline of stress: his heart frequently raced, he was constantly looking out for threats, and his body was primed to protect himself and escape, not for learning and connection. He sat in the classroom, waiting and watching for signs someone was going to hurt him or others. Dev's threat defense detector fired constantly, his stress response activated, and his body filled with stress hormones. A loud voice, a door slamming, someone yelling would activate his stress response and result in a shutdown.

The acts of violence Dev had witnessed were all perpetrated by people much bigger and stronger than him. Due to his extreme helplessness, Dev did not experience fight or flight; he had a freeze reaction. Dev's path towards survival was to disconnect from the moment—his response was to dissociate. Seeing Dev's unmet needs from this perspective helped us understand why he was often vague, foggy, and detached from the moment. Dev's physiological and nervous systems met his needs in the best way they knew how: prioritizing survival.

Dev was too dysregulated, stressed, and hypervigilant to form the sort of enduring relationship Mr. Freeman was trying to develop. Yes, Dev needed adults in his life who provided a sense of warmth, stability, and safety. However, he also needed these adults to go one step further and provide him with regular and repeated opportunities to de-escalate his stress response, and build his capacity for self-regulation. Furthermore, any top-down strategy for helping Dev develop insight into his thoughts, feelings, and behaviors was futile when he was in survival mode. In that mode, he did not have access to higher-order parts of his brain that enabled self-insight and perspective-taking.

We need to be clear here: Dev needed substantial professional clinical and therapeutic support for his symptoms of trauma and ongoing distress. However, we also advocate strongly that a lot could be done within the classroom to address his highly dysregulated stress response. The first step Mr. Freeman took was to create a safe space Dev could call his own and where he could feel safe and secure. Dev knew he was able to go to this safe space whenever he chose to do so. Together, Mr. Freeman and Dev developed a Ready to Learn Plan he could enact when he was feeling distressed or overwhelmed. In contrast to his initial impression that he was getting nowhere with Dev, Mr. Freeman realized it was huge progress when Dev began to identify early warning signs that he was feeling dysregulated, then proactively retreated to his safe space to listen to music on his headphones.

Mr. Freeman then turned his focus to whole-class strategies and implemented classroom rhythms through the school day that provided all students with soothing and regulating experiences. One of Mr. Freeman's great passions was music, and he created drumming patterns and brain breaks that involved the students clapping their hands, clicking their fingers, and drumming their hands on their desks. Mr. Freeman started the drumming rhythms at a fast rate and then reduced the pace until it mirrored a slow and regular heart rate rhythm.

Mr. Freeman understood the incredible importance of developing a strong relationship with Dev. However, he revised his approach. Mr. Freeman reflected that he was much bigger than Dev, and his size may be inherently threatening for him. He began to monitor Dev's signs of stress closely and to respond appropriately. When Dev was visibly stressed, Mr. Freeman reminded himself it was essential for him to draw out his skills in co-regulation. He kept his voice soft and calm. He approached Dev from the side, never from the front. He got down on one knee or kept his distance.

When Mr. Freeman could perceive Dev was having a moment of self-regulation, he used the opportunity to build rapport and connection through humor, or by giving Dev a high five or a fist bump. Mr. Freeman developed his mindfulness practice and rekindled a long-lost passion for weekend bike rides to bring his calmest self to the classroom. Several months later, Mr. Freeman contacted us to tell us Dev had approached him after class one day to show him a song he had produced using a musical software program on the school's computers. Mr. Freeman told us it took him everything he had to keep calm during the interaction; however, when Dev left the room, he fist-pumped the air.

SOME CONCLUDING THOUGHTS

It is important to keep in mind that the classroom can be a stress-inducing experience for most students. We think of all the cognitive tasks a child is asked to do in a school day—to concentrate, to remember, to think laterally, to sequence multi-step directions, to connect with others. Our experience is that stress impacts *all* these capacities. Through our work in Body, we aim to help students increase their ability to deal with the usual ups and downs of the school day. The strategies outlined in this chapter aim to equip teachers with a toolkit for placing the body at the center of their classroom and care.

We know that, for some students, the classroom is the most stable and predictable setting in their lives. We encourage teachers to see the many things they can do to help all students to meet the needs of the body proactively and pre-emptively. Through both bottom-up and top-down regulatory approaches, we equip students with strategies for soothing the stress response and strengthening their self-regulatory capacities. Even simple things can make an enormous difference, such as giving students regular opportunities to move, and empowering them with the language to recognize and communicate times when they are becoming stressed or their behavior is escalating. We want students to have thousands of experiences of moments at school in which they feel a sense of safety, predictability, and belonging.

We also remember it takes a calm regulated classroom for teachers to do their best work. Dysregulation demands a considerable proportion of teachers' time, resources, and mental energy. When a class is well regulated, and students are on task, the teacher has the time and space to spend with individual students and check in on their progress. When students are on task, the teacher can provide invaluable, individualized instruction tailored to their learning needs and goals. In this way, prioritizing the needs of the body is a foundation for learning and academic growth. Supporting students to soothe their stress response and build their regulatory capacities also enhances their opportunities for enduring and authentic connections—a topic we turn to next in Chapter 5, Relationship.

SELF-REFLECTION CHECKLIST

After completing this chapter, please check you can do the following:

- ✓ Understand the importance of both bottom-up and top-down strategies for student regulation.

- ✓ Identify signs of bodily dysregulation and escalation in your students.

- ✓ Consider age-appropriate strategies for explicitly teaching students about stress and the fight-flight-freeze response.

- ✓ Integrate mindfulness into your classroom and support students to bring their attention to the present moment.

- ✓ Use the language of present, centered, and ready to learn with students.

- ✓ Develop, use, and refine your recipe for co-regulation.

- ✓ Implement tools such as the Ready to Learn Scale and Ready to Learn Plans to build students' capacities to meet their unmet needs.

- ✓ Prioritize your wellbeing and minimize decision fatigue to bring your most regulated self to the classroom.

CHAPTER 5

Relationship

In this chapter, you will learn about:

- the role of strong student-teacher relationships in student learning and wellbeing

- pathways for cultivating secure attachments and unconditional positive regard with students

- strategies for nurturing enduring relationships with students.

Sasha was a Grade 11 student, aged 17, who was holding on at school. While the student support staff were unclear with the family's history, Sasha reported a great deal of conflict in her home. Sasha's teachers were also aware her housing could be unstable, and she often stayed with different friends for days at a time.

Many of her teachers had great admiration for Sasha. She put much of her effort into artistic pursuits and was constantly creating beautifully detailed sketches in her school notebooks. She was spirited, courageous, and highly opinionated on social issues. She was often the first to speak out about perceived injustices in the community and world. However, Sasha was involved in social drama—frequently. Her alliances seemed to shift on a daily, even hourly, basis. Often, she came back to class after breaks either furious at one of her peers or in tears. She was a leader in her peer group and fiercely loyal to her friends, but would often berate her friends or act in ways teachers perceived as demanding or manipulative. Sasha had also been at the center of several significant social media issues that were escalated to the school leadership team.

In addition to ongoing challenges in her social relationships, Sasha's academic progress was a cause of concern. She described a range of physical complaints such as headaches, stomach aches, and nausea. Her attendance was inconsistent, and she had missed a considerable amount of school. Often, she would arrive at school and then leave after an hour or so, saying she felt unwell. When Sasha did attend, she often refused to do the learning tasks, claiming she did not understand or was too far behind to catch up.

Our team attended a student study meeting at Sasha's school. During the meeting Sasha's teacher, Ms. Lee, asked our advice on working with Sasha and helping to shift her academic trajectory. Ms. Lee shared numerous strategies she had tried to support Sasha to engage in the work—asking her to try her best, promising rewards, sitting with her, and threatening the negative consequences of not trying. It seemed it did not matter what Ms. Lee did; once Sasha decided she was not going to do her work, nothing could convince her otherwise. Ms. Lee appeared exhausted, deflated, and at a loss about what to do next.

After hearing Ms. Lee's concerns, another teacher attending the meeting shared that he thought it was all about the relationship with Sasha. He said that in his own work with struggling students he focused first on building a strong relationship. Everyone in the meeting nodded in agreement: 'Yes, it is all about the relationship. Once students feel safe and secure in their relationship with you, then you can ask them to do the work.' Our team appreciated this advice, but we wanted to delve deeper, so we asked more questions. How should Ms. Lee build this relationship? What does she need to do? The teachers shared that Ms. Lee should spend time getting to know Sasha, find out her interests, and build the relationship from there. Someone in the meeting suggested Sasha loved art, so perhaps Ms. Lee could engage her by discussing her love of creative projects. Ms. Lee agreed to try this, and we decided to review progress in a few weeks.

The time came for our follow-up meeting, and the first thing we did was ask Ms. Lee about how things were going with Sasha. Ms. Lee reflected that her relationship with Sasha had come a long way. She had found out more about her love of art, and they had several constructive chats outside the classroom. Everyone in the meeting looked pleased and commended Ms. Lee on her excellent work. Amid all the positive responses it took a few moments to notice that Ms. Lee did not look happy at all. She looked even more deflated than when we had met previously. When we asked Ms. Lee to elaborate on what was going on, her voice trembled into tears. 'Yes, my relationship with Sasha has come a long way. However, I still cannot get her to do the work. What am I doing wrong?'

BEYOND STUDENT INTERESTS

The story of Sasha and Ms. Lee is one of many similar stories we could share. We regularly hear teachers keep saying the 'r' word: *relationship, relationship, relationship*. We have had countless conversations about the importance of strong relationships for students. And, rightly so—it would be impossible to understate the importance of nurturing school relationships for all children and young people, let alone those who have experienced early adversity, unstable attachments, and relational rupture. However, when our team asked teachers how to form strong, nurturing relationships with students, we heard the same thing repeatedly: 'Spend time getting to know the student's interests and build a connection from there.'

While we viewed this as a great start, we also had deeper questions. First, we observed that relationships with students could be highly contextual. We witnessed students and teachers having a great chat on the school grounds, but then the same student would quickly escalate half an hour later in a moment of learning stress in the classroom and they would resist teacher instructions. How do teachers ensure that their strong relationships translate to the classroom? Furthermore, many children have significant barriers to building trusting relationships with adults. What strategies can teachers use to connect with students who need more enduring connections?

Other concerns we had were pragmatic. Some teachers, in particular secondary and specialist teachers, can teach over a hundred students each day. Are these teachers meant to have opportunities to develop a relationship with *all* their students? We also know that some students we are most concerned about are the most transient—students with housing instability and those in out-of-home care can frequently move schools during the year. What does a teacher need to do to build relational safety and trust with students who relocate and transfer to new schools? How can teachers meet the emotional needs of students who may not be in their classrooms very long?

We knew we had to think beyond the approach of connecting with students over their interests. With this in mind, we spent time with clinicians and therapists exploring what they do to create a sense of relational safety with children and young people. We identified teachers who were renowned for their ability to connect with kids who resist school relationships—we asked them questions and observed them in action. We devoured the literature on attachment theory, school-based relationships, and school belonging. We identified strategies with both a robust evidence base and practical applicability. We were captivated by questions about how teachers can create nurturing daily interactions with students and how they can create enduring, trusting bonds.

In this chapter, we share what we have learned with you. We outline core concepts that have transformed our work and helped us create relational safety and connectedness with students across a variety of schools. We believe in the importance of a range of relationships within the school community—whole school relationships, student-student relationships, and staff-parent relationships. But in this chapter our span is narrower: we focus on student-teacher relationships as a central and primary driver of learning and wellbeing.

THE IMPORTANCE OF STUDENT-TEACHER RELATIONSHIPS

Can you remember your favorite teacher? We invite you to think about what it felt like to be in this teacher's presence and reflect on what made this teacher stand out for you. We have spoken to many people about this topic, and the answers are surprisingly similar. In essence, the teacher *noticed* them; students genuinely felt the teacher cared about them and believed in them; the teacher created a sense of community and connectedness at school; and these were the teachers who could give honest, sometimes confronting, fix-it feedback in valued and respectful ways.

Our observations on the vital importance of strong relationships are reflected in the literature base. Across a range of studies, strong student-teacher relationships are associated consistently with enhanced school motivation and improved academic performance (Cornelius-

White 2007; Klem and Connell 2004; Roorda *et al.* 2011). A review of studies found nurturing student-teacher relationships were related to student engagement and attendance at school, and inversely related to disruptive behaviors, suspensions, and dropping out of school (Quin 2017). Strong student-teacher relationships help students take risks in their learning, develop their passion for learning topics, and pursue ambitious goals. Knowing a teacher believes in them and accepts them allows students to recover from mistakes while maintaining a sense of integrity and feelings of self-worth and efficacy.

In addition to being imperative for learning, strong teacher-student relationships are essential for wellbeing. One of the most robust findings of the wellbeing literature is that social connectedness is related to psychological and physical health (Myers 2000; Uchino, Cacioppo, and Kiecolt-Glaser 1996). For children and adolescents, who spend a substantial proportion of their time at school, a sense of connection and relatedness to their teachers is of primary importance. For students, strong relationships with their teachers foster a sense of belonging and connectedness to the school community (Allen *et al.* 2018). Fascinatingly, strong student-teacher relationships are also important to teachers' wellbeing (Spilt, Koomen, and Thijs 2011).

💡 **KEY IDEA:** Nurturing student-teacher relationships are foundational for student learning, wellbeing, and feelings of belonging at school.

ATTACHMENT THEORY

To help us understand why school-based relationships are so central to wellbeing we turn to attachment theory, which serves as a conceptual underpinning of our relational approach. As we have noted briefly in previous chapters, attachment describes the special bond between an infant or child and their primary caregivers, such as parent, carer, grandparent, and other people involved in the child's care from a young age (Ainsworth 1964; Bowlby 1969). Here, we consider some fundamental aspects of attachment theory and then explore how they apply in the classroom.

Attachment theory proposes that a child's early relational experiences serve as a template for all relationships throughout life. To thrive in their physical, emotional, cognitive, and social development, an infant or child needs to feel safe and secure in the knowledge that their caregivers will meet their needs. They may be physical, such as the need for food and warmth. Equally important are emotional and relational needs, such as a child's need for adults to play with them, smile at them, and comfort them when they are distressed. When children feel confident their needs will be met, they feel safe to explore and learn in the world. Children who are treated with love and care come to see themselves as worthy and lovable, and the world as safe and exciting.

It is concerning then that some students' physical, emotional, and relational needs remain largely unmet (Pearce 2016; van der Kolk 2005). Students who have experienced relational instability, disrupted attachments, and violence often struggle to form enduring friendships and relationships. Students with unstable relationships may not have experienced the modeling of healthy relationships. They may not have an understanding of relational boundaries. Some children view adults as a source of threat and danger rather than a source of security and safety (Bath 2008). We must state that in no way do we blame adults within the child's home for their family's relational concerns. Instead we take a systemic approach. This helpfully suggests that family struggle is the result of many complex intergenerational and community factors. This approach urges that comprehensive supports for children and their families are nested in interdependent community systems (Bronfenbrenner 1979).

Knowing that some students may not have experienced care and safety in their primary attachment relationships helps explain why they may struggle to form enduring bonds at school, despite their teachers' efforts to connect with them. Observing students with empathy also helps us to understand that some students may resort to unhealthy or unhelpful ways of trying to get their emotional and relational needs met. To deepen our exploration of attachment theory, Box 5.1 explores the circle of security framework. In addition, Box 5.2 suggests excellent resources for teachers interested in further understanding the role attachment plays in the classroom.

:ؘؘؘO̗: **KEY IDEA:** Students with a history of relational instability may have a deep unmet need for secure and nurturing attachments, but have difficulty connecting with others in healthy or enduring ways.

BOX 5.1: Circle of security and the classroom

A model that underpins our work is the circle of security model of attachment (Hoffman *et al.* 2017; Powell *et al.* 2016). According to this approach, an attachment figure plays several key roles in a child's life. First, the attachment figure serves as a *secure base* from which to explore the world. When children feel safe and trust that an adult is there to nurture and protect them by establishing healthy boundaries, children feel confident to explore, take healthy risks, and engage in the environment. Adults must establish clear limits to ensure the safety and healthy development of children. When we apply this to the classroom, we see that students feel confident to engage in their learning when they feel a sense of safety, fairness, and security in classroom environments led by their teachers.

Attachment figures also serve as a *safe haven*. After a period of exploration, the child returns to their attachment figure to receive comfort, protection, and reassurance. We see safe haven behavior in the classroom when a student tries something new and looks to the teacher for validation or affirmation. We see it when students run to a teacher after a disagreement in the playground. We see it when a student is distressed or upset and the teacher acts in supportive ways until the student calms down. Equally, we see it when a student has a learning success and the teacher responds with pride and delight.

Once the student receives emotional and relational comfort—whether it is a five-second look of acknowledgment or a 20-minute chat with a calm, supportive teacher—they are ready to explore the world again. Throughout the day, children and young people repeatedly move through this circle of going out and exploring the world, encountering the boundaries and limits of the classroom, and then returning to trusted adults for comfort and co-regulation.

We find this framework particularly helpful when we consider the unmet needs of children who have experienced trauma and instability. Some children and young people may have little experience of adult figures serving as their secure base by maintaining consistent expectations at home or school. They may require substantial support from their teachers to feel safe enough to explore the world through their learning.

Other students may have had limited opportunities to develop their capacities to regulate stress as well as their emotions and feelings. They may need frequent co-regulatory experiences with their teachers to help them to make sense of what they are feeling, and to feel better. When we consider the circle of security, we see the importance of supporting students' exploration within healthy limits, and of helping them co-regulate their feelings and experiences. We find this framework is also invaluable in identifying students' moment-to-moment relational needs. In each moment, teachers can ask themselves if a student needs them to serve as an encouraging and supportive base for exploration, or as a safe haven of calm, comfort, and emotional safety.

BOX 5.2: Attachment resources

If you are interested in learning more about applying attachment in classrooms, we recommend the following excellent resources.

Bombèr, L. (2007) *Inside I'm Hurting: Practical Strategies for Supporting Children with Attachment Difficulties in Schools.* London: Worth Publishing.

Bombèr, L. and Hughes, D. (2013) *Settling Troubled Pupils to Learn: Why Relationships Matter in School.* London: Worth Publishing.

Brooks, R. (2020) *The Trauma and Attachment-Aware Classroom: A Practical Guide to Supporting Children who have Encountered Trauma and Adverse Childhood Experiences.* London: Jessica Kingsley Publishing.

Colley, D. and Cooper, P. (2017) *Emotional Development and Attachment in the Classroom: Theory and Practice.* London: Jessica Kingsley Publishing.

Delaney, M. (2017) *Attachment for Teachers: The Essential Handbook for Trainee Teachers and NQTs.* London: Worth Publishing.

Geddes, H. (2006) *Attachment in the Classroom: The Links Between Children's Early Experience, Emotional Wellbeing and Performance in School.* London: Worth Publishing.

Marshall, N. (2014) *The Teacher's Introduction to Attachment: Practical Essentials for Teachers, Carers and School Support Staff.* London: Jessica Kingsley Publishers.

Riley, P. (2010) *Attachment Theory and the Teacher-Student Relationship: A Practical Guide for Teachers, Teacher Educators and School Leaders.* London: Routledge.

ATTACHMENT AND CO-REGULATION

In Chapter 4, Body, we spoke about the importance of co-regulation in soothing students' dysregulated stress response systems. Here, we further explore the role of attachment, co-regulation, and students' ability to self-regulate their physical and emotional states. In particular, we shine a light on the role of attachment in building students' self-regulatory capacities and helping them to regulate stress (see Schore and Schore 2007).

First, consider that when an infant or child feels stressed or distressed, they seek closeness and comfort from an adult caregiver. If the adult responds in a comforting and soothing way, the infant or child comes to understand adults are there to meet their needs, and so the child begins to feel better. These nurturing and responsive interactions build both strong attachments and the child or young person's self-regulatory capacities (Schore and Schore 2007). Children and young people rely on nurturing and consistent co-regulatory experiences to develop their own capacity to regulate stress.

Without loving and supportive early experiences that help to scaffold their self-regulatory capacities, some students may have low levels of resilience, difficulties in impulse control, or display aggressive behaviors. Disrupted attachments and relational trauma can lead to an impaired capacity to regulate emotions, affect, and physiological states (Schore 2003; van der Kolk 2005). Consequently, some students have highly dysregulated stress response systems, and therefore do not have the tools they need to self-regulate their stress response or self-soothe.

Considering the role of co-regulation in meeting students' unmet needs is where we see the enormous value of attachment theory in the classroom. We are highly respectful of the bounds of the teacher's role. We do not propose that teachers aspire to fulfill students' unmet relational needs in the way parents or carers may do. However, we know teachers are important attachment figures. They can provide students with co-regulatory experiences that are exceptionally healing for young people. For example, when a student shows a fight-flight-freeze response, the teacher stays as calm as possible and communicates a sense of safety and acceptance, supporting the student to de-escalate. Similarly, when students challenge relational bonds with resistant behaviors, teachers can maintain a firm and calm presence. Every time a teacher provides a nurturing co-regulatory experience, they both support the student in the moment and strengthen the student's ability to regulate stress over time. The influence of being soothed and comforted in times of distress helps students build their own capacity for self-regulation (Brumariu 2015).

🔆 **KEY IDEA:** Nurturing student-teacher relationships help students regulate stress in escalated moments, and also build their own capacity to meet their unmet relational needs over time.

NEUROCEPTION AND POLYVAGAL THEORY

As we seek to further understand the relational needs of students in the classroom, it is helpful to reflect on the emerging science of neuroception and polyvagal theory. Professor Stephen Porges (2004, 2011) coined the term *neuroception* to describe the neural circuits and neurobiological processes that are activated as humans evaluate whether situations are safe or threatening. Imagine you walk into a room and encounter an unfamiliar person; your neural and physical responses will differ if the person appears angry to you compared to if the person appears calm and welcoming. Even before any words are exchanged, your neural networks are assessing the person's non-verbal cues, body language, and general physical presence. They are facilitating an appropriate response that ensures your emotional and physical safety. In particular, neuroception relies on neural circuits that regulate muscles of the face and head, the ability to make eye contact, to vocalize in a calm manner, and to discriminate the human voice from other noises in the environment. Your evaluation of the situation is immediate, and largely subconscious. This ability to scan people and the environment, and make an assessment of safety, forms the essence of neuroception.

As we seek to understand neuroception's underpinning mechanisms, we turn to polyvagal theory (Porges 2004, 2011). This is a complex and sophisticated theory, and exploring it fully is beyond this book's scope. However, we do want to highlight key ideas that are useful as we take a trauma-informed, strengths-based approach in the classroom. In essence, *poly* refers to 'many,' and *vagus* refers to the 'vagus nerve.' The vagus nerves are part of the parasympathetic branch of the autonomic nervous system. In particular, we are interested in the *ventral vagus complex*, which is strengthened when people are safe in their environment and connected with others.

Porges (2004, 2011) explains that strong ventral vagal tone leads to increased capacities of the *social engagement system*. This system is central to how people engage with their environments, connect with others, and take part in pro-social activities. Let's return to the situation where you walk into a room and encounter an unfamiliar person. If your neural and sensory networks detect a threat you may engage in defensive reactions and a fight-flight-freeze response is activated. When that unfamiliar person seems angry, you may prepare yourself for a difficult conversation, leave the room, or even experience a sense of immobilization. However, if your neural networks detect feelings of warmth and safety, and the environment is perceived as safe, the fight-flight-freeze response is inhibited, and pro-social behaviors—the social engagement system—are prompted, and so you may engage in a discussion or interact with the person in a warm, friendly manner. In this way, an activated social engagement system facilitates growth, fosters learning, and enhances social connectedness.

NEUROCEPTION IN THE CLASSROOM

We see countless ways in which an understanding of neuroception and polyvagal theory applies in the classroom. First, we know that students have the capacity to scan the room and assess who wants them there and who does not. We understand also that students with a history of violence, trauma, or disrupted attachments often have impaired neuroceptive capacities (Porges 2004). They may have limited capacity to read cues in facial expression, tone of voice, and body language. Similarly, their neural networks may be primed to detect risk and threat when interacting with adults, even if an adult is trying their best to communicate trust and safety to them. This underscores the importance of patience and empathy when forming connections with children and young people with complex unmet needs.

As we appreciate the role of neuroception and polyvagal theory in student learning, we prioritize communicating *safety* in our verbal and non-verbal interactions. This leads us to keep our face calm and remain aware of our tone and pace of speech. It leads us to treat students in an honest and genuine manner. If we try to mask moments of irritation or frustration in disingenuous ways, students often detect how we truly feel through their highly attuned neuroceptive capacities. A student may experience the incongruence between our words and our underlying feelings as confusing and destabilizing. A most effective way of fostering relational safety is to engage in play and genuine humor (not sarcasm). When we interact with others in playful, fun, and humorous ways, we send neuroceptive messages that the environment is safe.

🔆 **KEY IDEA:** Neuroception involves the sophisticated neural networks that interpret whether environments are safe or threatening. We aspire to provide students with relational safety and connection, so their social engagement systems are activated in the classroom.

UNCONDITIONAL POSITIVE REGARD

We once spoke with a highly experienced teacher who had a passion for connecting with students. He explained that sometimes teachers find it challenging to feel and think positively about some students and he shared some examples. It can be difficult, he observed, to feel warmth towards a student who damages school property, or one who provokes other students, or a student who never seems to listen—many factors may influence how teachers feel about students. The teacher's advice was that it is invaluable to form a positive understanding of the child, to see through surface behaviors and nurture genuine care and affection for each student. This teacher was espousing the value of *unconditional positive regard*.

We have adopted the concept of unconditional positive regard through our work with clinicians and therapists. Humanistic psychologist, Professor Carl Rogers (1961), popularized the term and credited Dr. Stanley Standal (1954) with first developing the theory.

Unconditional positive regard facilitates an environment in which the student feels valued and accepted regardless of their behaviors, emotions, failures, or successes in the classroom. When we act with acceptance and empathy towards students, we help them cultivate feelings of self-esteem and self-acceptance. Nurturing unconditional positive regard for students helps create highly relational classrooms built on acceptance, empathy, and trust.

As we introduce this approach, we want to be clear that unconditional positive regard does not mean being constantly positive or happy with students—a constant state of positivity is not helpful, nor even possible. A teacher can have deep feelings of warmth, empathy, acceptance, and respect for students, and still feel frustrated, confused, or even escalated when confronted with a range of behaviors students may enact in the classroom. What unconditional positive regard does entail is maintaining a sense of care, empathy, and respect for students, independent of what they might do or say in the classroom. Here, we describe four key pathways to creating conditions for unconditional positive regard for students. The pathways are represented in Figure 5.1.

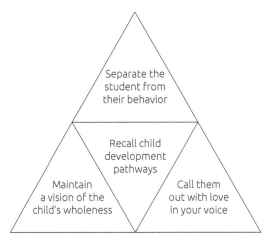

Figure 5.1: Unconditional positive regard triangle

PATHWAYS TO UNCONDITIONAL POSITIVE REGARD

Our first pathway to fostering unconditional positive regard is to separate students from their behavior. We have all heard examples of teachers referring to a 'crazy student' or a 'lazy class.' When we reflect on and plan for students, we shift our language from 'this student is really challenging' to 'this student's *behavior* is really challenging.' We remember that all students may have moments when they struggle to act in ways we hope or expect, but this does not define who they are as a person. In your thinking and communicating, we recommend separating a student from their behavior at all times—whether you are interacting with a student, speaking about a student with other teachers, or planning for a student.

Separating students from their behavior paves the way for the next aspect of unconditional positive regard: maintaining a vision of the child's wholeness. Time and time again, students who present escalated or disengaging behaviors are designated to a particular trajectory. When we do this, we lower our expectations for those students, who can often tell how we feel about them through observing our verbal and non-verbal communication. When we maintain a vision of a child's wholeness, we maintain our hope that the child can fulfill their academic goals, build their social and emotional capacities, and be a positive member of the classroom community. We remember that children often understand non-verbally which adults are in their corner and which adults want them out of the room. We also remember there may be only a small number of adults at this point in the child or young person's life who hold a belief in their potential. It is up to us to be the safe haven for them, and to maintain a vision that all our students are on a journey to meeting their own needs in healthy ways.

Our next pathway for unconditional positive regard is to remember the developmental gates the student may not have passed through. This pathway reminds teachers that some students' needs for care, safety, and stability remain largely unmet. Consider the unmet needs of a student presenting dysregulated behaviors—we see them from a unique viewpoint when we realize this student may not have received adequate co-regulatory experiences, nor been exposed to healthy role models for how to respond to stress. Considering students' unmet developmental needs reminds us that acting in dysregulated ways may not be the student's choice—nor their fault. Determining who to blame does not lead to proactive planning.

Separating students from their behavior, maintaining a vision of their wholeness, and remembering the developmental gates they may have missed—these three pathways lead to the final aspect of unconditional positive regard which is to call them out with love in your voice. When teachers have developed a relationship based on understanding and acceptance, they can be honest with students. Calling them out with a wink in your eye and love in your voice is when you sit down next to a student who is off task and say, 'Come on, buddy, let's get back to work.' Once we have built that foundation of acceptance and respect, students know that constructive feedback comes from an underlying assumption: 'I know you can do it.' In Box 5.3 we acknowledge the importance of recognizing that sometimes unconditional positive regard is hard.

BOX 5.3: When unconditional positive regard is hard

It is helpful to know when our unconditional positive regard is being tested. What challenges a teacher's capacity for unconditional positive regard? The range of teachers' reflections has surprised us. Some find it difficult to hold unconditional positive regard for students who have a distinct body odor or spit saliva when they talk. Others struggle to extend unconditional positive regard to those who make fun of others for their gender, identity, culture, or country of origin.

It is important for every teacher to identify and reflect on the students who make it difficult for them to hold unconditional positive regard. We invite you to take a moment and ask yourself two questions:

- When is it hard for me to have unconditional positive regard?

- When is it easy for me to have unconditional positive regard?

Becoming aware of your unconscious and conscious biases can help you develop awareness of when you struggle to maintain feelings of unconditional positive regard for students. Exploring situations that escalate your stress response helps you both prepare de-escalating strategies as needed, and maintain a calm and accepting classroom presence.

POWER WITHIN RELATIONSHIPS

As we turn to the topic of power within relationships, we want to first acknowledge that some people are uncomfortable with the word 'power' and may be more comfortable with the word 'empowerment.' However, we are intentional and thoughtful in using 'power' because we want teachers and students to understand how power can be used positively and negatively in relationships.

We would like to acknowledge explicitly that power is inherent in *all* relationships, including the student-teacher relationship. In particular, we consider that the relationship between a student and a teacher is not one of equals. Teachers hold positions of power and authority—their roles allow them to set norms, rules, and expectations for students in the classroom (Reid and Kawash 2017).

There are different ways teachers can approach power in the classroom, including permissive, authoritarian, and authoritative styles (Walker 2008). *Permissive* teaching involves a laid-back approach: standards are relaxed, and students experience imbalanced freedom and too much unhelpful control. Teachers who customarily use permissive styles may be popular on a surface level, but often students do not feel safe or contained and their behavior can become dysregulated. We liken this to the teacher giving their power to the students in ways that do not create a secure base within the classroom. By contrast, in *authoritarian* teaching the teacher holds all the power. Students are given little autonomy or voice. Rules are often enforced strictly. Authoritarian teachers can use power coercively, issuing threats to students and punitive responses for even minor rule breaches. We refer to this as 'dominator values of power'—that is, one person tries to dominate another.

Authoritative teaching is different. It involves a balance between high behavioral expectations and nurturing relational interactions. In our work, we refer to this pro-social or collaborative approach as *sharing power* with students. We share power with students when we develop a sense of belonging and community in the classroom. We share power when we genuinely listen to students and take on board their suggestions, concerns, and feedback. We share power when we involve students in decision-making and give them a voice in developing classroom rules and expectations. We share power when we acknowledge a community's culture and integrate students' and families' cultural practices in ways that recognize and honor diversity.

In addition to considering student-teacher relationships, it is also useful to consider students' unmet needs through the frame of power. Our aim is to have our students feel empowered in healthy relationships; however, many students who struggle with their behavior may not feel a healthy sense of personal power in the ways they feel about themselves or relate to others. We consider that students who have experienced trauma and instability may have had limited experiences of socially acceptable expressions of power; they may have been exposed to, or been victims of, dominator behaviors of aggression, violence, manipulation, or other maladaptive forms of power, coercion, and control.

As we consider power within the classroom, we see that when students feel threatened, stressed, or vulnerable, they can resort to many ways of regaining a sense of personal power and control. We see this concept in action when a teacher asks a student to do something and the student does the opposite. We see it when a student resorts to unhelpful actions when they feel a lack of autonomy and control. With this in mind, we recommend teachers be proactive and intentional about the role of relational power in their classrooms. This is particularly important when interacting with students who enact the same dominator values they may experience within their families or other classrooms. It is important for teachers to model healthy relationships through nurturing a shared, collective sense of power. Box 5.4 invites you to reflect on power dynamics within your own life and classroom. Box 5.5 provides an example of power in action.

🔆 **KEY IDEA:** Sharing power with students helps meet, in healthy ways, their needs for autonomy, control, and self-efficacy in the classroom.

BOX 5.4: Teacher reflection and discussion

Consider a relationship in your life where you and the other person are equals. You collaborate, make decisions together, and feel as if you can express your feelings and ideas in respectful and assertive ways. How is power shared within this relationship?

Next, consider a relationship you struggled to maintain because there was a power imbalance and the relationship felt unequal. Perhaps there were conditions that needed to be met for the relationship to survive. As an example, many of us, including our students, may have relationships built on a shaky foundation that follows this template: 'I will only respect you, *if* you respect me.' What effect did this unequal sense of power have on the relationship?

Consider power dynamics in your classrooms. Do you stand over students or crouch down and get on their level? Do you use a loud voice to exert your authority? Do you use a quiet voice that helps students to co-regulate and encourages them to listen? What kinds of things do you do to maintain power over students? In what ways do you share power with students?

Finally, how do you feel when students try to exert their power in their interactions with you? What do you notice in your body when a student competes with you for power in a moment? How do you respond in these situations?

BOX 5.5: An example of power in action

Take a moment to picture Felix, a student aged eight with a history of disrupted relationships and unstable attachments. Felix's teacher had worked hard to build a strong relationship with him through consistency, unconditional positive regard, humor, and playfulness. Felix and his teacher had a moment the teacher interpreted as a real connection when Felix opened up about some of his hopes and aspirations. The teacher left work that day feeling optimistic and hopeful there was meaningful progress in building a connection with Felix.

But the next day things did not go well. While the teacher was explaining a concept, Felix started kicking another student's chair. The teacher told him to stop and return to the learning task. Felix stopped when the teacher was looking, but a moment later started kicking the chair again. The teacher, feeling increasingly frustrated and disappointed, yelled: 'Felix! This is ridiculous. Stop it or get out!' Felix got up, threw his chair over, and walked out.

We can gain insight into this situation when we consider it through the lens of power. Felix was trying to gain a sense of power and control in a situation he perceived as threatening. His teacher escalated and reacted from a place of dominator values.

Instead of feeling empowered to de-escalate, Felix was left with one choice for maintaining his own self-concept in the power challenge.

Felix's teacher shared on reflection, 'I lost my cool and resorted to some of my past reactions.' The teacher then explained how he sat down with Felix the next day and apologized like this: 'I care about you, and I'm sorry I embarrassed you in front of the room. I can understand why you left in anger. What I did created a no-win situation for you. You and I have to figure out a way to communicate so you can let me know when you need support. I didn't take the time to understand why you were kicking the student in front of you. Was he bothering you? Or did you feel a little lost in the lesson? Let's start with two agreements. I will work on not embarrassing you. And I want you to consider how you can let me know when you need my help to figure things out.'

BUCKET AND DIPPER THEORY

Now we want to explore a strategy with positive outcomes in many of our classrooms—bucket and dipper theory (Rath and Clifton 2004). Bucket and dipper theory provides a simple metaphor for building strong relationships. It is relevant for people of all ages, and can be understood by the youngest members of the school community.

First, consider that everyone has an invisible bucket. When students experience enriching and nurturing social interactions their buckets become filled, and they feel filled. They have the emotional reservoirs needed to engage with others and their learning in meaningful ways. But when people's buckets are empty, they feel empty. Taking this one step further, we can link an empty bucket with hypo-aroused or hyper-aroused behaviors. When students have an empty bucket, they may appear flat and withdrawn (hypo-aroused), or may appear heightened, impatient, anxious, or shaky (hyper-aroused).

When we introduce bucket and dipper theory explicitly to students, we equip them with a simple tool that builds their social and emotional intelligence. We find immense value when students can self-reflect that their buckets are feeling empty and they proactively reach out to others for connection or to meet their unmet needs in other healthy ways. This metaphor also provides a shortcut for members of the school community to communicate with each other about how they are feeling. A student may comment to their teacher, 'My bucket feels empty today.' A teacher may share with a colleague, 'It has been a big day. I think I need to go home and do something that fills my bucket.'

In the next layer of the theory we consider that everyone has an invisible dipper. When we interact positively with someone, we fill their buckets. Bucket-filling behaviors include greeting students warmly first thing in the morning, sharing a smile, communicating empathy and safety, and treating students with kindness. In contrast, we dip from others' buckets when we speak harshly to them, when we are not mindful of their feelings, or when we treat them as if they do not matter. This simple idea helps even the youngest students in the school community reflect on how they interact with others, and how they can build positive relationships through nurturing daily interactions.

Our observations of some students moving through the school day inspire and motivate us to promote the bucket and dipper theory. Some students constantly receive critical feedback and negative comments: 'do this,' 'do not do this,' 'you did this wrong,' 'you need to try harder,' 'you did not remember to bring this.' We imagine how depleting it is for a child or young person to go through a school day continually hearing negative, destructive comments. We remember that some students arrive at school in the morning with empty buckets. They have significant unmet relational and emotional needs, and may have limited resources to draw from when called to perform all the tasks required of them in the school day.

From the moment students arrive at school in the morning—when we greet them with a warm smile, when we say how nice it is to see them—we have the opportunity to help fill their buckets. In doing so, we add to their emotional reservoirs. We invest in their capacity to regulate their behavior, to take risks in their learning, and to engage meaningfully with others. Box 5.6 provides examples of teachers filling their students' buckets in the classroom.

🔆 **KEY IDEA:** Filling students' buckets builds connectedness and invests in their capacity to stay present, centered, and ready to learn in the classroom.

BOX 5.6: Bucket-filling strategies for the classroom

- Doing 'shout outs' to students during morning circle time, recognizing birthdays and special events, highlighting student accomplishments and their use of character strengths.

- Making 'I notice' statements such as 'I notice that today you've shown so much kindness to your friends.'

- Having a bucket bulletin board for a month that involves a colorful visual display and celebration of bucket-filling behaviors.

- Having a special 'www' (what went well) circle at the end of the week that celebrates student achievements and their use of character strengths, with the aim of filling students' buckets before they go home for the weekend.

THE TRIAGE CONVERSATION

Let's consider how the language of the Relationship domain can be used in the triage conversation. In this example, the teacher is aware the student has struggled to form healthy classroom relationships and often enacts a dominator version of power:

> Today was rough in group work, wasn't it? I notice how much you usually do to empower your group. However, today when you did not let your group mates contribute to your plans for the project, things did not go well. Let's figure out some ways you can share power with your group tomorrow.

Here it is the teacher's responsibility to brainstorm different strategies that help the student redefine what personal empowerment means. Many students believe they are successful with their friends if they force others to agree with them. Moments like these are valuable opportunities for showing students new ways to understand the power of collaboration and to strengthen their own classroom communities. Building on these strategies, Box 5.7 provides an example that actively integrates concepts from the Relationship domain.

BOX 5.7: The Relationship domain in action

Imagine that the end of the school year is approaching. It is a time when some students' dysregulation escalates as they face changes in routine, shifting relationships with their teachers and peers, and unpredictability about what comes next. Imagine it is Monday of the last week of term. A student is having a difficult day. By lunchtime, his unmet needs are so extreme he starts destroying a classroom display of students' artwork, tearing down the posters and throwing them on the floor.

Here we outline two different responses to the student's dysregulation. Response A does not apply attachment and co-regulatory principles. Response B is based on an understanding of how the student's unmet needs may influence his behavior. We invite you to reflect on the two responses and consider similar or different ways you may respond if faced with a similar situation.

RESPONSE A

After repeatedly yelling at the student to stop destroying the classroom display, the teacher calls the assistant principal. The assistant principal takes the student to his office and reprimands him for his destructive behavior. The student is made to sit outside the assistant principal's office by himself while his parents are called and informed. The assistant principal decides the student needs to spend the next three recess periods inside.

RESPONSE B

The teacher reflects on how much the student must be struggling at this moment. He is not being intentionally defiant but has not yet developed the capacity to self-soothe when he experiences distressing or uncomfortable emotions. Taking a deep breath, the teacher calls the assistant principal for support so there is another adult in the room. The assistant principal sits quietly and side-by-side with the student, supporting him to de-escalate. The assistant principal trusts in the relationship they have with the student and knows the student will center himself with support.

After some time sitting together, the assistant principal shares his own feeling of being escalated about the end of the year and suggests they can create a picture together to remind them of the school year. The student agrees to this and they draw a picture of some of their favorite parts of the year. As they do so, they chat quietly about things that have happened, such as the sports day and class trips. When the student has calmed down, the assistant principal supports the student to repair the display of artwork by fixing the ripped paper with tape and sticking everything back on the wall. The assistant principal has a calm, firm, caring chat with him about why destroying the display requires restoration, and supports him to repair the ruptures to the relationships. The assistant principal and teacher agree that one of them will call the student's parents, so that school and home can work together to support him through this uncertain period of the school year.

REVISITING SASHA

Let's revisit Sasha and Ms. Lee, who we met at the beginning of this chapter. We remember that Sasha has many strengths, but she frequently missed school and on many days refused to do her work in class. Her teacher, Ms. Lee, was determined to build a connection with Sasha and was motivated to put trauma-informed, strengths-based strategies into action.

Ms. Lee started with the simple objective of filling Sasha's bucket to the point that she wanted to come to school. She began by looking at the micro-moments of connection throughout the school day—when she passed Sasha in the school grounds, she made sure to smile warmly, notice something positive Sasha had done, or ask her a question about the day. She told Sasha how wonderful it was to have her in the class that day—and meant it. She made sure to keep her expression warm and relaxed, not stressed or frustrated, which sent neuroceptive messages about safety and security to Sasha.

Ms. Lee strived to cultivate a sense of unconditional positive regard for Sasha. She shifted her intervention language to focus on the behavior, not the person. She maintained a vision for her wholeness; that is, she maintained hope that Sasha could successfully finish the school year and one day meet her own emotional needs in healthy and proactive ways. Considering Sasha's history of instability fostered a sense of empathy and care for her, rather than constantly feeling frustrated and hopeless.

Ms. Lee shared her surprise that the most significant difference came when she started to call Sasha out with love in her voice. She was consistent and explicit about having Sasha complete her learning tasks. 'I care about you enough to sit here with you until we get this work done.' 'I know you can move past this morning.' 'I believe in you enough to tell you that you need to put more effort in right now.' When Ms. Lee held Sasha to firm and fair standards, she began to slowly change her behavior. Ms. Lee had a realization: she may be the first person in Sasha's current school who communicated to Sasha a genuine belief in her potential for learning success.

For Ms. Lee, an 'aha' moment came when she reconsidered Sasha's refusal to do her work through the lens of power. There may not be much that Sasha felt control over in her life—each day was filled with volatility and instability. It could be that her refusal to do learning tasks was an attempt to fulfill her need for control and autonomy. While it impeded her learning in the long term, refusing to do her work in the short term allowed Sasha to feel she was in charge of her life at that precise moment. While Ms. Lee maintained control of her class, she took simple steps to share power with Sasha. She always got down low when speaking with her, rather than standing over her. She provided Sasha with choices about tasks or projects. She asked for Sasha's opinion on topics the class would be learning. Over time, she drew on Sasha's passion for social justice and encouraged her to pursue leadership opportunities in school community projects that provided her with feelings of self-efficacy and self-worth.

We received a call from Ms. Lee who told us Sasha would soon move to a kinship placement across the state, and would leave the school community. We responded with empathy. We knew Ms. Lee had put her heart into connecting with Sasha and it would be hard to say goodbye. Again Ms. Lee surprised us. Yes, she was disappointed that she had not had more time with Sasha. She was also proud of what they achieved together. Knowing she had persisted despite the barriers to connectedness Sasha put forward was a source of immense pride and meaning for her. Our team was especially moved on hearing this next bit—when Ms. Lee found out Sasha was leaving, she got a notebook similar to the one Sasha constantly drew on. She asked school staff to contribute notes and draw pictures for her. In her own message, she wrote what she hoped she had communicated during their time together: 'You matter. You can do this. Wherever you are, always remember there are people at this school who care about you and who believe in you. We will miss you.'

SOME CONCLUDING THOUGHTS

The research underpinning this work suggests that teachers want to teach because they want to nurture healthy relationships for their students (Brunzell, Stokes, and Waters 2018). Teachers find immense meaning and joy in interacting with young people, getting to know them, and knowing they have a profound impact on their current and future lives. However, some teachers we work with do not realize the huge barrier trauma can pose to developing enriching relationships with students. The sad truth is that often the students who need the most care and support are those who most test teachers' resolve. Aspiring to form meaningful connections with students can lead teachers to feel helpless, frustrated, and deflated. We see so many teachers' determination and patience start to wane as they pour their hearts into connecting with students, yet feel they are back to square one after a few weeks. When we build insight and empathy, and foster pathways for unconditional positive regard, we persist in developing relationships with students, despite the dysregulated or challenging behaviors they may enact at times.

We also remember that relationships with teachers have the potential to be enormously healing for young people. For some students with complex unmet needs, having an adult who interacts with them in a warm, positive, consistent way is a powerful pathway to self-worth and growth. One of the most healing things we can do for children is to provide them with a sense of safety, trust, and security at school. When we act in kind, respectful, empathetic, and even playful ways with students, we act as role models for healthy relationships. When children know that there are trusted adults to provide a secure base and safe haven it creates wonderful child development outcomes.

We encourage you to think that each interaction with a child or young person matters. You will have the opportunity to work with some students for months or even years, serve as a source of secure attachment, and see them grow in their capacity to meet their own unmet needs. Other students may cross your path for a short amount of time; however, even the briefest moments of filling students' buckets, and of sharing power, make a difference to many children and young people. Nurturing relationships are the center of our approach, and we are sure you agree that they are at the heart of great schools. Children and young people thrive when we invest in respectful, empathetic, and inclusive relationships at school—and, importantly, teachers thrive too.

SELF-REFLECTION CHECKLIST

After completing this chapter, please check you can do the following:

- ✓ Understand the importance of nurturing attachments and teacher-student relationships for student wellbeing and learning.

- ✓ Appreciate the value of co-regulation in supporting students' learning and growth.

- ✓ Consider pathways to unconditional positive regard, including focusing on the behavior, maintaining a vision of the child's wholeness, and remembering the developmental gates that students may have missed.

- ✓ Recognize the importance of calling students out, and of providing fix-it feedback with love in your voice.

- ✓ Attend to power dynamics in your classroom, and invest in simple strategies for sharing power with students.

- ✓ Explore ways that bucket and dipper theory applies in your classroom.

CHAPTER 6

Stamina

In this chapter, you will learn about:

- prioritizing stamina for academic learning

- assisting students in staying focused on growth and improvement

- using tools to track the increase in students' stamina in ways that support their academic growth.

Talia, aged 13, was in Grade 7 and had substantial caring responsibilities at home. Her mother had a physical disability, and she was the oldest child in a large, single-parent family. Over the previous year, Talia increasingly had disengaged from the school community and missed school once or twice a week. When she did attend, Talia appeared anxious and distracted. She was now socially isolated from her friends and instigated social media drama. Talia did not show a great deal of dysregulation or escalation in the classroom. However, her learning outcomes had suffered, and she was completing little work at school or at home.

Talia's teaching team was determined she show up at school. In an effort to set a possible goal, the teachers agreed Talia should have a positive attitude at school and they could enable that by not insisting she complete learning tasks unless she wanted to. The teaching team also agreed Talia did not have to sit tests or exams, and exempted her from homework. Talia's teachers sought our team's opinion about what to do next. When the teachers shared Talia's story, we realized they needed to do much more than have Talia show up. They needed strategies to prove to Talia her time in school mattered. They had to empower Talia with the belief she could increase her stamina for learning.

BUILDING STAMINA IN THE CLASSROOM: A SET OF TOP-DOWN STRATEGIES

It is vital that educators have high expectations for their struggling students' academic learning and growth. All students need to know their time in school matters, their time in school yields visible results. Students like Talia are fairly well regulated in class. They need strategies for their brains, their thinking. We call these top-down strategies. Students who successfully employ their thinking to identify goals for learning, and use thinking strategies to persist when they feel like giving up, are using their brains to self-regulate and learn. It is essential for students to have a whole toolkit of top-down strategies. This chapter, along with Chapter 7, Engagement, and Chapter 8, Character, explore this focus on learning.

We needed to shift the approaches of Talia's teachers so that they believe all students can achieve real growth in their learning within a developmental approach. Students who have a history of limited academic achievement must see real, concrete results from their efforts. We want to see and celebrate the growth and accomplishments of students who have a history of poor learning outcomes. Stamina, the focus of this chapter, is the foundation on which we scaffold academic rigor for students with even the most disrupted school histories.

💡 **KEY IDEA:** All students need to observe that their time in school matters. Teachers need to help students set high expectations for themselves.

THE EXPERIENCE OF LEARNING

Consider a recent time when you struggled reading a text. Was it a complex academic article? An instruction manual? Maybe a recipe that seemed to miss a crucial step? What did this feel like? What impact did this feeling have on your confidence, engagement, and motivation? To understand stamina, you need to understand that real learning involves being pushed into an uncomfortable state of mind. Often the students we work with are happy to sit and do addition worksheets. This is within their capacities—they feel confident and comfortable. Yet this is not real learning or new learning; this is repeating and rehearsing what they can do already.

The heart of the Stamina domain is the recognition that learning can be an uncomfortable process. Learning occurs one minute at a time, one step after another, through deliberate practice. Learning is also built on vulnerability—it requires students to be open to being wrong and making mistakes. It requires striving to understand—even when it feels as if their practice is not paying off. Learning requires students to sit with uncomfortable questions. Can I do this? Am I smart enough for this?

We need to be mindful that when students encounter difficulties in their learning, they can feel exposed in front of their peers and teachers; they can feel as if their failures and insecurities are on show. Like all of us, they often fall back on defensive behaviors or strategies they have developed on their own to compensate for feelings of inadequacy, shame, or embarrassment. These defensive behaviors often involve a student appearing disengaged, distracted, or disruptive. In Box 6.1, we invite you to reflect on stamina in your classroom.

BOX 6.1: Teacher reflection and discussion questions

Take a moment to picture a student in your life. This student may arrive at school with the best intentions of learning. At some point in the school day, though, the student starts an activity they do not understand, or they come across a difficult problem and get stuck.

- What might it be like for this student to face (another) difficulty in their learning?

- What might it be like for this student to look around and see their peers successfully working on the task?

- When faced with the choice of persisting with the challenge or disengaging, which path might this student take?

- What unhelpful or disruptive strategies or behaviors might the student use at this time?

- What impact does the student's dysregulation have on the rest of the class?

MICRO-MOMENTS OF EXPANSION

Through focusing on stamina we aim to support students to tolerate those times when learning is difficult. We know that it is in these moments of learning adversity that teachers have the potential to build students' capacity in overcoming the roadblocks that threaten to derail their learning. We want students to feel what it is like to struggle yet maintain effort and persist. We want students to be comfortable making errors, be willing to take risks, and feel confident to ask for help. We need to understand that stamina is built for our students— and all of us—literally one minute at a time. Maddie Witter (2013), an international author and expert on building stamina for academic success, likens building stamina to a bodybuilder who needs to set incremental weightlifting goals.

The purpose of our work in stamina is to give students the tools to stay with the tough task for another minute, another moment. If the student engages for that one extra moment, they have what we call a *micro-moment of expansion*. This occurs when a student feels that sense of stress and distress that comes with learning vulnerability but, taking a deep breath, the student persists. This is a cognitive or thinking skill (top-down regulation) that allows us to hold the complexity of a confusing situation. By staying with the difficult task, students build their capacity for persisting when things get difficult—they build their stamina.

🔆 **KEY IDEA:** Learning can be an uncomfortable process filled with struggle and doubt. For students who stop learning, as with all of us, stamina for learning is built one moment at a time.

WINDOW OF TOLERANCE

Let us revisit the window of tolerance framework introduced in Chapter 2, Understanding the Effects of Childhood Stress and Trauma in the

Classroom (see Ogden, Minton, and Pain 2006; Siegel 2020). When a student is within their window of tolerance, they can tolerate the level of escalation required for learning. A child needs to be within their window of tolerance to think clearly, to concentrate on their learning, and to connect with others in healthy ways. When a student is outside their window of tolerance, either in a state of hyper- or hypo-arousal, it is almost impossible for them to make progress in their learning. When a child has experienced trauma, chronic fear, or chronic stress, their window of tolerance can be narrow. Everyday moments in the classroom—such as not understanding a task or seeing an unfamiliar face coming into the room—can push students into a state where they struggle to tolerate and regulate their internal experiences.

It is also important to be aware that students often use unhelpful strategies to attempt to regulate their emotions and bring themselves back to within their window of tolerance. When a student instigates conflict, withdraws from the group, or leaves the classroom, it is often an attempt to regulate their distress. These behaviors can distract students from their learning. Stamina helps students develop healthy ways of returning to their window of tolerance, and in so doing enhances their capacity for staying with the learning task.

💡 **KEY IDEA:** It is difficult for children to learn when they are outside their window of tolerance. Students need support to develop healthy strategies for returning to within their window of tolerance so they can focus on their learning.

UNDERSTANDING STAMINA

The strategies in the Stamina domain help students develop the skills to have those micro-moments of expansion and persist. We have drawn on the wellbeing and educational literature to build explicit strategies for helping students to widen their window of tolerance, to have that expansive feeling that comes with saying, 'I can handle this, and if I can't I know how to get the support I need.'

Classroom strategies included in this chapter have both short-term and long-term aims. In the short term, the aim is to help students experiencing escalation to come back within their window of tolerance so they can re-engage in their learning. In the long term, the strategies for building stamina aim to help students expand their window of tolerance so they spend more of the day in a state where they are ready to learn, connect with others, and enjoy their time at school.

This chapter introduces you to four focus areas that are valuable for building students' stamina for learning:

- Helping students develop a growth mindset (Dweck 2008) and showing students that their effort pays off, even when learning is difficult.

- Helping students develop emotional intelligence and equipping them with skills for regulating their feelings in moments of learning discomfort.

- Helping students develop resilient self-talk and identify unhelpful mindhooks that can undermine their learning.

- Using tools that build stamina for independent learning across a classroom community.

GROWTH MINDSET

We would like you to take a moment to picture Michael. Our team first met him as a 14-year-old who struggled to read at a Grade 2 level. Michael had been brought up with consistent and negative messages about himself and his abilities—messages often given to him by frustrated teachers. He had been told he was at the lowest reading level in the class; he had been told his choices would never lead to success. When we dug deeper we realized Michael had also been hearing these messages from his older brother for more than eight years. Michael believed he was 'dumb' and he thought school was a complete waste of his time. Michael also believed trying at a learning task would entail everyone seeing he could not do it, exposing that he could not learn. Unfortunately, years of learning difficulty had reinforced Michael's negative beliefs about himself.

Given Michael's deeply held beliefs and history of difficult school experiences, it is perhaps unsurprising that his attendance was inconsistent. He was easily distracted. Every month he got older, his desire to strike out on his own surpassed his desire to finish the school year. However, Michael had many strengths. He was funny, with a subtle sense of humor that combined social intelligence and perfect timing. Michael loved cars. He could tell you specific details about hundreds of makes and models. And with time and some useful strategies, Michael learned to read, and became an avid consumer of blogs, books, and magazines.

SHIFTING MINDSETS

Michael's story is common. Many children who have experienced unstable environments have limited experiences of feeling successful when persisting in their learning. We can shift students' limiting self-concepts and beliefs by focusing on Professor Carol Dweck's (2008) theory of fixed and growth mindsets. According to mindset theory:

- A student with a *fixed mindset* believes intelligence and skill are stable; people are either born smart or dumb, and nothing they do will or can change it.

- A student with a *growth mindset* believes their intelligence and abilities can be changed with effort and persistence.

Let's take two students with different mindsets encountering the same, difficult problem. The first student, one with a fixed mindset, believes their difficulty in understanding the problem reflects their intelligence—they cannot understand because they are not smart enough. This student gives up; better to stop trying than attempt the problem and fail.

The second student has a growth mindset and understands that learning is difficult. This student knows that the more effort and practice they put in, the more likely it is that they will begin to understand. A student with a growth mindset has the confidence to ask for help, and actively seeks feedback that will help them grow and improve. For many students, learning growth mindset theory is the first step towards shifting their thinking in difficult moments from 'I am dumb' to 'I am stuck.'

Box 6.2 introduces our growth mindset hero, Kylie. Box 6.3 invites you to reflect on your own thoughts and experiences related to mindset theory.

BOX 6.2: Our growth mindset hero

My colleague, Maddie Witter, and I (Tom) first met Kylie when she was 14 years old and in Grade 5. Kylie was four years older than her classmates and physically well developed for her age. Understandably, Kylie found the physical differences between herself and her ten-year-old peers a source of great frustration and embarrassment. Kylie had several learning difficulties and had struggled to learn to read.

One day, Maddie and I took Kylie aside and said, 'We need you to know there is one way for you to be ready for Grade 6 and that is not to compare yourself to anyone else in the class. We will give you your own learning goals: these will be based on what you can do right now and what you need to develop next to continue becoming an excellent reader. To achieve this goal, we need you to focus on what *you* need to do, not on what the students around you are doing.'

Fast forward to the end of the year, I was turning the corner of the school and heard an argument break out between Kylie and a small group of students from her class. The students were saying, 'How could you go to Grade 6? You are still the lowest reader in our class.' At the top of her lungs, Kylie yelled at them, 'Well, you should see my individual education plan, and Ms. Witter and Mr. Brunzell said I needed to increase three reading levels, and I did it! So I am going to be in Grade 6!'

I went over to de-escalate the students and later, when Kylie and I had a moment alone, I quietly gave her a high five. I was so proud of her—she knew what her learning goal was, she knew it did not matter what anyone else in the class was doing. Kylie knew if she put her growth mindset to work she could achieve her goal—and she did.

BOX 6.3: Teacher reflection and discussion questions

- Can you think of students in your life who are big believers that they cannot change?

- How does this belief impact their learning and behavior in the classroom?

- Can you think of students in your life who have a growth mindset?

- How does this mindset impact their learning and behavior in the classroom?

SUPPORTING GROWTH MINDSETS

As we travel to different schools, we are continuously impressed by the creativity and innovation with which teachers apply the theory of growth mindsets in their classrooms. We have seen visual displays encouraging students to persist despite challenges. We have heard students singing songs and making up rhymes about the importance of effort in their learning. We have seen classroom cultures where it is encouraged to make earnest errors and where no one feels embarrassed or ashamed if they do not know the answer to a question. Time and time again, we have seen the enormous value of having the language of growth and fixed mindsets for students.

As evident in Kylie's story, understanding mindset theory helps students to focus on their progress, independent of what the students around them are doing or achieving. Focusing on their goals is particularly important when the differences between students are highly visible, such as when students are streamed into different reading groups, receive differentiated instruction, or are taken aside for additional support. We want all students to focus on their own learning goals and not to let unhelpful comparisons with their peers convince them they do not have the capacity to achieve in the classroom.

During our work with schools, we continually see evidence that growth and fixed mindsets are not simple. Even within literacy, a student may have a growth mindset towards non-fiction tasks but struggle with comprehension in fiction stories. A student may show a well-developed ability for mental arithmetic but quickly give up when faced with word problems. The challenge for the teacher is to be flexible in their understanding of their student's mindset and to continually revise and refresh their point of view.

💡 **KEY IDEA:** Supporting students to develop a growth mindset builds stamina so that when the student faces difficulty, they persist. When a student with a fixed mindset encounters a problem, they often disengage from the task: a fixed mindset is a barrier to stamina.

SELF-REFLECTION FOR GROWTH MINDSETS

A tool that we would like to introduce you to is our Self-Reflection for Growth Mindset Rubric (Figure 6.1). It is a simple tool that asks students to rate how they are feeling about their progress on a scale of 1 (feeling stuck) to 4 (making progress). Let's follow Brianna in a whole-class geography lesson. Brianna does not understand the learning task. She looks around and all the students around her seem to be making progress.

I am feeling stuck	I am making a little progress	I am learning	My effort and persistence are really paying off
1	2	3	4

Figure 6.1: Self-Reflection for Growth Mindset Rubric

Once the growth mindset theory has been scaffolded, Brianna has new pathways available to her. With a prompt from her teacher, Brianna uses the rubric to assess her progress in the moment. If she identifies that she is making little progress, she can remind herself of the importance of effort, with any luck have a micro-moment of expansion, and persist for a few more minutes. If Brianna identifies that she is stuck, the rubric can prompt her to ask her teacher for additional support. Here the responsibility is also on the teacher to scan and monitor the class for their ratings. Brianna's teacher monitors her growth mindset regularly and steps in with support and encouragement as needed.

PERSON AND PROCESS PRAISE AND FEEDBACK

One of Professor Dweck's key messages is that how teachers, parents, and other adults provide feedback and praise to students is instrumental in developing their fixed and growth mindset voices (Dweck 2007; Mueller and Dweck 1998).

- *Person praise* is directed towards students' attributes, such as their intelligence, abilities, skills, or talents. (Example: You are such a good reader.)

- *Process praise* is directed at the effort and work students put into a task. Process praise highlights students' persistence, their use of learning strategies, and their determination to overcome challenges. (Example: You have finished two chapters today!)

Person praise can lead to a short burst of good feelings; however, research has found it decreases effort and motivation over time (Mueller and Dweck 1998). In comparison, process praise helps students nurture a growth mindset and reinforces the effort they put into their work.

The distinction between person and process praise has particular relevance for students who have experienced conflict and instability. Well-meaning adults may try to counter the negative and harmful messages a child may have received in their upbringing with reassurances. There can be a temptation to provide students with compliments such as 'See, you are a great reader!' or 'You are so smart!' Adults who provide these messages to students have the best of intentions, but our experience is that such messages often have unintended effects. Students can view the feedback as inauthentic and manipulative. It often erodes the trust the student has in the relationship. Our goal is to give fix-it feedback to students that is true and undeniable. We strive to stop giving students reasons to argue with adults silently in their heads. Box 6.4 includes some examples of person and process feedback.

BOX 6.4: Examples of person and process feedback

Person feedback:

- You are a great student.

- You are artistic.

- You are kind.

- You are so good at athletics.

- You are great at numbers.

Process feedback:

- This is a strong piece of work. It is clear you put a lot of effort into it.

- You really persisted on this painting, and your effort shows.

- That was a very thoughtful act. It is wonderful to see you paying attention to other people's feelings.

- Your letter formation has really improved. I can tell you have worked hard at practicing your writing.

- Good result on this assignment. However, I am unsure about the level of effort you put in. Perhaps this was too easy for you. Can we talk about some ideas for extending and challenging you?

Notice that our examples of process praise focus on both the effort the student puts into the task, and acknowledgment of the outcome. Dweck (2015) reminds us that if you praise the effort a student puts into the task, even if they have not done the task properly, you may unintentionally reinforce ineffective learning strategies the student uses. When applying process praise, it is essential to connect student effort to outcomes so students make associations between how hard they have worked and what they have achieved. If the student has worked hard but not achieved the right outcome, it is important to acknowledge the student's effort but also to provide feedback on how to improve next time.

BOX 6.5: Beware the false growth mindset

We want to be transparent here. We see a danger in our work in growth mindsets, and in the Stamina domain more widely. Dweck (2015) writes that when a child is not learning well, it is tempting to attribute the cause of the student's difficulties solely to a fixed mindset, or lack of effort or stamina. This promotes the idea that if the child does not succeed it is because they did not try hard enough, persist long enough, or have the right mindset. Attributing poor learning outcomes in this way does not acknowledge the learning difficulties, special educational needs, or special learning supports some children require. It also does nothing to address the unmet needs of the community that pose significant barriers to the student's ability to learn.

For students who require targeted and individualized interventions, it is important to balance growth mindset feedback with differentiated instruction that supports them to overcome learning or behavior difficulties. When it comes to growth mindset feedback, we recommend fix-it feedback: individualized and differentiated instruction that provides students with clear information on things they may be doing wrong and areas for improvement. Fix-it feedback may entail gently letting students know about mistakes they are making, providing individualized strategies when students need more practice, or even showing students the steps needed to progress to a higher level of difficulty or challenge with a task.

EMOTIONAL INTELLIGENCE

We had the pleasure of running into a teacher we had worked with but not seen for a while. We had a great chat about how she was implementing our strategies in her classroom and across the school community. The teacher made one point that has stuck with us. She said her single most powerful takeaway from her work with our team was this: now when she sees a student struggling in a moment, she stops and asks two questions. What is going on for this student? How might he or she be feeling at this moment? Let's take a moment to imagine a workforce of teachers that can hold their students' emotional vulnerability like that, and respond to students with such compassion and insight. This is a huge step towards the goal of creating emotionally intelligent classrooms. Educators must be mindful that students who have experienced trauma, neglect, or mistreatment may have an underdeveloped capacity to manage strong emotions and distressing internal experiences (Schore and Schore 2007). For students who have been exposed to conflict and instability, the school or classroom environment can be rife with experiences that lead a child to become distressed, angry, anxious, fearful, or upset.

Emotional volatility can have a pervasive, detrimental impact on the classroom; it can disrupt students' learning and compromise their relationships with peers and adults. Unpredictable escalation or inconsistent emotional regulation leads to a volatile classroom culture in which students do not feel safe. In addition, dealing with angry or emotionally turbulent behaviors can be one of the most stressful aspects of a teacher's role. Constantly working with escalated emotions can quickly undermine a teacher's confidence and erode the meaning and satisfaction derived from their career (Brunzell, Stokes, and Waters 2018).

We interpret a student's emotional volatility as a sign the student requires both bottom-up and top-down strategies. Among bottom-up strategies is ensuring that the classroom environment is rhythmic and predictable, with plenty of opportunities for students to understand their own body in times of escalation. We stepped through these strategies in Chapter 4, Body. In this chapter, we want to share a top-down strategy that specifically focuses on students' ability to identify, understand, and de-escalate heated emotions.

Another common presentation we see in children who have experienced conflict and instability is a state of detachment from emotions. When thinking about students who have experienced trauma it is useful to draw on the literature on alexithymia, which is a reduced capacity to experience, articulate, identify, and think about emotions (Larsen *et al.* 2003).

We consider two types of alexithymia (Bermond *et al.* 2007):

1. Cognitive alexithymia, or challenges in thinking about and interpreting emotions.

2. Affective alexithymia, or challenges in experiencing, expressing, and sharing emotions.

It is useful for teachers to consider that students who have experienced trauma may not understand their feelings. They may have limited capacity to describe what they are experiencing, and may have little insight into what others around them are feeling. These children may not have been soothed or comforted by caregivers in a predictable way, and instead may have been punished or ignored for expressing their normal, natural feelings. Making an effort to build students' capacity for understanding emotions of the self and others is a valuable pathway to building stamina and wellbeing. You can use the questions in Box 6.6 to guide reflection on the experiences of students in your classroom.

BOX 6.6: Teacher reflection and discussion questions

- Think of a student in your life who often appeared confused, distressed, or dysregulated. What impact did this have on the student, the classroom community, and you?

- Think of a student in your life who appeared detached from emotions, or seemed numb and distant. What impact did this detachment have on the student, the classroom community, and you?

BUILDING EMOTIONAL INTELLIGENCE

A promising wealth of research over recent decades has shone a light on the importance of schools in helping students develop emotional and social intelligence (Payton *et al.* 2008). There is convincing evidence that schools investing in social and emotional wellbeing programs experience positive academic gains and enhanced student wellbeing (Durlak *et al.* 2011). We believe building emotional intelligence is important for all students.

Building on theories of emotional intelligence, we suggest implementing strategies that help students to:

- recognize the emotions of themselves and others

- manage emotions effectively

- respond to complex social situations in helpful ways

- identify times when their emotions might be shifting

- apply self-regulation strategies before they reach a state of heightened stress or distress.

One strategy for building students' capacity for emotional regulation is to invite students to make their own toolkit for 'turning down the volume' on strong emotions. Box 6.7 offers prompts for designing that toolkit. We aim to have students reflect on the intensity of their heated emotions as a strategy to both pause and de-escalate. Teachers can weave prompts into their debriefing with students, which might sound something like 'Wow, lunch looked intense for some of you on the football field. A lot of you appeared frustrated. Can I ask: Out of a possible 10, how frustrated were you?' Engaging in self-reflection and proactive planning assists students in creating a list of prepared strategies that help them de-escalate when they are feeling strong, distressing, overwhelming emotions. This also overlaps with the concept of Ready to Learn Plans introduced in Chapter 4, Body.

BOX 6.7: 'Turning down the volume'— student reflection prompts

- What activities help you when you are feeling strong and escalated emotions?

- What songs help you feel calm?

- What are some healthy distractions for you?

- Who can you call to talk to?

- What exercise/body movements work for you?

- What else helps you feel calm?

EMOTIONAL INTELLIGENCE THROUGH SAVORING

In my (Tom's) first year of teaching in the Bronx, my Grade 4 students and I went for our first field trip excursion to the Museum of Natural History. We spent a few hours racing through the museum looking at the beautiful animal dioramas lining the halls. At the end of our time at the museum, I tried to remember what my parents had said to me after family trips. My mother is a paragon of savoring, and she has always supported my siblings and me to collect mementos to savor from our special family events and holidays. With this in mind, I marched the students into the gift shop and said, 'I want you all to have something that helps you to remember our special day. Carefully choose a pencil, bookmark, sticker, eraser, or a ruler that reminds you of our learning so we can always have this souvenir.'

The next moment was absolute chaos. Thirty-two little people were running around and scrambling to find something they wanted, and there was me trying desperately to keep them under control, ensure they did not break anything, and prevent scuffles. Finally, we all had our little mementos from our first excursion together and started to walk the five blocks back to the subway train station. We were crossing Central Park when I looked back and saw a trail of bookmarks, erasers, and stickers all along the sidewalk. In the middle of Central Park, I started to yell at my students, 'Get back there and pick up those things! I bought them for you, and you are not taking care of them!'

This was a moment of absolute frustration for me. I felt unappreciated and undervalued. I felt like a failure. Later, once we were safely back in the classroom, a student approached me. 'Mr. Brunzell, why were you yelling at us? Yes, littering is wrong, but really, you just bought us school supplies. We already have pencils. Why do you care so much about pencils?'

My frustration turned to rumination, evolved into self-reflection, and became a profound 'aha' moment. I realized I had not deliberately taught these children how to savor their positive emotional experiences. To me, the pencil was a special physical reminder of our first excursion together, something to treasure for years. My pencil was going to be stored in my box of special things and looked at often and fondly! To my students, the pencil was just a pencil. I realized we had some work to do.

Over the next week, I had all the students bring in shoe boxes. Together we decorated the boxes. In big, colorful letters we wrote on them, 'We love Grade 4!' Together we started to collect special memories and stories. Together we built the students' capacity to treasure and savor their positive and meaningful experiences. I learned that savoring, just like any other capacity, is a skill that can be deliberately taught and practiced to capitalize on and extend wellbeing.

BUILDING SAVORING CAPACITY

When working with students who often feel no durable bond yet to the school or classroom community, we spend a lot of time supporting them to regulate negative emotions and states. We must remember that many vulnerable students have not had opportunities to develop their capacity to savor or regulate their positive emotions and experiences. When a child has experienced conflict, violence, instability, and stress, they often become hypervigilant and highly adept at scanning the environment for threats (Dalgleish *et al.* 2001; De Bellis and Zisk 2014). Their amazing brains can be so skilled at protecting them from danger that they can find it difficult to enjoy or savor positive emotional experiences.

Here are some examples where students may have an underdeveloped capacity to regulate positive emotions:

- A student appears to be excited about the upcoming school camp and then is purposefully absent on the day and misses out.

- A student goes on a school excursion, has a wonderful time, and then implodes with anger on the bus ride home.

- A teacher asks a student to recall one good thing he has enjoyed about the last year of school, and the student cannot think of a single thing.

- A student has successfully finished the aims of a lesson but, when asked, genuinely does not think they have completed the task correctly and cannot think of anything they have learned that day.

We believe strongly that having a reservoir of positive emotional experiences and memories is an important foundation for resilience and wellbeing (Jose, Lim, and Bryant 2012; Quoidbach *et al.* 2010). We work extensively on helping educators to apply the skills of savoring across classroom and school communities. When integrating savoring strategies, we draw on the work of Professors Fred Bryant and Joseph Veroff (2007), who define savoring as intentional actions or thinking strategies that generate, enhance, intensify, or prolong positive emotions and positive experiences.

Savoring can be directed towards the external environment, such as when a person savors the view of the beach or relishes the moment their football team wins an important match (Bryant and Veroff 2007). Savoring can be directed towards the internal environment, such as when students celebrate growth in their learning, or experience joy and pride in their accomplishments. Savoring strategies can also be directed towards the past, present, or future. Savoring the past, or reflective savoring, may entail treasuring mementos or photos, or sharing experiences and successes with others. Savoring in the present might involve mindfully focusing on an experience, such as sharpening the senses when eating a delicious meal. Savoring directed towards the future, also known as anticipatory savoring, might be looking forward to a school event, camp, or excursion. We include some strategies for savoring as a classroom intervention in Box 6.8.

💡 **KEY IDEA:** Students may struggle to regulate their positive emotional experiences, just as they struggle to regulate their negative or painful mood states. Intentionally building students' savoring capacity creates a reservoir of positive emotions and memories that serves as a useful resource in difficult times.

BOX 6.8: Savoring strategies for the classroom

- Support students to predict how they might feel during upcoming positive events.

- Work together to create a classroom calendar of future events to look forward to.

- Reflect on 'what went well' (www) as a classroom ritual.

- Take photos or create artwork to encourage students to reflect on their experiences.

- Create a yearbook of signatures and messages. Provide students with time to reflect on the yearbook and share aspects that are meaningful to them.

RESILIENCE

Bella had survived more in her ten years than any student should have to. Bella's mother passed away when she was young. She was not in contact with her father. Bella had moved between different caregivers in her extended family. Despite moving school numerous times, Bella was deeply committed to her learning and always tried her best. She showed many character strengths, including kindness, social intelligence, and persistence.

It was fascinating to us that Bella would take moving houses (again) with remarkable composure; however, she would become distressed and anxious at the smallest of moments. Bella would experience waves of distress when she forgot her pen or when asked to answer a question in front of the class. This is a common pattern in our work: students who have experienced instability and inconsistency have underdeveloped skills in self-regulation when they encounter everyday challenges. Building students' resilience is a process through which we support them to become better at dealing with daily stressors and difficulties they face.

For adults who work with vulnerable children, the conversation around resilience can be tricky. We want to avoid the misconception that supporting resilience in children who have survived trauma and hardship is akin to telling vulnerable kids to 'toughen up' or just 'try harder.' We define resilience as a person's ability to think clearly about the next helpful step forward. We have found that this definition of resilience applies when a child is having a dispute with another child. It applies when a student is struggling with a learning problem. It applies as a teenager searches for a way forward when they feel their reputation is at risk.

🔆 **KEY IDEA:** Resilience is thinking calmly about the helpful next step, especially when faced with stressful situations.

RESILIENT SELF-TALK

Our team believes that some of the most important work we do is helping students identify and challenge negative and unhelpful thoughts they can have about themselves. This belief was reinforced when doing a resilient self-talk exercise with a cohort of Grade 11 students. We invited students to reflect on their self-talk for a few minutes and asked them to finish the sentence 'My self-talk is…' A girl sitting in the front row looked up and said, 'Brutal. My self-talk is brutal.' Her peers nodded in acknowledgment.

This student's comment reflects the reality that so many young people are experiencing frequently crushing, negative self-talk. These adolescents were heading towards the stressful final year of their schooling, plagued with a barrage of often destructive social media messages, the pressures of performing in their studies, and frequent and consistent doubts about themselves and their learning abilities. We aim to help students turn down those loud, critical internal voices, and develop more flexible, resilient, and compassionate self-talk.

INTRODUCING MINDHOOKS

Acceptance and commitment therapy (ACT) literature uses the term *cognitive fusion* to refer to times when a person is experiencing unhelpful thoughts that distract them from taking that next helpful step forward (Harris 2007). Cognitive fusion is like being stuck on a thought. A student we worked with provided the example of feeling as if your mind was a washing machine, going around and around without getting anywhere.

Say a student has the thought 'I am stupid, I cannot do this.' The student's attention is on those unhelpful statements, not the task in front of them. To support students to create more flexible self-talk, we have found it useful to create a classroom language around what we call 'mindhooks,' or common ways the mind becomes stuck or fused. We base this activity on an adaptation of strategies we learned about in *The Resilience Factor*, an excellent book by Dr. Karen Reivich and Dr. Andrew Shatté (2002).

The aim is to support students to have distance from their unhelpful thoughts, to have that micro-moment of expansion, and to focus on the work at hand. With teacher support, students can identify mindhooks that have the potential to derail them from being on task, and can then refocus on the important task in front of them.

We provide a summary of common mindhooks in Table 6.1. Box 6.9 invites you to reflect on students in your life who may demonstrate different mindhooks.

Table 6.1: Me, them, always, and everything mindhooks

Mindhook	Explanation	Examples
Me, Me, Me	Blaming the self without considering external or uncontrollable factors that may have contributed.	'Kelly is away today. *I* must have upset her.' 'It is all my fault my team lost.'
Them, Them, Them	Blaming others or external forces without considering how one's actions may have contributed.	'I did not do my homework because she did not explain it properly.' 'He made me do it.'
Always, Always, Always	Thinking negative events are permanent.	'I am terrible at fractions. I will never understand.' 'He is never going to speak to me again.'
Everything, Everything, Everything	Seeing negative events as pervasive and related to all aspects of life.	'Everything I do is useless.' 'Kara isn't speaking to me today. Everyone must hate me.'

BOX 6.9: Teacher reflection and discussion questions

- Think of a student in your life who often gets stuck on a particular mindhook. Perhaps a student thinks in a 'Them, Them, Them' way and does not take responsibility for themselves. Or a student falls into the trap of thinking that 'Everything, Everything, Everything' they do is useless. What impact does this unhelpful self-talk have on the student's emotions, behaviors, and learning capacity?

- Can you think of a time when unhelpful thinking has caused you stress or distress? Do you see yourself in any of the mindhooks? You should! All of us get caught in mindhooks. Perhaps you take full responsibility for misunderstandings or problems ('Me, Me, Me'), or fall into the trap of thinking difficulties are permanent ('Always, Always, Always').

When identifying mindhooks, it is important to remember that sometimes our mind gets hooked because of something we did or said in a moment of stress or escalation. We wish we could take it back. Are we suggesting that if your mind gets hooked about something you need to restore or resolve, you should just move on or push away personal responsibility? Quite the opposite.

Remember the definition we used for resilience: thinking calmly about the helpful next step, especially when faced with stressful situations. With this in mind, identifying mindhooks builds our resilient thinking because it helps us identify when we start ruminating. Instead of holding on to the rumination, we want people to breathe and take the next step forward through calm thinking. That next step may be proactively addressing the situation, one action at a time.

In summary, we have explained strategies used in successful top-down resilient thinking. It is important to remember that resilient people are resilient for many reasons. They can be resilient in their bodies and resilient in their relationships. They can be resilient in their family, cultural, and community connections, and resilient in many other domains within their lives. Thinking resiliently is just one part, but an important area to focus on with students in the classroom.

STAMINA FOR INDEPENDENT LEARNING

Introducing students to concepts of growth mindset, emotional intelligence, and resilient self-talk paves the way for widening their window of tolerance and creating essential micro-moments of expansion. Here are some strategies for bringing it all together and developing stamina across a classroom community.

When introducing these stamina strategies, we would like to acknowledge the invaluable contribution of Maddie Witter (2013). Maddie developed these strategies on the understanding that growing student stamina for learning does positively impact achievement. Growing a student's stamina can be compared to working out a muscle in the body. We certainly could not immediately lift a heavy weight without first deliberately practicing with lighter weights. The same is true with minutes on task. To help our students maintain learning stamina for 20 sustained minutes, we need to start with small, achievable goals.

The ability to stay on task provides students with opportunities for deliberate practice over longer and longer periods of time, and deliberate practice is key to academic mastery (Duckworth *et al.* 2011).

The strategies that follow help students identify stamina goals and reflect on how their practice is paying off. We want students to make predictions about their ability to learn and prove to themselves they can exceed their own expectations. Students develop high expectations for themselves when they can see their growth in visual, clear, and concrete ways (Hattie 2012).

STAMINA GRAPHS

The first tool for independent learning is a stamina graph. Figure 6.2 depicts the use of a stamina graph over two weeks by a student named Lisa. When using this tool, the first step is for the class to brainstorm responses to the question 'What does excellent stamina in reading look like?' We also encourage the teacher to work with students to list pre-emptively all the potential distractors students may face. Students might volunteer reasons such as 'when you are unsure about the meaning of a word' or 'when a friend distracts me.' After the students have brainstormed barriers to stamina, the group works together on creating class strategies that enable them to support one another in overcoming the barriers.

Worksheet: Stamina graph   **Name:** Lisa

Mark how many minutes of stamina you did in class today. Connect it to yesterday's mark.

Reflect on how well you think your stamina effort was today on a scale of 1–10 (10 is high)

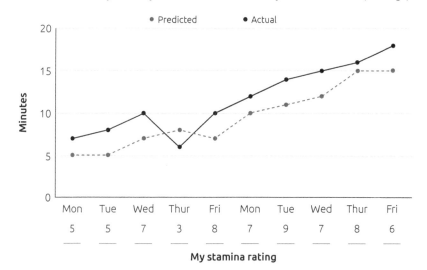

Figure 6.2: Stamina graph

Once the students have been supported to come up with a range of barriers to stamina, and what they might do to overcome those barriers, it is time for students to predict how long they think they will maintain their stamina. For example, on the first day Lisa predicts she will be able to read for five minutes. She marks this prediction on her individual stamina graph.

Next, students use a timer to track how long they can read with excellent stamina. Lisa can read for seven minutes before she becomes distracted. She marks this achievement on her stamina graph and can compare her prediction to her actual result. In this way, students begin to set high and realistic expectations for themselves. It is also helpful for students to self-assess how well they did on a scale of 1–10.

As students each have their own stamina goal, the teacher needs to have alternative activities ready for students once they finish the reading task. The class repeats the process each day, and the stamina graphs provide students with visual reminders of their progress and concrete evidence that their efforts are paying off. As students' stamina builds, they can see and celebrate their achievements. Over time, students also become more accurate and deliberate in their self-evaluations.

STAMINA THERMOMETERS

The second tool we would like to introduce you to is stamina thermometers, depicted in Figure 6.3. When using this tool, the first step is for students to anticipate or predict how many minutes they will remain focused on a task. A student who has struggled to read in the past may predict they can read independently for three minutes. Students record their estimates on the 'predicted' thermometer. Having a specific, measurable, achievable, realistic goal builds motivation (Locke and Latham 2002).

Teachers must be ready to celebrate when students exceed their goals. The student who predicted they would read for three minutes can celebrate if they read for three-and-a-half minutes. The students record their performance on the 'actual' thermometer, and they experience pride at exceeding their goal. This is repeated over several days and weeks. While some days are always more successful than others, in most cases the student's achievement builds over time.

Stamina thermometers are a practical tool because students often think the teacher's expectations are unfair or impossible. With these tools teachers can help students set realistic goals within the confines of the lesson. Most independent reading periods are 10–15 minutes long, so students can build stamina for on-task behavior while the teacher helps other students. Some students may have a five-minute goal while others plan to work for the full 15 minutes, so it is important that the teacher has alternative tasks ready for students when they finish so they do not become distracting to other students. Box 6.10 includes a case study of a school that showed dramatic increases in its literacy levels with the help of our independent learning tools.

Worksheet: Stamina goal

My predicted stamina for _____

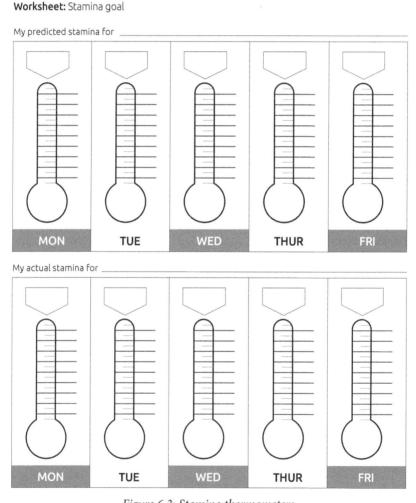

My actual stamina for _____

Figure 6.3: Stamina thermometers

BOX 6.10: Case study: Western Primary School

Western Primary School is a relatively small school with dedicated teaching staff. The school is in a community with many intergenerational and systemic unmet needs; more than one-third of the children are known to child protection services. The weather was a considerable barrier to stamina at the school, which had several old buildings. Every time the wind blew—which was often—the roof shook, and it was loud. With the roof shaking and rattling, the kids became escalated and just could not concentrate.

When we first went to Western Primary, we found some students would arrive on their first day and give up. The teacher would try to encourage the students to read or join in a song, and they just would not do it. Together with the school staff, we set a shared goal for the whole school community of building stamina in reading. We tackled this goal in a range of ways. We introduced explicit lessons on growth mindsets, resilient thinking, and social and emotional intelligence. We implemented stamina graphs and stamina thermometers.

Slowly, the language around growth mindsets, resilience, emotional intelligence, and stamina spread throughout the school community. The students developed strategies they could use to persist with their learning. The teachers developed concrete tools they could use when they saw a student's emotion shifting, or when a student disengaged from the learning task.

Notable was the change in the teachers' expectations of students' stamina. Before our work together, teachers could often be heard lecturing the students: 'I told you to ignore the sound of the rain and read for ten minutes, and you gave up. Get back on task!' After our work together, the language changed to: 'When we set our stamina goal for today, you said you could only read for four minutes. But you read for five minutes. Awesome! I noticed that when it started raining loudly, most of you chose the strategy we brainstormed yesterday. I saw students looking up at the ceiling once, smiling, and then looking down at their books. Let's see if you can beat your prediction tomorrow.'

Together the whole school community built stamina for reading to approximately 20 minutes. For 20 glorious minutes, every student was reading. This meant teachers now had time to sit side-by-side with individual children and provide one-on-one help and support. Over the next ten months, the students increased their reading level to double their achievement of the previous year (Stokes and Turnbull 2016). The school then turned its attention to student writing. Across this community, in a myriad of ways, students are reaching and exceeding the high expectations teachers hold for them.

THE TRIAGE CONVERSATION

Embedding the language of stamina in the classroom paves the way for an essential aspect of our work—the triage conversation. As you may remember from Chapter 4, Body, the triage conversation is where we apply our learning and strategies to the times when students are experiencing distress or dysregulation. In this way, the language of stamina we have worked hard to develop facilitates that micro-moment of expansion for students.

Opening sentences like these show how the language of stamina is helpful in the triage conversation:

I can see you are having a hard time remembering your resilient self-talk. That's okay; everyone finds learning difficult sometimes. Let's work together to sort this out.

You've worked really hard on your growth mindset thinking lately, and I recognize your effort. But we didn't see that today. That moment when you gave up on the task and pushed your chair over, I could hear strong fixed mindset thinking. Something like 'I am giving up, this is useless.' I know we can try again tomorrow.

I think I noticed your emotion of frustration when you saw everyone else doing the activity, and it was hard for you. Am I right? Let's talk about that moment. It didn't feel good, did it? It felt frustrating. That's okay; we all feel frustrated sometimes. I wonder if we can try together for one more moment.'

That was a complicated problem. I can hear you saying it's useless, you'll never get it. I am wondering if you may have some 'Never, Never, Never' mindhook thinking? I think more time and practice will help. Let's come up with a plan together.

REVISITING TALIA

You may remember Talia from the beginning of this chapter; she struggled in her attendance and had a number of complex unmet needs within her family. Her well-meaning teachers initially thought getting her to school more frequently was a solid goal. They came to us seeking support because when Talia did attend class, the quality of her work was far below her potential and her teachers had begun to excuse her from assignments and assessments.

We helped Talia's teachers understand that coming to school was an important first step. The next important step needed to occur within the teachers' own mindsets. They needed to believe, one step at a time, that they could create the conditions to improve Talia's stamina for learning. This was a slow and steady journey. The change first occurred in the language teachers used to encourage Talia: 'Great to see you today! We're going to do this one day, one minute at a time together.' Her teachers started using the language of academic stamina. They helped Talia determine her own stamina goals and ensured Talia would beat her own goals. They set up strategies in Talia's reading journals where Talia could visually record her successes—and they celebrated when Talia's goals become more ambitious.

Another key learning for her teachers was their own change in language when encouraging Talia. Instead of simply giving her reading advice, they began to notice when Talia's own self-talk could be heard out loud in moments of her frustration. They were quick to gently catch her mindhooks, then redirect and reframe them in resilient ways. Talia's own frequent mindhook was 'Them, Them, Them,' as in 'This book is stupid!' Her literacy teachers knew to take a breath, encourage Talia to take a breath, and connect back to her goal. These tools required hard work from both Talia and her teachers. Together, they had much to celebrate at the end of the year.

SOME CONCLUDING THOUGHTS

If you take one message away from this chapter, let it be this: for students, it is not enough for them to just 'show up' at school. From a trauma-informed perspective, students must witness the outcomes of their effort in the classroom. From a wellbeing-informed perspective, students must see the results of their social and emotional learning. For all students in the school community, we need to move the needle on academic growth. Academic rigor—and supporting students to set high expectations for themselves—is a foundational underpinning of trauma-informed, strengths-based classrooms.

As educators, we need to remember that students who have experienced trauma, conflict, and instability may have barriers that negatively impact their capacity for learning. We need to commit to helping students develop skills and strategies that overcome roadblocks to their learning. We want to be clear here: promoting stamina is much more than telling a student to 'try harder.'

We encourage you to consider top-down stamina strategies to help students widen their window of tolerance and persist with their learning. Too frequently in classrooms, a student gives up when they come to a moment that is hard for them—a time when their self-talk says, 'I cannot do this. It's pointless.' As educators, we need to reframe this experience with the understanding that stamina is built in those times of learning adversity. In those difficult moments, we want students to connect to their growth mindsets, to connect to their emotional life at the time, to connect to their resilient self-talk, and to connect to their independent learning goals. We want a struggling student to think, 'I can achieve this thing one minute at a time, I just need to get to the next minute.' And, in doing so, they prove to themselves they can do this, that their time at school matters.

SELF-REFLECTION CHECKLIST

After completing this chapter, please check you can do the following:

✓ Understand the idea of micro-moments of expansion.

✓ Articulate the difference between growth and fixed mindsets.

✓ Use process praise and fix-it feedback to build students' capacity for stamina.

✓ Prioritize building students' emotional intelligence.

✓ Support students to turn down the volume on strong, distressing emotions.

✓ Explicitly use savoring activities to help students develop a reservoir of positive emotions.

✓ Bolster resilience through recognizing mindhooks in the self and others.

✓ Implement tools for independent learning, such as stamina graphs and stamina thermometers.

CHAPTER 7

Engagement

In this chapter, you will learn about:

- identifying intentions and counter-intentions to student engagement through motivational interviewing techniques

- strategies for applying flow theory to maximize student engagement and learning

- how positive emotions broaden students' awareness and build enduring resources.

Riley, aged 14, was a Grade 8 student with an inconsistent school history. Some weeks, Riley appeared motivated and interested. During these weeks, he put a lot of effort into his work. Then for days at a time Riley would hardly attend school. When he did he seemed to pick public arguments over small things, then withdraw and disconnect for the rest of the lesson. At times, it seemed he chose obvious school rules to challenge, like taking his phone out in class to text someone else in class. However, Riley was often reserved when interacting with adults in the school community. His English and homeroom teacher, Ms. Smith, had worked hard to form a strong relationship with him but noticed that during rough weeks, Riley would resist classwork from the beginning of each new task.

At the beginning of one week, Riley's class prepared to write a non-fiction essay as an assessment task. Ms. Smith discussed the importance of this essay and encouraged all the students to try their best. During the week, students carefully chose their topics, researching their positions, and creating an essay plan. Riley decided to write about his favorite subject—motorbikes and, specifically, the usefulness of helmet laws. Ms. Smith had several students with complex unmet needs in the class and was often busy responding to a range of behaviors. Despite many competing demands for her attention, Ms. Smith was aware the essay might be challenging for Riley and had quietly monitored his mood and behavior all week. She was pleased he seemed to be approaching the task with interest and determination.

On Friday, the day of the writing assessment, Riley had a good morning. He arrived at school on time and prepared for the day. The time came for students to write their essays. Ms. Smith handed out the paper and instructed the class to get out their pens, portfolio materials, and laptops. When she gave Riley his essay planning paper, he sat there for a moment and then pushed the paper away. Ms. Smith gently asked him to please do his best, and he threw the paper on the ground. Flustered now, Ms. Smith raised her voice and told Riley to sit down and at least try the essay. At this point, Riley stood up and walked out of the room. Unable to leave her class to follow him, Ms. Smith called the assistant principal. The assistant principal caught up with Riley and walked with him to the wellbeing office, but could not get him to return to class. Despite the assistant principal's best efforts, Riley did not return to any class that day.

In the staffroom during the break Ms. Smith was upset. She shared with a trusted colleague she genuinely believed Riley would do the essay; they had been working towards it all week. Riley seemed interested in writing about motorbikes—she had primed him with news stories, pictures, and other source material. Ms. Smith's colleague consoled her and said, 'I have taught him before; he is just a difficult, disengaged kid.' Ms. Smith nodded in agreement, but deep down she knew there must be more she could do to support Riley and help him overcome the speed bumps getting in the way of his learning potential.

STUDENT ENGAGEMENT

In our experience, adults often label students as disengaged, much like Riley. Students are called disengaged when they do not want to do their work, when they appear to be bored or uninterested, and when they have inconsistent attendance at school. We also meet teachers who are committed to doing everything they can to engage these students.

Teachers tell students how important it is for them to come to school and try their best. They espouse the importance of education for students' futures. Teachers invest in getting to know students' interests and passions—media culture, music, sports, cars—and use these interests to capture their attention. They focus on developing their relationships with students and hope this will be enough to keep them interested in school.

We have seen these approaches have positive results—sometimes. Some students do connect meaningfully with their teachers and become engaged, motivated, curious members of the school community. However, we see too many students remaining disconnected, despite their teachers' very best efforts. We see too many students make progress and then have weeks or months where things seem to go backward.

Motivated by our desire to help reach *all* students, we knew we had to go deeper into student engagement. We dug into the literature in both therapeutics and wellbeing science and used our learning to reconceptualize student engagement. We learned that engagement is so much more than a student's motivation or interest to do something. Engagement requires top-down regulation. Just like stamina for learning, engagement requires a well-regulated brain to understand and make decisions to pursue learning. If a student has the opportunity to build bottom-up regulation within their own bodies, then engagement strategies have real opportunities to bolster learning.

Engagement is a state of peak concentration, interest, and enjoyment when students are absorbed in intrinsically motivating tasks and challenges (Shernoff *et al.* 2003). Within this chapter, we would like to share our learning on three key topics that have expanded our understanding of student engagement:

- Motivational interviewing

- Flow theory

- Broaden-and-build theory.

UNCOVERING OUR STUDENTS' TRUE MOTIVATIONS TO CHANGE

As we began our quest to further our understanding of student engagement, we became increasingly intrigued by a pattern we kept seeing in the classroom. Students arrived at school eager to learn and determined to do their best. Within an hour or two, they were distracting other students in the classroom. Often, neither the teacher nor the student were sure why the student's behavior had gone off track. We genuinely believed these students did want to do well at school; however, something was negatively affecting them. It was when we started to explore the therapeutic modality of motivational interviewing that we began to appreciate the complexity of factors influencing student behavior and engagement.

Motivational interviewing is a person-centered process of helping people to change their behaviors in healthy directions (Miller and Rollnick 2012; Miller and Rose 2009). While motivational interviewing is used predominantly in health and therapeutic professions, we have seen teachers gain positive insights when it is applied in educational contexts (Rollnick, Kaplan, and Rutschman 2016). There are several concepts that inform the approach (Matulich 2013):

- *Partnership:* motivational interviewing is a collaborative approach where the teacher and student work together.

- *Acceptance:* the teacher respects the student's autonomy, perspectives, needs, and strengths.

- *Compassion:* the teacher has the student's best interests at heart and responds with empathy and understanding.

- *Evocation:* the best motivations for change come from the student, not from the teacher.

A central tenet in motivational interviewing is the idea of ambivalence (Miller and Rollnick 2012). Ambivalence is defined as a state of having mixed feelings, motivations, needs, and desires at the same time. When we apply this concept to education, we see that students can experience a range of often contradictory feelings about school. On one level, they know their learning is important. However, they may have other ideas, beliefs, and desires—sometimes conscious and sometimes subconscious—that pose barriers and obstacles to them engaging in their learning in meaningful ways. This a key idea for teachers to remember: students often do not understand the drivers of their own behavior, and when adults make assumptions about student motivation we deny the student the opportunity to gain understanding about themselves.

Take a student who missed a science class. On a surface level, it might seem the student did not want to attend the class and made a poor decision. As we dig deeper, we identify that the student felt significant confusion and ambivalence about attending. We understand the student does value learning and had intended to attend class and do their best. They did not want to disappoint their teachers or get into trouble. Yet they also wanted to spend time with their friends and did not want to miss out on a shared experience with their peers. In their world, the pressure to stay connected, and their fear of peer-bullying for not keeping up with their friends, far outweighed the long-term gains of attending a science lesson.

We must note that, all too often, well-meaning teachers respond to disengaged behaviors by giving their students a motivational lecture on high expectations and making better choices. We suspect most of these lectures are given for the benefit of the rest of the class and for teachers to feel that they are doing something to motivate a change in behavior. However, these kinds of lectures do not get under the surface. If we are going to truly influence student behavior, we need to go deeper.

Terms we find helpful in understanding students' ambivalence are *intentions* and *counter-intentions*. An intention is a desired goal or behavior. In this case, the students' intentions may be to try their best in class and do well at school. Counter-intentions are thoughts and beliefs that are inconsistent with desired goals and behaviors—they often hold us back from achieving our goals. As we explore counter-intentions, we can see that students may derive great benefits from disengaged behaviors.

We empathize with this ambivalence. It can be anxiety-provoking for students to want to engage in learning and at the same time experience complex feelings, desires, and motivations that distract them from learning. For children and young people, mixed and sometimes contradictory feelings can lead to stress, confusion, and uncomfortable feelings and internal states. When this ambivalence is present, what students may need most is a caring, listening adult to help them better understand these confusing and competing priorities. Students often say to us that teachers don't understand them. We have to agree, particularly when teachers have not taken time to understand the motivation behind the potentially significant challenges of changing one's behavior. The personal examples in Box 7.1 may help you grasp the concepts of ambivalence, intentions, and counter-intentions.

🔆 **KEY IDEA:** Students can feel ambivalent about their learning. When we respect and explore their intentions and counter-intentions, we significantly enhance our understanding of student engagement and gain greater insight into how to communicate with them effectively.

BOX 7.1: Reflecting on ambivalence

We often see people have an 'aha' moment about ambivalence when they find a way to apply it to their own lives. Perhaps you can relate to one or more of the following examples of ambivalent feelings, intentions, and counter-intentions.

- You want to make healthy food choices (intention), but you love baking cookies and cakes and sharing them with your friends and family (counter-intention).

- You feel professionally ready to go for a promotion at work (intention), but you are also worried about how the extra workload will impact your partner or family (counter-intention).

- You know spending your weekends resting and recharging would be good for your wellbeing (intention), but going out and staying busy with your family and friends is an important part of your life too (counter-intention).

THE DECISIONAL BALANCE FRAMEWORK

As our understanding of motivational interviewing grows, we look to concrete tools for applying these concepts to the classroom. The Decisional Balance Framework is a motivational interviewing technique we have amended for use with students (see Figure 7.1). Working through the Decisional Balance Framework helps students explore their intentions and counter-intentions and uncover the complex feelings they have in different situations (Matulich 2013). This technique has a variety of uses with students; we find it is especially helpful when students show disengaged behaviors, such as not attending school, being disruptive in class, or not completing assigned homework.

Question 1: What are the benefits of continuing your behavior?	**Question 2:** What are the disadvantages or downsides of continuing your behavior?
Question 3: What are the disadvantages or downsides of changing your behavior?	**Question 4:** What are the benefits of changing your behavior?

Figure 7.1: Decisional Balance Framework for students (adapted from Matulich 2013)

The technique involves the teacher asking the student four questions, in the context of a supportive and empathetic relationship. The overall approach should be one of collaboration and partnership, where the teacher and the student work together. It is important to note that the teacher does not provide the student with reasons for change, nor the consequences of continuing with their current behaviors. Instead, the teacher evokes the student's ambivalence and motivations. In other words, this is not the time for the teacher to do most of the talking!

In the first question, the teacher asks the students about the benefits of staying the same, referring to the benefits of continuing their current behavior. Starting with this question opens up the conversation in a non-threatening way. It encourages the student to start talking in a non-defensive manner. For many, many reasons, the student will have a vested interest in *not* changing their behavior. The second question the teacher asks is about the disadvantages or downsides for students of continuing their current behavior. This is where the students' ambivalence starts to emerge as they can see the costs of continuing their current behavior.

In the third question, the teacher asks the student about the disadvantages of changing their behavior. This question encourages students to start thinking about what change would be like. It gives the teacher insight into a student's hesitations and concerns. The final question explores the benefits of changing. This is when you hear the most 'change talk' from students as they recount their reasons, motivations, needs, and desires for change (Miller and Rollnick 2012). Once this process is completed, the teacher and student can move on to problem-solving, goal-setting, or planning for the future. We provide an example of the decisional balance technique in Box 7.2.

BOX 7.2: Decisional balance example

Mr. Diaz sat down with a student, Lucy, aged 16, who had been loudly talking and disrupting the lesson. After a general check-in, Mr. Diaz thanked Lucy for joining the meeting. Next, Mr. Diaz asked Lucy to share some benefits of not changing her behavior in class. Lucy was not expecting this question. She answered that the advantages were that she enjoyed talking to her friends and keeping up with the latest news. Mr. Diaz accepted this answer in a supportive and non-judgmental manner. He replied, 'You know, I get it. I completely understand why talking to your friends is important.'

Then Mr. Diaz asked Lucy about the disadvantages of not changing—in this case, what were the downsides of continuing to talk in class? Lucy thought about this for a while and then suggested the disadvantages of talking in class were that she would miss out on learning, and also she might get in trouble. Mr. Diaz again thanked Lucy for her honesty.

Next, Mr. Diaz asked about the downsides of changing. This was a surprise to Lucy. She had never been asked this before. Lucy responded that her friends might become frustrated at her or think less of her if she ignored them and concentrated on her work. Mr. Diaz responded with empathy: yes, he could see those were important and valid points. Mr. Diaz reflected later that this was the first time he could see why Lucy had more at stake than simply making a choice to concentrate.

Mr. Diaz then asked Lucy what the advantages would be of working hard during the lesson. Given that Mr. Diaz had given Lucy time and space to explore her counter-intentions, Lucy was open to this question and readily responded. Lucy volunteered that she did feel good about herself when she tried hard at her school work, and she knew she had to do her best to create opportunities for her future.

Mr. Diaz summarized the situation to Lucy (in motivational interviewing, the act of reflecting the student's feelings and descriptions is called a *summary* or *complex reflection*). He said, 'I would like to check my understanding. You do want to do your work, because you want to do well in class and you know learning is important to your future. But talking to your friends is important to you too. You want to share your news and keep up with what is going on. You've been friends with them for a long time and I get that you can't suddenly change your reputation with them. Does that sound about right?' Lucy nodded in agreement.

Mr. Diaz suggested they brainstorm ways Lucy could get her work done and also have opportunities to connect with her friends. They focused specifically on how group work in class could facilitate both connection and work. However, Mr. Diaz requested that if Lucy did group work with one of her friends, she would be open to regular check-ins from him to ensure that the learning aims were accomplished in a given class session.

You will notice two important things in this example. First, Mr. Diaz did not show judgment about any reasons Lucy provided for talking in class. He showed respect, empathy, and acceptance for her ambivalence. Second, Mr. Diaz did not offer solutions, make recommendations, or lecture Lucy on how important her education is. He listened to Lucy's responses and thought processes, then helped her reach a solution to try for the coming week.

After reflecting on the possible applications of motivational interviewing with your students, we encourage you to adapt this strategy to your own context. Motivational interviewing takes practice and requires playing around with the wording of the questions to best suit individual students. When comfortable with listening with empathy to student insight, some teachers can jump authentically into the prompt 'I've been wondering about the benefits for you not participating in class. Let's brainstorm those again.' This opens up a new conversation, and a new way for a student to see themselves, without fear of adult judgment.

FLOW THEORY

As we delved into student engagement we also turned to the concept of flow (Csikszentmihalyi 1990, 1997). To understand flow theory, we invite you to think about how you feel when you are doing your favorite activity—swimming perhaps, or reading, dancing, playing games, having an exciting conversation, teaching a favorite lesson. Take a moment to reflect on how you feel when you are engaged in this activity. If the task is highly enjoyable and rewarding, if you lose track of time, and if nothing else seems to matter in that moment, it may be that you are experiencing *flow*.

Professor Mihaly Csikszentmihalyi (1990, 1997) was fascinated with the experience of people engaged in highly valued tasks. Csikszentmihalyi studied artists, scientists, athletes, and authors engaged in their favorite activities. He found that when people were asked to reflect on their experiences they often used similar language: 'I lost track of time,' 'nothing else seems to matter,' 'the task felt rewarding,' 'I could have kept going for hours,' 'I was in the zone.'

Csikszentmihalyi (1990, 1997) coined the term flow to describe the optimal experience of being engaged in a highly motivating task. A flow state is one in which a person is so involved and absorbed in an activity that nothing else seems to matter. When in flow, people are unaware of their surroundings and their sense of time is distorted. The activity is rewarding and fulfilling for its own sake and not pursued for external rewards or validation from others. We love it when students have activities or hobbies that bring them flow and engagement outside school. However, we strive to see flow in the classroom. In Box 7.3, we invite you to reflect on your own experience of flow and on observing students in flow in the classroom.

💡 **KEY IDEA:** A flow state is the height of interest, effortless concentration, and engagement.

BOX 7.3: Teacher reflection and discussion questions

- In which activities do you experience flow or peak engagement?

- What does it feel like to be in flow?

- Can you think of different times when you have observed your students in flow?

- What do students look like when they are in flow?

APPLYING FLOW THEORY TO THE CLASSROOM

Through understanding flow, teachers can effectively plan classroom activities for optimal student engagement. For students to be in flow, the challenge of the task and the perceived skill of the student need to be closely matched; this is referred to as challenge-skill balance (Csikszentmihalyi 1997; Nakamura and Csikszentmihalyi 2009). If the task is too hard, students can become anxious or overwhelmed. In comparison, if the task is too easy, students can become bored and disengaged (see Figure 7.2). We understand that challenge-skill balance is a complex goal in a class of many students with different capacities, and instruction needs to be highly individualized.

To achieve challenge-skill balance, teachers need to engage in regular assessment to ensure they have up-to-date information on students' current capacities. For instance, many students struggle because the reading level of the text in front of them is beyond their independent or instructional level. An independent level is where the text can be read and understood by the student without assistance from the teacher. We know that independent reading level is important to readers because if they do not experience success they will not continue reading. Instructional level is the level of reading the student can do with some support, perhaps from the teacher, or a peer coach assisting them in a reading conference (a reading or writing conference is a short, individualized meeting between a student and a teacher wherein the teacher discusses the student's progress to collaboratively set new goals for learning). Teachers need to be mindful of assessing both independent and instructional reading levels: assessing what our students can do at the independent level is the first step to ensuring that they are in flow when reading (Witter 2013).

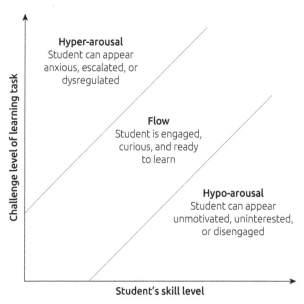

Figure 7.2: Flow in the classroom (adapted from Csikszentmihalyi 1990; Nakamura and Csikszentmihalyi 2009)

Clear and immediate feedback is vital to achieving a flow state (Csikszentmihalyi 1997). A person receives information from their senses on how they are doing at a task and adjusts accordingly. A skateboarder in flow can quickly tell whether they are well balanced on the skateboard, and continually adjusts their positioning. Similarly, an artist can see the quality of their work on the canvas, which generates further effort.

It is important to keep in mind that students with disrupted school histories may have received inadequate individualized and specific feedback about their strengths and areas of deficit. This may mean their capacity to self-assess how they are doing at different tasks is underdeveloped—we liken this to skateboarding or painting while blindfolded. Feedback offers a valuable pathway to student engagement, and it builds students' capacities in accurately self-appraising their performance at learning tasks. Therefore, we recommend that teachers provide ongoing, regular feedback to students. The more 'disengaged' the student is, the more they require moment-to-moment feedback until they can work independently. Too often we see well-meaning teachers purposely ignore the student for a variety of reasons. Box 7.4 outlines the importance of pre-planned systems or mechanisms for providing feedback for students.

BOX 7.4: Pre-planned feedback systems

We are aware that there are substantial barriers to providing students with ongoing, regular, and meaningful feedback. Primary school classroom teachers, who teach the same students all day, may have more opportunities for giving feedback to each of their students than secondary school or specialist teachers, who often teach more than a hundred students during the day. We are aware that providing so many students with meaningful fix-it feedback on their classwork, homework, assignments, and assessments may be an unrealistic target. However, to create engaged learners, students need regular feedback that motivates them to complete the task.

We have had substantial success in turning around some students' academic trajectories when we have implemented pre-planned mechanisms or systems for providing feedback. In one class, the teacher knew that to keep one of her students engaged she needed to put her pen on his paper at least once every ten minutes. Therefore, every ten minutes she circled around the classroom, put a tick on his page, and provided a meaningful comment such as 'Great, I notice you have used today's vocabulary. Nice job for editing your own work. Well done.' The teacher would then resume walking around the class before circling back ten minutes later and repeating the process.

Another teacher successfully implemented a 'weekly conference schedule' and let students know when they had regular one-to-one time with their teacher to discuss strengths and receive fix-it feedback for their work. Students were on different schedules depending on their own differentiated needs for completing learning aims.

We know that this level of individualized attention is a big ask for teachers. Sometimes, it feels as if one or two students take up all your time and attention. However, we have seen some classrooms where the teacher spends so much time focusing on a student's behavior that the student's work is essentially ignored. In other classrooms, the teacher intentionally ignores a student, believing that providing attention to off-task behaviors rewards the student and reinforces the behavior pattern. In these situations, students receive no indication their work matters, and in part this contributes to their low motivation and engagement levels.

We advocate strongly that struggling students need extra care and attention through regular, predictable, and supportive feedback. Students need to know that their work matters and their teachers are paying attention to their effort and achievement. Students with inconsistent academic histories need individualized fix-it feedback that helps them make progress in their academic goals. We know this approach is working when we see a struggling student who is keen to show their teacher they are putting in the effort. We always feel a sense of achievement when a student approaches the teacher with his work and asks for feedback in an excited voice: 'Here, look at this! Do you have any fix-it feedback for me today?'

THE IMPORTANCE OF GOALS

Clear goals are another prerequisite for flow (Csikszentmihalyi 1997). In the classroom, explicit goals provide students with structure and direction. They also facilitate a sense of progress and achievement. Similarly, to reach a flow state, students need explicit and fair expectations. Explicit expectations are especially crucial for students as they provide them with a sense of comfort, safety, and containment.

In the language of curriculum, we provide clear goals and expectations through *learning intentions* (Hattie 1998; Wiliam and Leahy 2015). Learning intentions are descriptions of what a learner should be able to do, learn, or know by the end of a lesson or learning period. *Success criteria* scaffold learning intentions and are indicators or measures teachers and students use to track students' progress. Learning intentions and success criteria should be shared with students at the start of a learning period, and then revisited frequently. We have provided an example of learning intentions and success criteria in Box 7.5.

BOX 7.5: Learning intentions and success criteria

Learning intention:

- Students will be able to draft a five-paragraph persuasive essay.

Success criteria:

- The essay has a galvanizing topic sentence stating the author's intention.

- The essay includes at least three well-structured supporting paragraphs.

- The essay has a conclusion that concisely summarizes the key points, with a call to action.

FLOW CHECKLIST

We have created a Flow Checklist for teachers (see Figure 7.3). It can be used to reflect on any classroom activity to ensure that lessons are conducive to flow. The last row in the checklist records the extent to which the tasks completely absorb the students' attention, and the extent to which time stops for the students while on task. We find that if other flow conditions are met, then the classroom is set up for this last descriptor to merit a 'definitely there' rating. In Box 7.6, we invite you to reflect on how you can support students' needs by implementing these concepts in your classroom.

BOX 7.6: Discussion and reflection questions

- Looking at the checklist, what are your strengths in creating conditions for flow?

- Looking at the checklist, what are your areas for improvement?

- What three goals can you set to create conditions for flow in your classroom?

Flow conditions	Not there yet	Getting there	Definitely there
Students' skill level matches the task at hand. The task sits within the students' pre-assessed independent to instructional level (the task is pitched high enough to challenge students, but not too high to overwhelm them)	☐	☐	☐
Students receive immediate, ongoing, and meaningful feedback about their performance: from teachers, from peers, or through the task itself	☐	☐	☐
The task has clear goals, or the task allows the students to set their own goals and meet them within the session	☐	☐	☐
Clear and fair rules define the task	☐	☐	☐
The task completely absorbs the students' concentration. Time stops for students while on task	☐	☐	☐

Figure 7.3: Flow Checklist

THE TRANSFORMATIVE POWER OF POSITIVE EMOTIONS

Next, we turn to the third core topic in our engagement chapter—the transformative power of positive emotions. When we first speak with teachers, often we find they have spent little time thinking about the explicit role of positive emotions in teaching and learning. Of course, teachers want students to feel happy, joyful, interested, curious, and hopeful. However, these emotions are often viewed as the result of a thriving classroom and not as vital drivers of student engagement and learning. We challenge this idea and advocate that positive emotions have transformative effects. They are central to classroom teaching and learning. Here are some examples:

- A child who feels inspired and hopeful engages in a learning task differently from a student who feels defeated or distressed.

- A student who feels interested and connected interacts with peers and teachers differently from a student who feels nervous or anxious.

- A student who feels calm and curious approaches a challenge differently from a student who feels frustrated or angry.

As we explore the transformative effects of positive emotions, we need to be clear—we do not wish to imply that students can or should be in a continuous state of positivity. We hope we have communicated effectively throughout this book that we believe in the importance of supporting students' self-regulatory capacities across the spectrum of affective experiences. However, we also believe intentionally and thoughtfully integrating positive emotions into the school day has transformative effects.

We see many successful teachers prime their classrooms with positive emotions all the time: when they start the day with a positive and upbeat greeting, when they share a joke with their students, when they celebrate students' successes, when they encourage moments of play and fun throughout the school day. What we want to do is move the conversation about positive emotions and student learning from something great teachers do naturally, to an intentional and strategic component of trauma-informed, strengths-based classrooms. In Box 7.7, we invite you to reflect on positive emotions in your classroom.

💡 **KEY IDEA:** As positive emotions are key drivers for student engagement and learning, intentionally priming the classroom with positive emotions has transformative and therapeutic effects.

BOX 7.7: Teacher reflection and discussion questions

- Can you think of a time when positive emotions led to transformative effects for your students?

- How do you integrate positive emotions into your classroom to support students' healing, learning, and growth?

BROADEN-AND-BUILD THEORY

Professor Barbara Fredrickson's (2009) broaden-and-build theory is a useful framework for understanding how and why positive emotions are transformational. First, we consider that negative emotions narrow attention. When a person encounters a threat or difficulty, their attention focuses on it to enable them to respond safely and effectively. Perhaps you can think of a time when you have had a conflict with a friend or colleague. You might have had difficulty thinking about anything else and found yourself constantly brainstorming ways of dealing with the situation. Narrowing attention when negative emotions are experienced is a highly adaptive response. It equips people to respond to threats, solve problems, and act in ways that ensure their safety.

In contrast, when people experience positive emotions, their awareness broadens and they take in more information from the environment (Fredrickson and Joiner 2002). Positive emotions are associated with flexible thinking and creativity (Ashby, Isen, and Turken 1999). When in a positive state, people can integrate information from various sources. They also connect meaningfully with others and engage in collaboration. We all know of exceptions, such as times when grief or loss fuels creativity or when a difficult experience shared with others creates a lasting bond. Another common exception is times when students are too positively escalated to focus on their learning tasks. However, overall, there is convincing evidence: positive emotions broaden attention and fuel creativity (see Fredrickson 2013 for a review of research supporting this theory).

The second important aspect of broaden-and-build theory is that positive emotions build resources over time. A student who experiences the positive emotion of curiosity engages with the learning material and develops new intellectual resources. A student who feels satisfaction after successfully completing a learning task builds confidence for future lessons. A student who speaks to someone new while in a happy, playful state may make a new friend.

We see upward spirals for wellbeing when increased psychological resources lead to an enhanced capacity to generate positive emotions. In turn, these spirals create more opportunities for building even more psychological resources (Burns *et al.* 2008; Fredrickson and Joiner 2002). The broaden-and-build effect creates an upward spiral of positive emotions that facilitate enhanced learning, engagement, resilience, and wellbeing. There is also evidence that positive emotions have beneficial effects on physical health. Frequent positive emotions are associated with reduced stress hormones, enhanced immunity, lower levels of inflammation, and even increased longevity (Howell, Kern, and Lyubomirsky 2007; Ong, Mroczek, and Riffin 2011; Pressman, Jenkins, and Moskowitz 2019).

In our classrooms and communities, time and time again we see the value of positive experiences for students. Children and young people who have had more than their fair share of difficulty, stress, hardship, and instability deserve our best efforts to help them cultivate positive memories and experiences. Furthermore, as we discussed in Chapter 6, Stamina, savoring positive emotions takes on special relevance. Having a reservoir of positive emotional experiences and memories helps protect students' sense of self-worth and reminds them that difficult situations are often temporary. In this way, positive emotions are both pathways to student engagement and learning, and can be drivers for resilience and coping.

💡 **KEY IDEA:** Intentionally weaving positive emotions into the school day cultivates student engagement and creates broaden-and-build pathways for growth.

POSITIVE PRIMERS

Teachers can employ strategies to foster positive emotions in the classroom and across the school community. Fredrickson (2009) recommends increasing the quantity and frequency of positive emotions through a positivity toolkit. Fredrickson's toolkit for positive emotions comprises 12 strategies: being open and curious about surroundings and experiences, cultivating nurturing relationships, engaging in acts of kindness and altruism, developing healthy distractions, visualizing best possible futures, applying strengths, disputing negative thinking, spending time in nature, cultivating mindfulness, practicing loving-kindness meditations, practicing savoring, and reflecting on gratitude.

We recommend that teachers develop their own toolkits of strategies for integrating positive emotions into their classrooms. In particular, positive primers are activities that prime students' brains for engaged, creative, and flexible thinking. Starting a lesson or school day with a positive primer invests in student connection, collaboration, and enjoyment. There are thousands of positive primers. We encourage you to create and explore strategies that work for you. We would like to share some positive primers that form part of our toolkit. In addition, Box 7.8 provides an overview of the value in building positive emotions through positive circle routines.

Best, worst, funniest

Encourage students to take turns to ask each other these questions:

- What is the best thing that happened today?

- What is the worst thing that happened today?

- What is the funniest thing that happened today?

In sharing the worst moments, it is important that the focus is on identifying moments of disappointment and sadness, not on blaming others. Finishing on the funniest things turns attention to light-hearted moments. This activity underlines that, while 'worst' moments might happen, there are always good and funny moments.

Comic strip creations

Find a comic strip your students may enjoy and remove the final frame. Invite students (either in groups or individually) to create their own punchlines. Alternatively, you can use photos or images from a newspaper or magazine and ask students to add a caption or voice bubble to create a funny joke or story. Invite students to share their creations with the rest of the class.

Lottery winners

Divide the class into groups and explain you will give each group some good news. Explain that the group should listen carefully to the good news, and then respond exuberantly, as if they have just heard the best news in the world, or that they have found out they won the lottery. They can whoop, cheer, jump in the air, and give each other high fives. Whisper a different piece of news to each group. Examples could include 'Today is Tuesday' or 'I am not wearing a hat.' The more ordinary the statement, the more hilarious it can seem to elicit such enthusiastic responses.

BOX 7.8: Positive circle routine or meeting

Circle routines are nurturing classroom practices that support student engagement, build wellbeing, and create positive classroom communities (Roffey 2006). In addition to creating a sense of safety and belonging, a predictable circle ritual evokes positive emotions. It primes students for open, flexible, and engaged thinking.

Here we share our approach to circle time that includes intentional strategies for cultivating positive emotions. In many classrooms, teachers and students start every day of the school week with this circle routine. If it is practiced each day in a consistent way, students can eventually lead this routine themselves, with adult coaching. There are six steps.

1. GREETING

To commence, students sit or stand in a circle shape. Once students are in position, the circle routine begins with a greeting. For example, students go around the circle and say good morning to each other in turn. Students are encouraged to use each other's names, maintain good eye contact, and perhaps give each other a handshake or fist bump.

2. VALUES

The teacher states the school values. This statement of values connects students to the school community and fosters a sense of belonging.

3. EXPECTATIONS

The teacher shares an expectation for positive behavior for the day, such as setting the students the goal of raising their hand before they speak.

4. ANNOUNCEMENTS

The teacher shares the class news and announcements, such as acknowledging any birthdays or letting students know about any upcoming events.

5. POSITIVE PRIMER

The next step is a positive primer game. This may be an activity described earlier in this chapter, or something as simple as singing a song or playing silent ball.

6. WHAT WENT WELL

The circle routine finishes with a reflection on 'what went well' (www). Students share three things they did well during the morning circle. They may share that they showed respect to each other during the greetings, listened attentively during the statement of the school values, and had fun during the positive primer game. These www reflections provide an opportunity for teachers to emphasize and encourage positive behaviors for learning the students have shown.

THE TRIAGE CONVERSATION

Remember that engagement strategies are top-down strategies. They require a well-regulated thinking brain that can listen, understand, and reflect if students are to make positive classroom choices. When considering the state of total engagement, or flow, teachers can use the conditions of flow to prompt meaningful dialogue in the triage conversation. We know these conversations can be quite escalating for many students at first, particularly if they feel they are about to be blamed for not finishing the assignment. Remember, the goal is for the student to feel insight, not guilt.

Here are some ways to use the language of engagement in the triage conversation. Helpful prompts can start with acknowledging the assignment may not have been scaffolded for student success. For example: 'I noticed today you were struggling to make a "galvanizing" topic sentence. Tomorrow, I'm going to show you three examples so you can have a strong start to your essay.'

The teacher can acknowledge the student was not in flow because the learning intentions were unclear or required adjustment for the individual student's goals. For example: 'Tomorrow, let's focus on just one supporting paragraph to convince us on one of your points. I will show you how to structure this paragraph first thing during the work period.'

Finally, we urge teachers to make feedback conversations with students a regular and expected occurrence. In the hustle of the lesson, if feedback conversations do not happen (and the student loses motivation that day), the teacher can say to the student, 'Hey, I realized today it looked as if I was ignoring you and spending far too much time with students on the other side of the room. How about tomorrow, you will be the first student I have a conference with? We can do a quick check-in at the end of the lesson too.'

REVISITING RILEY

Let's revisit Riley and Ms. Smith, who we met at the beginning of the chapter. Ms. Smith had prepared her class to write an essay, but when the moment came to start that task Riley pushed his paper away and walked out. In her next quiet moment during a busy day, Ms. Smith sat by herself and considered the barriers to Riley's engagement. Ms. Smith could see Riley showing a lot of concerning behaviors. His inconsistent attendance was a priority, and it was difficult to know what to do when he refused to do his work. Like many of her students, Riley had a disrupted educational history. She had incredible empathy for how hard it must be for him to take risks in his learning when it was likely he had deeply embedded beliefs that he was not smart enough to do well. Ms. Smith was also acutely aware that in Riley's peer group no one wanted to appear as if they tried hard at their school work. They certainly did not want to be seen asking for help when they found something difficult.

However, Ms. Smith believed this was only part of the story. She could also see that Riley had a deep desire to learn and wanted his teachers to be proud of him. He craved a sense of achievement and feelings of belonging to the school community. She put herself in his shoes and considered how difficult and confusing it must be to experience such different feelings and motivations, all at the same time. From this perspective of empathy and compassion, it was easier for Ms. Smith to see positive ways forward.

When Riley returned to school, Ms. Smith set aside time and together they went through the Decisional Balance Framework. They focused on his behavior of leaving school when things got difficult. Riley was surprised at this collaborative approach; he assumed he was going to get into trouble. As they worked through the process, it emerged that Riley had wanted to write his motorbike essay. He had spent the whole week prior rehearsing what he wanted to say in his head. However, when he sat down to write it, his mind had gone blank. All he could think of was that he could not possibly write that much, and his mind filled with negative self-talk: he was useless, worthless, and dumb. Instead of activating his focus plan or asking for help, he left the classroom—after all, it was better not to try at all than to try his best and fail.

This is a complex state to disentangle. Students like Riley frequently do not believe they can succeed each day in the classroom. However, working with the Decisional Balance Framework was a profound first step. It provided Ms. Smith with tangible evidence that Riley cared deeply about his education; he really did want to do well. Ms. Smith took a mental snapshot of this moment and intentionally recalled it whenever Riley acted in ways that on a surface level seemed unmotivated or disengaged: 'This is not the behavior of a student who does not care. This is the behavior of a young person who is confused, overwhelmed, stressed, or struggling. This student does not need another adult to label him as disengaged, lazy, or difficult. This student needs understanding and support.'

Ms. Smith believed that Riley could write the non-fiction essay. Riley was not sure about his capacities to write that much or for that long. Ms. Smith realized that at this point in time the perceived challenge-skill balance was not quite right. Together, they agreed that Riley was going to try again, but they amended the success criteria. This time, Riley had to focus more attention on the essay planning paper and then draft two strong paragraphs. She reminded him that if his negative self-talk resurfaced, he could always ask for her help in the form of a writing conference. Together, they developed subtle ways for him to communicate that he needed her attention, without an overt request for help made in front of his peers.

Now Ms. Smith and Riley had a plan in place, Ms. Smith moved on to areas for growth in overall classroom engagement. Ms. Smith went through the Flow Checklist and identified two areas for improvement. First, she set the goal that she would do more regular assessments of her students to know where they were at with their literacy levels. Second, she set the goal of providing fix-it feedback more often. In this case, she set the goal of correcting a sample of students' writing each week.

In addition, since she was Riley's homeroom teacher, she implemented a regular circle routine first on the agenda each morning, including positive primers. While students were a little hesitant to start with, after a few weeks they were laughing and connecting well most mornings. It was a good circuit breaker from the students' hectic arrival at school and a positive way to start the school day. She could tell the circle time was having the desired effect when one morning she intentionally 'forgot' to start the class in this way, and Riley was one of the first students to remind her.

SOME CONCLUDING THOUGHTS

Engagement can be a buzzword in education. All teachers want students who are engaged, curious, motivated, and enthusiastic. Teachers certainly do not want students who are disengaged, unmotivated, uninterested, and disconnected. Here, we have not tried to tackle the breadth of perspectives on human engagement. Rather, we have tried to reframe the concept of engagement as a top-down capacity. We distilled three rich areas of exploration that provide, in our opinion, great insights into student engagement—areas that greatly help students in our school communities.

By delving into the motivational interviewing literature, we can explore and respect the complex intentions and counter-intentions that influence students. We can learn from the conditions for peak engagement—the idea of flow—and apply this learning to the classroom. We can intentionally weave into the school day activities that are fun, positive, and enjoyable. We can prime students for flexible thinking, leading to upward spirals of learning and wellbeing over time.

Often when a student appears disengaged, teachers may think the student is unmotivated. Many teachers stop in frustration once they hear students declare, 'This is boring!' However, we have never met a student who did not want to do well in the classroom, nor one who did not understand that the reason they go to school is to learn. However, we have met many students who have a desire to learn but who also find the learning experience escalating, or not adjusted to their learning needs. We have met students whose self-esteem and confidence were challenged to the point that they disconnected from learning tasks. We have certainly met students who wanted to do well, but who talked through lessons to connect with their friends or to protect their identity, or because their daily survival needs far outweighed the long-term investment of education. These reasons may seem superficial, but the truth is they are influential motivators for young people. Students— especially those who sit at the edges of the classroom community— experience complex and often conflicting emotions about their learning. When we respect the complexity and ambivalence that surrounds student engagement, we can create pathways to learning and growth.

SELF-REFLECTION CHECKLIST

After completing this chapter, please check you can do the following:

- ✓ Understand the complexity of student engagement and the ambivalence students may feel about their learning.

- ✓ Use tools such as the decisional balance technique to uncover student intentions and counter-intentions.

- ✓ Use the Flow Checklist to reflect on classroom activities and ensure they are designed for optimal engagement.

- ✓ Appreciate the importance of positive emotions for student engagement, growth, and learning.

- ✓ Prioritize integrating positive primers and circle time rituals as ways of embedding positive emotions in the classroom.

- ✓ Develop a toolkit of activities for cultivating positive emotions and priming students with creative and flexible mindsets.

CHAPTER 8

Character

In this chapter, you will learn about:

- developing students' psychological resources and cultivating growth-orientated ways of thinking

- identifying, nurturing, and celebrating students' character strengths

- building character strengths of gratitude and hope.

Zane, aged 13, arrived at his new school after being excluded from his third school in four years. He came with a thick file and a comprehensive list of mental health concerns. Zane often referred to himself as worthless; he spoke about hating himself. Zane rarely smiled. He spent most of his time at school alone.

A team of teachers and wellbeing staff met to explore steps they could take to support Zane's positive transition to the school. Members of our team attended the meeting to see how we could help. Together, we went through the standard admission paperwork, writing down Zane's personal details, emergency contacts, medical history, allergies, learning difficulties, and academic goals. At the bottom of the admission form was a small box in which to describe Zane's strengths. In this box, the teacher completing the paperwork wrote one word: skateboarding. Everyone seemed content with this, and the discussion quickly moved on to the next topic.

We politely stopped the discussion and asked the team to return to the section on Zane's strengths. We commented that skateboarding was a good start, but we needed to go deeper. To us, skateboarding sounded like a talent, which we define as a natural ability for an activity. In contrast, character strengths are a subset of morally valued personality traits that provide people with a sense of identity and meaning (Park, Peterson, and Seligman 2004). We needed more information on Zane's positive attributes and qualities. We believed a focus on character strengths was particularly crucial given Zane's low sense of self-worth. The already frustrated and rushed team gave us incredulous looks and the head of campus responded, 'We have to start where he is, and what he can do is skateboarding.'

In addition to other academic assessments, before Zane started at the school, we suggested he complete an online inventory of VIA Character Strengths.[1] One teacher vocalized substantial resistance to this idea. In his opinion, Zane was never going to agree to complete the character strengths assessment, it was a waste of time, and the last thing the team needed was more stress and paperwork. After some further discussion, and gentle persistence on our behalf, Zane's teacher, Ms. Brown, agreed to spend time with him exploring his character strengths.

STARTING WITH STRENGTHS

On Zane's first day, Ms. Brown gave him a tour of the school and introduced him to some members of the school community. As standard practice, she then completed a brief assessment of his reading level. Next, Ms. Brown let Zane know they were going to do an exercise about his strengths. Before they started the online character strengths assessment, Ms. Brown asked Zane what he thought his strengths were. Zane responded, 'Well, that is obvious. Clearly, I don't have any strengths, and if I did I wouldn't be at this stupid school.' However, he agreed to give the character strengths assessment a try, and Zane and Ms. Brown completed all of the questions together. Altogether, the exercise took more than an hour, and Ms. Brown was surprised at Zane's interest and persistence.

After they completed all the questions, Zane received a summary of his character strengths. Right at the top of the list was the strength of humor. On receiving this result, Ms. Brown looked closely at Zane's face and saw what she perceived as something between confusion and

---

1   www.viacharacter.org

recognition. Knowing Zane's crushing sense of low self-esteem, she said, 'Zane, this is just a simple test, and if you do not think that humor is your top strength, we can always do this again, or we can explore your strengths in different ways.' Zane turned to her and said, 'You know what? We don't have to do this again. Humor is my top strength. I always thought that, but no one knows it. You see, I am a funny person inside my head. I just never say the funny things out loud. No, I do not need to do the strengths test again.'

Knowing a little about Zane's history, Ms. Brown's eyes started to well up. She did not want to cry in front of Zane on his first day, so she turned slightly to the side, brushed away her tears, and said what she was meant to say: 'Humor is a valuable signature strength, Zane. Now we have this important piece of information about you, we have to work on this strength all year. We will give you lots of opportunities to put your strength of humor into action. We are going to apply it in all sorts of ways. You better get ready. We have a lot of work to do.'

DEVELOPING CHARACTER

When students like Zane come into our classrooms and communities, it is easy to be consumed by their difficulties. We worry about the areas of concern, and we set goals for areas of improvement. We think that by helping them to address their challenges we do the best job we can of preparing them for the future. Some students have clear unmet needs that must be met for success at school, such as regulating their emotions and behaviors, staying on task, and controlling their impulses. Again, we refer to these concerns as bottom-up concerns. As our work turned to Stamina, Engagement, and now Character, we view these three developmental capacities in line with building psychological resources (Fredrickson 2001). These resources require top-down regulation: the ability of a well-regulated thinking brain to call on the right strategy at the right time to learn. We also might think if we focus on strengths we will not give enough attention to students' unmet needs. In our experience, some students have never had a conversation about their strengths with a trusted adult. Some students have never even thought about their strengths. Some do not believe they have any strengths at all. Box 8.1 invites you to reflect on the students in your life.

BOX 8.1: Teacher reflection and discussion questions

- Consider your students of concern.

- What messages were you told about these students before you taught them?

- Can you name three strengths for each one of them?

A FOCUS ON STRENGTHS

This chapter aspires to communicate how important it is to focus on students' character strengths. We want teachers to see what is right with students as quickly as they see what is wrong. We want the conversation about students' strengths to be one of compassion, commitment, and rigor. By rigor we mean that teachers make intentional moves to extrapolate strengths from talents, and that they ensure students specifically learn about and can define their own strengths. When a student has a deep passion for skateboarding, like Zane, what strengths are they nurturing through their talent? We know many students who spent years at skate parks, and every day they practiced their strengths of resilience, kindness, curiosity, bravery, and social intelligence.

We want to move conversations about strengths from a rushed add-on or afterthought to the center of how we approach students' education. Teaching through strengths is a lens through which to see the classroom—and in particular, to see students who may use their strengths in both helpful and unhelpful ways. For example, we hope students practice the strength of self-regulation in classrooms; but when a student is too self-regulated, they may not take creative learning risks, allow themselves to open up, or collaborate with others.

This chapter gives an overview of strategies based in positive psychology, which is the study of wellbeing, human strengths, and positive emotions (Gable and Haidt 2005; Seligman and Csikszentmihalyi 2000). All young people need regular and explicit opportunities to explore their strengths and build their psychological resources. Through integrating strengths-based and trauma-informed approaches, we create more opportunities to support students' academic, social, and emotional development. We know that even young people with the most severe emotional and behavioral challenges have strengths that are useful in their growth and recovery (Cox 2006). Box 8.2 provides an overview of the importance of considering journeys of both healing and growth for students.

🔅 **KEY IDEA:** Teachers need to help students by supporting their bottom-up unmet needs for self-regulation and relational repair. They also need top-down, growth-orientated ways of thinking, such as building strengths.

BOX 8.2: Journeys of healing and growth

In his dual state continuum model, Professor Corey Keyes (2002) describes mental ill-health and wellbeing as different (although related) concepts. In our work, we talk about taking students on journeys of healing and journeys of growth. Underpinning this approach is the idea that you cannot build people's strengths by addressing their weaknesses. Here are some examples that demonstrate this concept:

- A student does not grow their passion and aptitude for mathematics by receiving support for their literacy difficulties.

- A student does not learn about or celebrate their strength of kindness by focusing on overcoming their challenges in self-regulating their behavior.

- A student does not build their strength of appreciation of beauty and excellence by focusing on their difficulties in being honest with others.

THE VIA FRAMEWORK OF STRENGTHS

As we have discussed throughout this book, it is important for schools to develop respectful ways of talking about students who may regularly present dysregulated behaviors. We know that even subtle shifts in language can change how teachers see students and how students see themselves. To fully support students' healing and growth, we also need to unify our language across all staff in the school around students' strengths. Developing a shared vocabulary for strengths helps schools identify and celebrate ways in which members of the community are similar and ways in which they are different.

The strengths framework we recommend is the VIA classification of strengths (Peterson and Seligman 2004). We introduced this framework in Chapter 3, A Developmentally Informed Approach to Learning, and would like to elaborate on it here. The VIA is based on a historical study of positive personality traits valued across time and cultures (Dahlsgaard, Peterson, and Seligman 2005). The VIA works well in school settings due to its accessible language that is relevant to all year levels. Furthermore, it has a robust evidence base for use in schools (Lavy 2019). Under six virtues, the VIA lists 24 strengths which are described in Table 8.1. While this list is not exhaustive of the strengths within humanity, we believe it is an invaluable framework for exploring strengths in schools.

Table 8.1: Character strengths and virtues

Strength	Description
Strengths of wisdom and knowledge	
Creativity	Thinking of new and creative ways of doing things.
Curiosity	Being interested in and curious about the world.
Open-mindedness	Thinking about things from many different approaches and angles.
Love of learning	Being passionate about new ideas, education, and knowledge.
Perspective and wisdom	Having a mature and wise view of life and the world; being able to see the bigger picture.
Strengths of courage	
Bravery	Being courageous when faced with threats, challenges, or difficulties.
Persistence	Working towards goals despite challenges.
Enthusiasm (zest)	Being high on vitality and having a passionate and energetic approach to life.
Honesty	Being genuine and speaking the truth.

Strengths of humanity	
Love	Valuing loving and close relationships.
Kindness	Being thoughtful, going out of the way to do things for others.
Social intelligence	Having insight into the motives and feelings of yourself and others.
Strengths of justice	
Teamwork	Working well in a group or team.
Fairness	Treating people equally.
Leadership	Having vision, organizing, and leading people.
Strengths of temperance	
Forgiveness	Forgiving people who make mistakes.
Modesty and humility	Letting accomplishments speak for themselves.
Prudence	Acting carefully and exercising caution.
Self-regulation (self-control)	Having discipline and regulating your feelings and actions.
Strengths of transcendence	
Gratitude	Being thankful for good events and the kindness of others.
Hope	Thinking hopefully and optimistically about the future.
Humor	Appreciating humor and having the ability to make others laugh.
Appreciation of beauty and excellence	Noticing, appreciating, and valuing excellence and beauty.
Spirituality	Having a strong sense that there is a higher purpose to life.

The strengths of wisdom and knowledge are thinking strengths involved with acquiring knowledge and seeing things from different perspectives. When we use strengths of courage, we are brave and work towards meaningful goals despite setbacks or adversity. The strengths of humanity connect us to others; they are often referred to as heart strengths. Strengths that promote citizenship and strong communities are recognized in the virtue of justice. We use the strengths of temperance when we exercise our self-regulation and prevent excesses. Finally, the strengths of transcendence fill our lives with meaning and connect us to things beyond ourselves.

Imagine the possibilities when all members of the school community understand the 24 strengths, can use them in a range of ways, and can spot them in others. We want even the youngest children in the school community to think deeply about what it means to be fair. We love it when all students have a well-developed understanding of concepts such as teamwork and leadership. We are dedicated to helping students recognize and appreciate moments of kindness and social intelligence. We want students to be able to spot strengths like curiosity and humility in others. We invest in helping students develop their understanding of quite complex ideas, such as prudence and persistence. We aspire for all members of the school community to have a well-developed understanding of all 24 strengths, to be able to use them themselves, and see them in others. Box 8.3 summarizes the research evidence on the benefits of strengths.

BOX 8.3: The benefits of strengths

The 24 character strengths are psychological resources that have benefits for individuals, relationships, and academic outcomes (Park *et al.* 2017). Here is a snapshot of some of the strengths research:

- Character strengths are associated with subjective wellbeing and reduced depression (Gillham *et al.* 2011).

- Character strengths are related to positive peer relationships in adolescence (Wagner 2018).

- Character strengths are associated with positive feelings towards school (Weber, Wagner, and Ruch 2016) and increased classroom participation (Park *et al.* 2017).

- Character strengths are associated with superior academic performance (Park *et al.* 2017; Weber and Ruch 2012).

- Character strengths support students during school transitions (Shoshani and Sloane 2012).

BUILDING UNDERSTANDING OF CHARACTER STRENGTHS

Once introduced, the character strengths are invaluable resources that can be used to build positive classroom communities (Fox Eades 2008; Quinlan *et al.* 2014). We asked some teachers to share specific examples of how they use character strengths in the classroom. One teacher encouraged a student who was anxious about a school performance to draw on her strength of bravery. Another asked her class to use their strengths of kindness and social intelligence to be welcoming and inclusive when a new student arrived at the school. A third teacher encouraged two students having a difference of opinion to apply their strength of curiosity to see what they could learn from each other, rather than focusing on how they were different.

Having a strengths-based language shared by all members of the class (or school) community takes substantial investment and commitment. We encourage teachers to look for ways of introducing their students to different VIA strengths and encourage depth of understanding. We also recognize the importance of building a diverse and culturally responsive language for strengths. Box 8.4 discusses this point. Here are some ideas for integrating character strengths into the classroom and curriculum:

- Consider that every academic lesson is an opportunity to have students name and practice their strengths.

- Have visual displays that depict each of the 24 VIA strengths.

- Invite students to select one strength that is important to them and create a piece of artwork that reflects this strength for them.

- Work together to brainstorm synonyms for each strength.

- Create profiles of teachers, students, and other members of the school community that recognize their different strengths.

- Explore the strengths used by various characters in different texts and stories.

- Identify the strengths epitomized by leaders and historical figures.

- Integrate the language of strengths into student awards, recognitions, and records.

- Have assemblies or events that celebrate one or two strengths.

-ᆞᆼᆞ- **KEY IDEA:** A foundation of a strengths-based approach is nurturing students' strengths vocabulary, and their understanding of each strength. There are many ways teachers can build students' strengths knowledge—the more creative and varied the strategies, the better.

BOX 8.4: Diverse strengths

We would like to reiterate that the 24 strengths in the VIA framework do not comprise an exhaustive list of the strengths within humanity. Frequently, students connect strongly with strengths not represented in the VIA, such as love of nature, patience, punctuality, initiative, and calmness under pressure. A worthwhile class exercise may be to brainstorm strengths that are not part of the VIA framework. We have also seen schools create words or phrases for unique strengths important to their school community.

Every culture and community has unique and important strengths. When responding through a culturally responsive approach, it is valuable to encourage students to think about strengths reflected in their culture and community. Students can be encouraged to consider how their own culture's strengths overlap with the VIA framework, and how they are different. Many students traverse a number of different cultural expectations from their own home, extended family, communities, and schools. Identifying strengths within each of their cultural affiliations can build both understanding and connections within the classroom.

SIGNATURE STRENGTHS

We recommend supporting students to develop their understanding of a wide range of character strengths. We also recommend encouraging students to reflect on their unique character strengths profiles through exploring their signature strengths. Signature strengths are the subset of character strengths that come most readily to a person (Park and Peterson 2009). Within your school community, some students may be high on the strength of kindness, others may be known for their leadership, and others known as beacons of zest and enthusiasm.

Dr. Ryan Niemiec and Professor Robert McGrath (2019) describe the 3Es of signature strengths:

- *Essential:* the strength is a core part of who you are.

- *Effortless:* using the strength feels natural; it comes easily to you.

- *Energizing:* using the strength leads to a sense of happiness, vitality, and authenticity.

Identifying and using signature strengths is associated with increased wellbeing and decreased symptoms of depression (Schutte and Malouff 2019). Many students (and many teachers too) find exploring their signature strengths is a pathway towards self-awareness and growth. Proyer *et al.* (2015) found that people who benefit the most from identifying and using their signature strengths are those who initially do not think they have many strengths at all. We found this to be an encouraging finding as, like Zane, many students we work with have had few opportunities to identify and grow their strengths.

🔆 **KEY IDEA:** Our aspiration is that every student leaves a classroom able to articulate, develop, and employ their signature strengths, both now and in the future.

IDENTIFYING SIGNATURE STRENGTHS

We have carefully considered how to help students identify their signature strengths. One approach is for classes of students (or individual students) to complete an evidence-based strengths assessment. There is a range of online character strengths assessments that are relevant for people of different age groups, including younger children, adolescents, and adults (Park and Peterson 2006; Rashid *et al.* 2013; Shoshani 2019). Another valuable idea is for the entire school staff to complete a VIA strengths assessment and compare and contrast their character strengths profiles as a group of teaching professionals.

When working with students, it is also important to consider methods of exploring signature strengths that do not rely on high levels of literacy. In one school, each week the teacher would write two strengths on the whiteboard. The teacher would then provide these instructions: 'Today we are going to study a story that describes a difficult social situation between two friends. Now, I have written two words on the board: curiosity and fairness. I want you to think carefully about which of the character strengths you would use to manage the situation if you were involved.' Once the text had been introduced, students spent time in individual reflection, speaking in pairs, or engaging in a whole-class discussion, exploring how different strengths may be applied to the scenario. Throughout the year, the students expanded their strengths vocabulary and developed their understanding of how strengths are reflected in texts as well as their own lives. In Box 8.5, we outline important points to be aware of when considering a strengths approach.

BOX 8.5: Important points about strengths

- All VIA strengths exist to varying degrees in all of us and are useful in different situations.

- It is important to nurture a growth mindset about strengths—even if a strength is identified as a signature strength, there is still room to grow.

- Identifying and using signature strengths is important; however, sometimes the greatest growth comes from building character strengths that come less easily to us.

SPOTTING STUDENTS' STRENGTHS

Teachers can take an active role in helping students build awareness of their character strengths by being attuned to times when students are using their strengths throughout the school day. Strengths spotting is the skill of noticing and communicating the strengths used by the self and others (Linley 2008). Teacher strengths spotting has benefits for students' wellbeing and classroom engagement (Quinlan *et al.*

2018). Strengths may be evident in students' work, in their actions and behaviors, and during their interactions with others. For example, teachers may notice students using the strength of creativity when innovatively approaching a problem, or the strength of forgiveness after a conflict with a friend. Once the teacher sees a strength in use, it is valuable to provide this feedback to the student. To illustrate this, we provide an example of strengths spotting in Box 8.6.

You may find it easier to spot strengths in some students compared to others. At times, it may be difficult to see past a student's difficulties to notice and appreciate their strengths. It is useful to be aware that it can be easier to be attuned to the strengths you regularly use, compared to the strengths you underuse. An enthusiastic, zestful teacher shared the example of seeing countless examples of zest, humor, and bravery in action, but having to work hard to spot strengths of humility and prudence in their students. One idea is to spot and write down a character strength used by each student in your class each day for a couple of weeks. This helps gather information on students' signature strengths, and ensures that all students are recognized regularly for their positive qualities.

💡 **KEY IDEA:** Strengths spotting (the skill of noticing and appreciating strengths in use) has benefits for student-teacher relationships.

BOX 8.6: Strengths spotting example

Some students may find hearing about their strengths unfamiliar, confusing, manipulative, or inauthentic. Many students resist hearing about their strengths due to ruptured relationships with past teachers. We also understand that each culture has different ways of approaching this conversation. A teacher, Ms. Williams, shared a story about Katie, a student who had experienced little warmth or encouragement from her past teachers. Ms. Williams observed that Katie appeared highly uncomfortable whenever the concept of strengths came up. With the concept of *unpredictability = risk* in mind, Ms. Williams approached Katie carefully during quiet moments of the school day and pointed out her use of strengths. Ms. Williams would say, 'Katie, I noticed when you helped your friend at lunch today;

I noticed the character strength of kindness.' Ms. Williams would then move on and give Katie time and space to process this information privately while monitoring her reaction from across the room. Ms. Williams' hope was that, one day, Katie would recognize these strengths in herself. Katie knew Ms. Williams was looking for her strengths. Katie also knew she could trust Ms. Williams not to make her feel exposed or vulnerable. Over time, and as Katie's self-worth developed, she became more comfortable in strengths-based conversations, and Ms. Williams and Katie spoke more openly about her character strengths and positive qualities.

USING CHARACTER STRENGTHS

Once students have a well-developed understanding of strengths, and have had opportunities to identify their own signature strengths, we take the next step—putting strengths to use. Research has found that using strengths enhances wellbeing and positive emotions (Linley *et al.* 2010; Wood *et al.* 2011). Using character strengths also helps students develop resilience and provides a positive lens through which students can consider problems and challenges. Box 8.7 discusses using the language of strengths when providing feedback to students. Here are some ways of encouraging students to use their character strengths:

- Allocate small groups of students one of the VIA virtues. Ask students to brainstorm different ways of using each of the strengths included in this virtue. Have each group share their ideas with the class in a creative way.

- Allocate groups of students a different strength. Give students time to create a role play that depicts actively using the strength. Have the groups share their role plays with the rest of the class.

- Invite students to identify three strengths they used yesterday, and three strengths they plan to use today.

- Work together as a class to create a list of challenges common to students of a similar age. Encourage students to explore character strengths that may be useful in these situations.

- Have students think about one of their goals. Invite students to identify specific ways in which their strengths may support them as they work towards this goal.

- Have dual-purpose lesson plans that meet curriculum objectives and support the development of character strengths. For example, a lesson with the learning intention of writing a persuasive essay is an excellent opportunity to help students develop the strengths of curiosity and perspective.

BOX 8.7: Strengths and process praise

In Chapter 6, Stamina, we provided an overview of the importance of process praise and feedback (Mueller and Dweck 1998). Praise or feedback directed towards the effort the student has put into their work builds further effort, motivation, and growth mindset thinking, whereas person praise directed towards the student can undermine motivation and contribute to fixed mindset thinking. Integrating character strengths language is an excellent way of providing process feedback. The aim is to identify how students have applied their strengths in their work. For example, 'I noticed you using your strength of persistence here,' or 'Nice work on applying your strength of creativity to solve this problem.' In this way, integrating strengths-based language into feedback helps students develop their character strengths vocabulary, and helps build their effort and motivation.

STRENGTHS IN BALANCE

While we encourage students to develop confidence in applying their strengths, we also want them to think deeply about using strengths in balance. Dr. Ryan Niemiec (2019) observes that strengths can be overused or underused. Overuse occurs when the use of a strength goes too far and is unhelpful, and there are detrimental consequences for the self or others. Think of a student who perseveres with a goal to the point of exhaustion and burnout, or of someone who is kind to others to the point of neglecting their own needs. Another example may be a student who uses the strength of humor in a serious situation and upsets or offends others with sarcasm. Box 8.8 describes a time when considering the overuse of a strength was life-changing for a student.

Underuse of a strength occurs when *not* using a strength, or perhaps not using it enough, has costs for the self or others (Niemiec 2019). Underusing the strength of humility may lead to talking over other students and not allowing them the opportunity to share their news. Similarly, underusing the strength of teamwork may mean not pulling one's weight in a group assignment. Underuse of strengths is a pattern we often see in our students as they might have had few opportunities to develop their strengths in the context of consistent and nurturing relationships. Considering overuse, underuse, or misuse of strengths provides a wealth of opportunity for self-reflection and growth. Encouraging students to think deeply about strengths also develops their invaluable critical thinking and analysis skills. These questions can help students explore each of the 24 VIA strengths in balance:

- Can you think of ways in which this strength may be overused?

- Can you think of ways in which this strength may be underused?

- What are some situations where using this strength may be appropriate or helpful?

- What are some situations where using this strength may be inappropriate or harmful?

BOX 8.8: Intense risk management thinking

Nick was a senior student with a clinical diagnosis of depression and anxiety. His family had diligently overseen his professional treatment for years. Nick worried deeply about the risks in every situation. If the class was going on an excursion, Nick would think of a range of things that could go wrong. If he had to do a presentation at school, he would worry about leaving the materials at home, about the technology not working, about forgetting what he wanted to say while standing in front of the class. Nick's teachers tried a range of strategies for supporting him, but his negative thoughts and internal distress persisted.

One day, while looking at character strengths, Nick and his teachers had an epiphany. What if Nick's ability to think of all the different risks and outcomes was actually a strength? He was overusing his character strength of prudence—his extreme cautiousness. Nick and his own mother went one step further and created a special name for the overuse of his strength: intense risk management thinking.

Reframing Nick's experiences in this way was life-changing for him. He could still become highly distressed when his brain went into overdrive, but he was better able to recognize what was happening. He was able to see that by focusing on the risks in each situation, his brain was trying to protect him from negative outcomes. With this top-down insight, he could apply a mindfulness or resilience strategy that helped create distance from his negative self-talk and constant rumination. He began to fortify his bottom-up regulation and management of physical escalation in many more situations. Eventually, the school community recognized that Nick was a valued member of any team due to his capacity to pre-empt different outcomes and potential obstacles. He was excellent in an emergency as he had had so much practice coming up with contingency plans and possibilities. Nick has since gone on to finish school and pursue a career in emergency services. He knows he has to remain mindful of his mental health (and engage with professional help when needed), but he has recognized that his intense risk management thinking can be a tremendous asset when used in balance.

STRENGTHS-BASED QUESTIONING

One conversation we had with a team of teachers began with a student who consistently refused to start his classwork. After a time, we asked the teachers to name one or two of the student's strengths. One teacher commented, 'Well, he has potential, but…' The teacher then provided more examples of dysregulated behaviors. All of the other teachers joined in, reiterating their perceptions of the student's unmet needs. Again, we asked the teachers to think of one or two strengths. This time, they were stumped.

Professor Lea Waters (2017) recommends an approach she calls the 'strengths switch.' When we see children and young people through the lens of their difficulties or challenges, we can get stuck in a cycle of trying to remediate their unmet learning needs. We want to do our best to prepare students for the future; we focus on areas of improvement because we are motivated by a desire to give students the best chance of success. However, we can become so concerned about how to address students' needs or areas of difficulty that we can lose sight of their strengths and positive qualities. Here is the switch. When we see students through the lens of their strengths—and help them to connect with these strengths—we maximize and make the most of what they have. In helping students to connect with their strengths, we empower them and support their wellbeing and growth.

Strengths-based questioning is an invaluable tool for identifying and connecting with students' strengths. This strategy involves intentionally reflecting on times when students are succeeding in the classroom. Imagine you are working with a student who struggles with dysregulated and defiant behavior. We would recommend asking a series of questions like this: When is the student on task? When is he in flow? When is he connecting with others in meaningful ways? When is he using his character strengths? In which pockets of time is this student present, centered, and ready to learn?

Through strengths-based questioning, we may see that a student who struggles to stay on task is at their best when they have ample opportunities to move. Or a student who appears reticent to join in group activities opens up when they start the day with a small ritual that provides a sense of belonging and responsibility. Similarly, we may become attuned to the fact that a student who often shows signs of hypo-arousal lights up when the school therapy dog is around or when they spend time in nature. When we have a good understanding of moments when students are at their best, we can take steps to replicate conditions that ensure these moments happen as often as possible. Box 8.9 poses strengths-based questioning you can practice when considering a student you are concerned about.

🔅 **KEY IDEA:** Strengths-based questioning involves identifying when students are succeeding and capitalizing on this information, and supporting their learning and growth.

BOX 8.9: Teacher reflection and discussion questions
Bring to mind a student you are concerned about...

- Can you think of a time when the student was present, centered, and ready to learn?

- Can you think of a time when the student was in flow?

- Can you think of a time when the student connected meaningfully with others?

- Can you think of a time when the student positively contributed to the classroom community?

- What was happening in the student's routine or environment that enabled the student to thrive in these moments?

- What insights can you derive from these reflections to replicate conditions of success and help you support the student's unmet needs in other ways?

GRATITUDE

All 24 character strengths are valued pathways towards wellbeing and growth. We would like to shine a light on two strengths that have the potential to transform school communities—gratitude and hope. Gratitude involves being aware of and appreciating the good things in life, and taking time to express one's appreciation to others (Emmons 2007). Dr. Kerry Howells (2012) defines gratitude as acknowledging what we receive from others, and being motivated to express our appreciation and give back.

Over recent decades, gratitude has gained increasing recognition in the scientific community for the role it plays in wellbeing—and rightfully so. Gratitude is consistently associated with wellbeing and mental health (Wood, Froh, and Geraghty 2010). Cultivating gratitude is an especially powerful strategy in young people who experience low levels of positive emotions (Froh *et al.* 2009). Gratitude is associated with pro-social behaviors (behaviors intended to benefit others), and the drive to contribute to society (Froh, Bono, and Emmons 2010; Ma, Tunney, and Ferguson 2017).

There are many creative ways to embed gratitude into daily classroom routines. Here are some ideas:

- Greet students warmly by name when they arrive at school and thank them for joining the classroom community each day.

- Have a 'what went well' (www) board in the classroom (or even the staffroom) where students or staff can note good things that happen.

- Create gestures of appreciation for classroom guests and visitors.

- Develop rituals for thanking students who contribute to co-maintaining learning spaces.

- Encourage students to action gratitude for members of the school community, or even their families.

We have also found that students often surprise themselves when given time and support to develop their own gratitude interventions. In one school, a group of students worked together to make the principal the target of a gratitude project. Throughout the week, they left her thankful notes, recognized her efforts at meetings, and accumulated positive messages about her from members of the school community, including staff, students, and parents. At the end of the week, the project was revealed. The principal was immensely touched by this gesture. The students described being surprised at how good this made them feel. This is a powerful reminder that gratitude affects both the giver and the receiver.

> 💡 **KEY IDEA:** Embedding gratitude into the class and school community in thoughtful ways has meaningful consequences for wellbeing and relationships.

HOPE

Alongside gratitude, the character strength of hope is integral to trauma-informed, strengths-based classrooms. Hope involves expecting the best for the future and working to achieve it (Park *et al.* 2004). Young people's future beliefs are psychological resources that play a protective role against mental ill-health (Hamilton *et al.* 2015). Students' thoughts, feelings, and expectations about the future also play a central role in shaping their life paths (Seligman *et al.* 2013). Everyday decisions students make—from selecting their friends to deciding their classes and extra-curricular activities—are influenced by their aspirations (Callina *et al.* 2017). Students who struggle with low self-concept and self-efficacy may feel they have limited options for the future, or experience a sense of inevitability regarding their future life pathways. We want to support all students to be hopeful about the future, have confidence to pursue ambitious goals for themselves, and develop life strategies that enable them to exceed their own goals.

Snyder's (2002) hope model is a useful framework for helping students develop confidence in the future. Snyder describes hope as a positive motivational state that comprises three parts: goals, pathways, and agency. Goals are mental targets or representations that guide human behavior. Pathways (also referred to as *waypower*) involve the capacity to generate multiple strategies to achieve the goal. Agency (also known as *willpower*) is the motivation to implement the pathways. Hopeful people have a thinking style that integrates both waypower and willpower; they know how to set attainable goals that are intrinsically motivating to them, and mobilize multiple pathways to reach those goals. We have provided some examples of willpower and waypower in Box 8.10.

BOX 8.10: Examples of hope mindset in action

GOAL

- I will finish 20 minutes of reading independently at home each day this week.

WILLPOWER (IDENTIFYING ONE'S INTENTIONS AND COUNTER-INTENTIONS)

- I am motivated to do my independent reading homework because I know it will help increase my reading level in class. I also can predict that there are many distractions at home that may be speedbumps to my goal.

WAYPOWER (BRAINSTORMING THREE 'IF...THEN' PLANS)

- *If* I get home and my brother is bothering me, *then* I will go to my mother's room and close the door.

- *If* I don't understand a vocabulary word in the text, *then* I will circle it and ask an adult for help.

- *If* I go home and I start my reading and my best friend calls me, *then* I will not answer her call, but I will text her back and say I will call her in 20 minutes after my reading is done.

DEVELOPING WAYPOWER AND WILLPOWER

Pathways (waypower) and agency (willpower) are highly teachable capacities that serve as valuable psychological resources throughout life. To foster waypower, we recommend providing students with regular opportunities to brainstorm different strategies for achieving their goals. When a teacher hears about a student's goal (big or small), the next prompt should be: 'Let's brainstorm different ways to get there.' Our experience tells us that students who struggle with goal attainment certainly make goals for themselves, but often do not have a 'plan B' when 'plan A' doesn't work. Students do well when they assume they will need multiple plans to get to the same goal. Students also benefit from generating alternative strategies when barriers are encountered (we refer to this as '*if...then...*' thinking). Other strategies for building waypower include breaking large goals into smaller steps and using stretch goals (i.e. goals that are progressively more challenging).

Willpower—the motivation to stay with the goal—can often be uncovered by motivational interviewing (see Chapter 7, Engagement, for a discussion of this). Often, student willpower is increased if students uncover their intentions and counter-intentions towards completing an ambitious goal. In addition, working in teams, sharing stories of success, and providing regular feedback are strategies for encouraging willpower. We also recognize that willpower is influenced by relationships; in particular, nurturing student-teacher relationships are imperative in providing students with the confidence to achieve their goals and the motivation to do so.

💡 **KEY IDEA:** Cultivating waypower and willpower helps students to develop hope and to feel confident about future life pathways.

THE TRIAGE CONVERSATION

As you may recall from previous chapters, the triage conversation is the respectful and restorative conversation that happens between teachers and students to explore areas for growth. Here are some ways in which the language of character strengths may be useful in the triage conversation:

> Humor is one of your strengths, and you often put it to great use making us all laugh. However, when you made that joke about the way another student looked, it was actually an overuse of humor. I am wondering if we can combine your strength of humor with your strength of social intelligence and look for ways we can use your strengths to make other people feel good about themselves.

> You have the strength of fairness, and you were using your strength of fairness on the soccer pitch today. And you are right—your team did deserve that goal. However, arguing with the referee, and making a big drama of things with your team, clearly didn't work out well for you. While I appreciate that you were trying to use your strength of fairness, we've got to brainstorm how to use your strength of perspective for next time.

> You have the strength of honesty and you use that strength in a lot of helpful ways in this classroom. However, today you were overusing your honesty by telling your friends what you really thought of their art projects without considering the effort and care they put into their own work. We also need to think of kindness when you are giving that fix-it feedback to your friends.

REVISITING ZANE

Let's revisit Zane, who we introduced at the beginning of the chapter. You may recall that Zane had many complex unmet needs—his behavioral dysregulation was so extreme that he had been excluded from three schools. On his first day, his teacher, Ms. Brown, had sat with

Zane and completed an online assessment of VIA character strengths with him. Ms. Brown finished that first day with a lot of work to do, and a great deal of hope. She had one invaluable piece of information about Zane—he had identified that he had the signature strength of humor. She also knew that he had never been given the opportunity for that strength to shine.

This information about Zane's strength of humor was key to opening up all sorts of growth pathways for him. Ms. Brown used this knowledge to develop her relationship with Zane, through sharing jokes, funny pictures, and stories. She used humor to defuse situations when she saw that Zane was showing early signs of becoming escalated and dysregulated. She developed a collection of funny pictures and clips that she could show to the whole class as needed. Ms. Brown also shared Zane's strengths with the whole school staff. She identified staff members who were known for their humor and asked them to look for opportunities to connect with him.

Ms. Brown realized that Zane had a lot going on in his mind that he was not sharing with the world. She deliberately created opportunities for him to open up. She created group work opportunities where he was paired with students who also had the signature strength of humor and watched quietly from a distance when he started to engage in the humorous banter. She molded the curriculum to capitalize on this strength and created opportunities for students to write funny stories, develop comic strips, and even research the history of comedy. Building on this, she next extended his focus to another one of his signature strengths: bravery. She was also deeply respectful of his talent for skateboarding and looked for books, resources, and learning resources that could draw on this special interest.

Like many of our students, Zane had real and complex difficulties. He needed the best of all of the strategies covered in our book so far. He needed bottom-up activities for soothing his dysregulated stress response systems. He needed time and space to develop enduring attachments with adults who treated him with warmth and consistency. We also recognize and respect that Zane needed specialized therapeutic care from qualified health professionals. He deserved the best healing approaches that the school and community could offer him. However, Zane also needed the adults in his life to go one step further. He needed teachers to focus on his strengths and see the best in him. This focus on strengths made all the difference in terms of changing the trajectory of Zane's life.

When we last spoke to Ms. Brown, Zane was thriving. Over the space of two years, he had made significant progress in his literacy and numeracy goals. He had several strong relationships with staff members across the school community. He had a solid group of friends and had joined a sports team. Ms. Brown was again brushing away tears when she told us this next bit—Zane had recently successfully applied for a part-time job at the local cafe. Apparently, during the interview, the manager had asked Zane to describe his strengths. Zane was more than ready: 'I skateboard. Skateboarding has helped me to develop my strengths of humor, bravery, teamwork, kindness, and persistence. I will bring these strengths to your team and customers.'

SOME CONCLUDING THOUGHTS

When we first met with Zane's teachers, they voiced concerns that focusing on his strengths was somehow less important or valid than addressing his regulatory and relational needs. This conversation is both familiar to us and deeply respected. We have had many robust discussions on how to integrate strengths-based and trauma-informed teaching approaches. Our comprehensive focus on strengths has been critiqued for being simplistic or insufficient when considering the needs of students who have experienced complex trauma and disrupted attachments.

We persist in our mission to bring rigorous strengths-based conversations to classrooms because we have seen promising things happen when teachers and students are focused on their strengths, which in turn builds their own ability to employ top-down regulation for psychological resources. Yes, a student may have had a dysregulated morning in the context of an escalated home environment, but a teacher who is continually thinking of ways to help students to live in their character strengths—and reconceives the curriculum as a strengths-based way to communicate—can open up wonderful pathways towards self-knowledge, self-worth, and growth for their students. Our children succeed when both their unmet needs for healing and pathways to growth are considered in the classroom.

SELF-REFLECTION CHECKLIST

After completing this chapter, please check you can do the following:

- ✓ Understand the importance of a strengths-based approach for all students.

- ✓ Integrate the VIA language into your classroom and curriculum in ways that are suitable for your students and context.

- ✓ Encourage your students to identify, use, and grow their character strengths.

- ✓ Use strengths-based questioning to see students through the lens of what they do well.

- ✓ Appreciate the value of gratitude in creating positive emotions and nurturing feelings of connectedness and belonging in the classroom.

- ✓ Support students to develop hopeful mindsets through a focus on cultivating willpower and waypower.

CHAPTER 9

Moving Forward

We have explored with you the developmental domains of Body, Relationship, Stamina, Engagement, and Character. In conclusion, we would like to return to the purpose we attach to these domains. We invite you to recall Jalen, who we introduced in Chapter 3, A Developmentally Informed Approach to Learning, and the 'big moment' we observed during our visit to his school—the moment he broke into the school's shed, took a bike, and rode it across the school yard, disrupting many students playing at recess time. Jalen demonstrated many unmet needs resulting in behavioral, emotional, and relational dysregulation. Jalen's teachers and staff across the school community worked collaboratively over three school terms to meet his needs within the school. Slowly, and with determination and patience from both Jalen and his teachers, he began to experience positive shifts in his behavior, learning, and relationships.

Here, we would like to focus on one teachable moment with Jalen and use it to draw together key messages from our journey. We invite you to imagine the scene that took place one day after lunch when the class commenced a sustained reading activity. With support from one of his teachers, Jalen selected a text well matched to his independent reading level. As the teacher scanned the room within the first two minutes, she observed Jalen was on task and focused on his chosen story. A few moments later one of his classmates leaned over and loudly commented, 'Why is Jalen reading a baby book? I read that book last year!'

The teacher knew this comment was going to escalate Jalen's behavior. It challenged his self-concept and identity in front of his peers. She could see Jalen's body change, his muscles tense, his hands scrunch, his shoulders stiffen. The teacher reflected that her old approach would have been to quickly reassure Jalen the book was fine in an effort to prevent him from spiraling towards dysregulation. However, she now understood that for Jalen to be receptive to that conversation he would have to be in his 'thinking brain.' That approach would not work: his functioning was oscillating between his 'thinking brain' and 'survival brain.'

As she moved quickly to support Jalen, the teacher immediately thought of bottom-up and top-down regulation. In particular, the first question she asked herself was: 'What does Jalen need to regulate his body right now?' After substantial groundwork, the teacher had a range of strategies available to her that may help to de-escalate Jalen and soothe his firing fight-flight-freeze response. She could encourage Jalen to do some deep breathing, practice mindfulness, activate his focus plan, or invite him to come over to the de-escalation (calming) station at the back of the classroom. The teacher made a judgment that she wanted to preserve Jalen's sense of connectedness to the group. She stood close to Jalen and informed the class it was time to pause and take a brain break. She decided on a call and response game because she knew Jalen responded well to these activities. Furthermore, a call and response pattern would be rhythmic, soothing, and regulatory; and the whole class needed a quick break because all eyes had turned to the drama at Jalen's table.

Throughout this process, the teacher was also thinking bottom-up regulation through Relationship. After numerous months together, the teacher now had a well-honed strategy for co-regulating Jalen. When she got a moment, she crouched down next to Jalen, side to side and shoulder to shoulder, and kept her voice low as she spoke calmly with him. As she crouched down she was mindful of her own stress response, knowing the most effective thing that she could do was to send neuroceptive messages of safety: I am here, you are safe; together, we've got this. Simultaneously, she looked at the other student to non-verbally convey the message, I'll have a word with you in a moment—please continue reading.

At the same time, the teacher was thinking about Jalen's top-down regulation. The teacher drew on her strategies in the Stamina domain. In particular, she was aware of the importance of fostering Jalen's growth mindset and his belief that 'My effort matters, I am improving every day.' She also knew she had to listen carefully for Jalen's common mindhooks of 'See! He's distracting me!' and 'I will never get this.' As she co-regulated Jalen through a calm and supportive presence, she also gently challenged these unhelpful thoughts that posed barriers to his stamina for reading.

As Jalen's teacher considered the Engagement domain, she scanned the Flow Checklist in her mind. She knew she had to provide regular feedback to Jalen to keep him in the game. As the class resumed their sustained reading after the brain break, the teacher walked in a circle around the class, providing Jalen with feedback on every circle—helping him with a trickier word, giving him a quick thumbs-up. She made a commitment to herself, and to Jalen, that she would source more books, particularly graphic novels, that were both age and reading-level appropriate for him. She knew the de-escalating and nurturing power of positive emotions, so after the conclusion of the activity she had the class reflect on 'www' and share three things they did well during the lesson.

As the class transitioned to the next activity, the teacher found a moment to have a one-to-one triage conversation with Jalen, in which she ensured she drew out his character strengths. She shared with Jalen that she was aware the comment may have distracted him from his learning, but she was so proud he did not respond immediately. He allowed her to deal with the other student, and he was able to maintain his stamina for reading through the remainder of the lesson. She told Jalen she noticed the strengths of persistence, love of learning, and forgiveness, through his actions. She also asked Jalen whether he could identify any character strengths he used during the lesson. With his big smile, Jalen identified his use of the strength of love of learning.

A DEVELOPMENTAL JOURNEY

What we observed in the teacher's work with Jalen, and what we aspire for teachers to achieve, is a flexible and nuanced balance between bottom-up and top-down regulation. Often, teachers start with a top-down approach—providing directions, offering choices, or asking students to explain their actions. When students are well regulated and in their thinking brain, a top-down approach works for most. However, developmentally we need to shift this mindset so that teachers are

233

mindful of both bottom-up and top-down strategies being in place for some students.

We see bottom-up regulation as Body. When students are demonstrating complex behaviors in the classroom, we want teachers to consider whether they have unmet needs in their stress response systems. We want teachers to hone their skills in detecting early changes in students' behavior, emotions, and physiological states that indicate they may be on a trajectory towards hyper- or hypo-arousal. When students show signs of dysregulation, teachers can ask themselves several questions: What does this child need right now to regulate their body? How can I support this student to understand their stress response? How can I integrate mindfulness and breathing strategies and help the student to de-escalate? How can I provide calming environments, and the routines, rituals, and rhythms that widen students' window of tolerance and help them to be present, centered, and ready to learn?

We also see bottom-up regulation as Relationship. We continually remind ourselves that strong student-teacher relationships are co-regulatory (Schore and Schore 2007). When teachers keep their voices calm and their non-verbal cues soothing, they help students come back to within their window of tolerance (Siegel 2020). In moments of dysregulation, teachers have an opportunity to serve as a safe haven for students and send neuroceptive messages of warmth and safety (Porges 2004). Teachers can communicate unconditional positive regard through the pathways of separating students from their behavior, maintaining a vision for the child's wholeness, and remembering the developmental gates students may have missed. When all these conditions are in play, we encourage teachers to address and intentionally call students out with love in their voice. When teachers use the pathways to unconditional positive regard, they send the message 'I will be there for you, accept you, and support you, even in the difficult moments.'

💡 **KEY IDEA:** Teachers support students through bottom-up regulatory strategies that focus on the body and co-regulating students through nurturing relational interactions.

FROM BOTTOM-UP TO TOP-DOWN

As we focus on students' bottom-up regulatory needs, we also consider top-down regulatory strategies that address students' cognitive and thinking needs. We conceptualize top-down capacities as increasing students' own abilities to identify and make positive choices featured in the developmental domains of Stamina, Engagement, and Character. These domains highlight strategies with a top-down focus that supports students' own decisions to self-regulate and to learn.

In Stamina, the focus is on building students' capacity to sustain on-task behavior. The Stamina domain is based on the understanding that learning can be an uncomfortable process, especially for students such as Jalen with histories of unmet learning needs. Through the Stamina domain, the goal is for students to identify moments when they are finding learning difficult and, taking a deep breath, connect with a strategy that helps them persist. This strategy may be to use their knowledge of fixed and growth mindsets (Dweck 2008), or understanding their resilient self-talk and identifying unhelpful thoughts that pose a barrier to their engagement in the moment. Stamina also focuses on developing students' emotional intelligence and helping them to identify, understand, regulate, and communicate the myriad feelings they may experience throughout the school day. Building on this foundation is a focus on classroom strategies for students to deliberately practice their independent learning, such as stamina graphs and stamina thermometers, that build stamina on a whole-class level.

When thinking of top-down regulation, we encourage teachers to consider engagement. Students are empowered when teachers consider—both explicitly in their conversations with them, and implicitly in their planning for them—that students may experience substantial ambivalence towards their learning. Through considering students' intentions and counter-intentions, teachers help their students uncover more complex barriers that detract from students' natural desire to put forth effort in the classroom. Teachers also support students when they cultivate conditions for flow in the classroom: when they ensure students' skill level matches the challenge level of the task; when they provide feedback in immediate and meaningful ways; when the task has clear goals and fair expectations known to each student (Csikszentmihalyi 1990). Through intentionally weaving moments of

235

fun, playfulness, and respectful humor through the school day, teachers create broaden-and-build pathways to growth for students (Fredrickson and Joiner 2002).

The developmental pathway of Character further supports students' top-down regulatory needs. Helping the school community to develop a thriving language of character strengths serves as a valuable foundation for identifying the strengths of the self and others. Reconceptualizing the curriculum as a strengths-based way of communicating (e.g. encouraging students to read a text and identify strengths in different characters) helps students develop insight and wisdom into how people are similar and how they are different. Encouraging students to explore the strengths reflected in their own cultural and community groups helps build their self-awareness and self-concept, and serves as a respectful way of bringing culture into the classroom. As we recognize the value of character strengths for students, we also consider the strengths of hope and gratitude as particularly valuable pathways to growth and healing.

:Q: **KEY IDEA:** The developmental pathways of Stamina, Engagement, and Character help to support students' top-down regulatory needs.

BOTTOM-UP AND TOP-DOWN INTEGRATION

When thinking of the developmental pathways of Body, Relationship, Stamina, Engagement, and Character, we invite you to consider the term *integration* as both a metaphor in your work with students and an actual goal within the body itself. It is an overarching goal of trauma-informed, strengths-based classrooms to support students' holistic development in ways that support their brain, sensory, and body integration.

First, we consider that when a student's brain is not well integrated (also known as dis-integration), the different parts of the brain do not function in a coordinated way, and the student's behavior can become confused and chaotic (Siegel and Payne Bryson 2012). When a student's brain is well integrated, the different parts of the brain work well together, and the student develops a coherent understanding of themselves within their environment.

Sensory integration is also essential to holistic child development. Sensory integration is when the physical and neurological processes involved in organizing and modulating sensory input obtained from the body and the environment work in coordinated ways (Abraham *et al.* 2015). When students can process sensory information in integrated ways, they experience feelings of confidence and safety. When students struggle with sensory integration, they may become hypo- or hyper-sensitive to input from their environment, and the world can feel like an overwhelming or confusing place.

We also consider the importance of integrating the brain with the body. As a child's development progresses, neural connections between body and brain strengthen, facilitating more refined fine and gross motor coordination. While brain-body integration is important to all children, it is especially important for young people who have experienced adversity and who may experience, as a consequence, a disconnect between their brains and their bodies (van der Kolk 2014). For example, the trauma symptom of dissociation is characterized by feelings of numbness and lack of awareness of bodily states (Ogden, Minton, and Pain 2006). Similarly, students who have experienced adversity may have difficulties in interoceptive awareness, and in detecting and interpreting physiological cues essential to emotional awareness and regulation (Price and Hooven 2018). Therefore, we consider nurturing brain-body connections as imperative for all students, particularly those who have experienced stress and trauma. In Box 9.1, we provide an example that explores dis-integration and integration in more detail.

Keeping the importance of brain, sensory, and body integration in mind, we look continually for ways of nurturing students' neural networks in ways that enable them to heal, learn, and grow. Dr. Dan Siegel and Dr. Tina Payne Bryson (2012) use the metaphor of the whole-brain child to convey that the goal of healthy child development is for the different parts of the brain and body to work together in well-functioning ways. The key to this holistic development is experience—when students' neurons fire together, new connections between them grow, paving the way to integrated brain architecture. As students have enriching and nourishing experiences in safe environments, they strengthen their brain architecture. While daily outcomes may be small, they add up over time through repeated nurturing experiences. Therefore, every day, as teachers support students through the domains of Body, Relationship, Stamina, Engagement, and Character, we believe they nurture an integrated brain.

Here are examples of ways we believe strategies across the developmental domains support students' integration:

- Activities involving a balance between bottom-up and top-down regulatory strategies strengthen neural pathways between the 'survival brain' and the 'thinking brain.'

- Nurturing relational interactions with their teachers supports the healthy development of students' brain architecture.

- Providing opportunities for students to modulate and discriminate different sensory input supports their sensory integration.

- Helping students develop emotional awareness and literacy helps build connections between bodily awareness and the brain.

- Encouraging students to move their bodies creates neural networks for brain-body connections; for example, movement-based brain breaks both support students' brain-body integration and increase their physical activity levels throughout the day.

- Inviting students to consciously reflect on what is going on in their bodies strengthens brain-body awareness and connections.

💡 **KEY IDEA:** Providing students with nourishing activities and attachment-rich interactions nurtures an integrated understanding of the self, others, and the world.

BOX 9.1: The integrated student

Consider a moment of stress in the classroom, first through dis-integration and then through integration. In this moment, two students are sharing a pair of scissors for a craft activity. They reach for the scissors at the same time. One student snatches them, even though it was the other student's turn to use the scissors. Here, we look at the experience of the student who quickly escalated because she did not grab the scissors first.

RESPONSE A

In a state of dis-integration, the student's stress response begins to fire, and she feels increasing and confusing waves of distress and discomfort. The student slams her work on the desk and retreats to a corner. She sits down, folds her arms across her body, and starts to cry. The student is aware that everyone is looking at her. Crying over some scissors appears trivial; even she does not quite understand why she is so upset. Her interpretation of the situation escalates to justify her extreme reaction to herself and others—the student claims the other student always treats her badly and this class is never fair. At this point, the other students are becoming escalated. The teacher is flustered about how to contain so much emotion in the room at once.

RESPONSE B

Let's look at the same moment, through the lens of integration.

After her classmate took the scissors, the student attends to her body cues that her stress response is beginning to fire. She can identify and label that her heart is starting to race, and her face is starting to feel hot. She knows these are key signs of a fight-flight response for her. Because her teachers have intentionally given her the vocabulary of her stress response and heated emotions, she can also identify the feelings she is experiencing with words—confused, frustrated, angry. She takes some deep breaths, as she has been practicing with her class for the entire school year, and this calms her stress response enough so she can stay in her thinking brain and make a plan. She is able to shake it out (literally through the movement of a brain break). She realizes that while it does not feel nice when someone snatches something from you, it is just a pair of scissors. She can easily do something else while she waits for her turn. She has the thought that her character strength is kindness, and she is going to activate her strength right now by stepping away and not acting in ways that further escalate this situation.

The teacher has observed the situation unfold from a distance. Later, quietly, she commends the student for stepping away, noting her strength of kindness and also her use of the strength of leadership. Knowing the importance of building fairness and belonging across the whole class, the teacher later revisits the classroom values of fairness and sharing with others. She does not name or shame the student who took the scissors in the first place.

LIMITATIONS OF THIS BOOK

This book shares a developmental journey through the five domains of Body, Relationship, Stamina, Engagement, and Character. This chapter introduces the idea that approaching student learning through these domains supports students to become more integrated. That is, when students' bottom-up and top-down regulatory needs are met, they can respond to the world in a balanced, coordinated, and growth-focused manner. We are also aware of both the limitations of our approach, and the topics we have not covered in depth.

We are aware this book does not adequately cover how to involve parents, carers, and families. Similarly, we have not focused explicitly on the importance of school-community partnerships, nor how to apply strategies with students with special educational needs. We also acknowledge that our team is committed to a journey towards culturally responsive pedagogies and placing students' cultures at the center of school practice. We will also discuss limitations in our interpretation of the evidence base, specifically that we often discuss inherently complex ideas and topics in simple ways that can be effectively integrated into the classroom. We will now discuss these limitations in turn.

INVOLVING PARENTS, CARERS, AND FAMILIES

We have prioritized classroom strategies as a practical and priority starting point for creating trauma-informed, strengths-based schools. What we have not covered is the role of parents and families in nurturing students' holistic development. While strategies for involving parents and families is beyond our scope here, it is important to acknowledge the best outcomes for students always come from strong school-home partnerships. Students benefit greatly when teachers and parents work as a team in nurturing their academic, emotional, and social growth.

Best practice in trauma-informed, strengths-based schools involves creating a shared language so students hear the same messages at home as they do at school. It is incredibly valuable for parents and carers to be empowered with terms such as 'escalated,' 'de-escalated,' and 'centered' to describe their children's experiences and behavior, rather than resorting to unhelpful labels sometimes used to describe young people's behavioral and emotional struggles. Furthermore, when schools share effective strategies with families, they help build parents' toolkits of strategies that support their children's healing, learning, and growth.

We encourage all schools to prioritize home-school partnerships. With this in mind, one of the schools we work with has created a library of video clips that showcase trauma-informed, strengths-based strategies featuring their own students to share broadly with parents, families, and the wider community. This is a powerful teaching tool. Families can see the strategies across the developmental domains in action, explained by staff they are familiar with, and modeled by students within their own campus. As schools progress on their journey towards trauma-informed, strengths-based communities, we encourage them continually to ask how they can effectively bring parents, carers, and families along for this journey.

SCHOOL-COMMUNITY PARTNERSHIPS

We have not addressed the importance of school-community partnerships in meeting the needs of all students within the school community. We are inspired by schools that serve as the hub of the community; for example, schools that nurture strong connections with local health services, psychological services, services for families from cultural and linguistic diverse backgrounds, and early childhood services.

We want to acknowledge the importance of home, school, and community organizations working together when supporting students with complex learning, psychological, or developmental needs. In Chapter 3, A Developmentally Informed Approach to Learning, we discuss the importance of the three tiers of intervention (Victoria State Government Department of Education and Training 2020). We would like to reiterate that this book focuses on Tier 1 (universal interventions that support all students), and on Tier 2 (targeted classroom interventions for students considered at risk). We have not focused on Tier 3 interventions, which provide specialist support for students with complex needs. Tier 3 interventions may involve ongoing therapeutic supports from a school counselor, psychologist, health professional, and clinical care team. This level of individual intervention is not the core focus of this book, but we want to acknowledge explicitly the importance of targeted interventions delivered by qualified learning, health, and wellbeing professionals in providing trauma-informed, strengths-based care for students.

SPECIAL EDUCATIONAL NEEDS

We believe a strength of the developmental domains of Body, Relationship, Stamina, Engagement, and Character is that they can be used with students with a range of behavioral, developmental, and learning needs. However, we acknowledge that a shadow side of our desire for wide-ranging applicability is that we have not covered with depth or consistency strategies for students receiving special educational intervention. For example, we have not explicitly addressed how our strategies can be adapted for students with learning difficulties, autism spectrum disorders, attention deficit hyperactivity disorders, or other mental health or developmental needs. We invite you to share, and collectively adapt and scaffold, these strategies with allied education professionals who support your students.

We acknowledge that our strategies have been developed with input from therapeutic specialists, including psychologists, occupational therapists, wellbeing workers, and teachers, who have substantial experience in working with students with a range of special educational needs. We are also learning all the time as students teach us so much about supporting their growth. A more nuanced discussion of how to implement the strategies with students with special educational needs remains necessary, though it is beyond the scope of this book.

CULTURALLY RESPONSIVE PEDAGOGY

As we consider limitations that we were not able to adequately cover within this book, it is important to acknowledge our continued journey towards culturally responsive pedagogy. Culturally responsive pedagogy is defined as identifying, acknowledging, and embracing cultural backgrounds represented in the school as valuable resources within the school community—with intentional focus on the emancipatory power of education (Morrison *et al.* 2019). It acknowledges the impacts of systemic institutional racism within our communities and emphasizes first creating an environment of cultural safety within schools. All school communities benefit when they embrace inclusive practice to support students' own cultural identification, race, ethnicity, religion and spirituality, gender expression and sexual orientation, and geographical location when planning, implementing, and evaluating trauma-informed interventions (de Arellano and Danielson 2008; de Arellano *et al.* 2008).

To be culturally responsive and respectful is to acknowledge that culture impacts every aspect of a school. Even the simple idea of how different emotions are expressed and regulated varies substantially across cultures. We know that if we do not center students' cultures in our practice, we are missing valuable opportunities to engage both students and their families. Our team will always be on a journey towards establishing cultural safety in schools when learning about, respecting, and inviting people from different cultures to engage in education. Particularly for families that have experienced ongoing negative impacts of systemic institutional racism within education systems and within their communities, we urge schools to consider how to intentionally address these barriers—and the impacts of these barriers on learning. We remain committed to developing our culturally responsive pedagogical practices, recognizing our own subconscious biases, and showing our respect for the diverse voices and cultures that comprise our community.

A SIMPLIFICATION OF SCIENCE

We want to acknowledge that, at times, we do not do justice to the complexity of topics. In working with schools, we strive for applicability—we want strategies teachers can use every day in their classrooms, starting today. With this in mind, we take sophisticated and complex concepts and distill them into heuristic models that have utility in the classroom. As we shape evidence-informed concepts into classroom strategies, we are aware that at times we have not done justice to the complexities of ideas. This limitation is particularly relevant to our discussion of topics such as neurodevelopmental models, models of attachment, interpersonal neurobiology, and biological processes.

As an example, we write about the stress response system, aware that the human stress response is an incredibly complex system. We have been intentional in our decisions not to go into great depth about the underpinning neurological, biological, and hormonal processes involved. Our overview of the stress response may be a simplification, but we do know the heuristic model of the fight-flight-freeze response is extremely helpful for our students. We remain committed to psychoeducation suited to even the youngest members of school communities. At the same time, we acknowledge explicitly the limitations of simplifying complex concepts.

BIASES IN THE RESEARCH

In creating our trauma-informed, strengths-based strategies, we draw heavily on the peer-reviewed literature in the fields of neuroscience, traumatology, positive psychology and education, child development, and the science of learning. We would like to acknowledge the inherent limitations of the research methods most prevalent in these fields of inquiry. These disciplines often depend on quantitative methods based on numerical patterns across large samples. They may not adequately represent individual differences or the lived experiences of participants. Consequently, often they do not attempt to explain the ideographically unique experiences of each individual embedded within their own cultures and communities. We encourage our research peers to maintain focus on both quantitative and qualitative methods of inquiry. In particular, we would like to recognize that often the research literature does not adequately represent student voice.

To illustrate this complexity, we would like to draw your attention to the adverse childhood experiences (ACE) body of research which has been informative in shaping our approach. The field is certainly stronger because of the large-scale research studies that continually show the significant and lasting impact of early adversity across health, mental health, educational, and occupational outcomes (Anda *et al.* 2006; Hughes *et al.* 2007). However, we remember that ACE research focuses on a limited number of adverse childhood experiences. We know that many students' experiences of early stress and adversity may not be captured neatly by such a limited range of definitions or categories (see Kelly-Irving and Delpierre 2019 for an informative critique and exploration of the ACE research). While we pay attention to emerging research, we remain mindful that individual-level experiences may be inadequately reflected in studies based on patterns across large samples.

FUTURE DIRECTIONS FOR THE FIELD

We would like to note directions for the field of trauma-informed, strengths-based schools. Once teachers have strategies for transforming their classrooms through the developmental domains of Body, Relationship, Stamina, Engagement, and Character, we ask the next imperative question: how can we move towards systemic ways of working?

A systemic approach appreciates that students function within multiple and intersecting levels of community and culture (Bronfenbrenner 1979). A student may be a part of a family, an extended family, a school community, sporting teams, and extra curriculum organizations, as well as influenced by the geographical, political, and social environments in which they live. All these intersecting systemic factors play vital roles in children's development, health, learning, and resilience. A systemic approach recognizes that to truly shift behavioral, emotional, relational, and learning outcomes for students, the work cannot end when students leave the school gate. It must involve families, allied community organizations, access to health care and other supports, and cultural practices.

Once teachers feel confident in their capacity to support students in their classrooms, the next step is to ask further questions. How can we involve families in building trauma-informed, strengths-based communities? How can we form community partnerships that support students with diverse needs? What can we continue to learn from culture and community to better serve all children and young people? How can we leverage the power of a systemic approach to truly create community change? In Box 9.2, we consider the speedbump we often encounter in our work, when a teacher aspires to apply the strategies independently in their school, without being part of a whole-school or systemic commitment to change.

We see the power of a systemic approach when all schools within a geographic vicinity work in an aligned way. This is apparent when a family moves and is welcomed into a school community that shares similar language, strategies, and values to the school they have left. We see the value of a systemic approach when teachers arrive at a school bringing a foundation of knowledge and a wealth of ideas from how they have applied the developmental domains within their previous schools. An area for growth for our team is our increasing involvement in pre-service teacher training and our ongoing mentoring support for graduate teachers. We also join our colleagues and institutional partners to advance advocacy with local and national government about maintaining focus on the importance of trauma-informed, strengths-based teaching and learning standards, and supporting policy.

BOX 9.2: Managing the speedbumps

One of the biggest speedbumps we encounter in our work is hearing from teachers who initiate trauma-informed, strengths-based strategies by themselves in their schools. We are aware it can feel lonely when teachers are working individually in their schools and are not part of a whole-school journey towards change. In these situations, whole-school systemic change may seem a distant goal. We also recognize that creating trauma-informed, strengths-based communities can require a seismic culture shift. It may take several years within a school's strategic plan. Changing culture also requires buy-in from many levels of the school—the principal and leadership team, teaching and non-teaching staff, parents, carers, and members of the wider school community.

We do not want teachers to feel disheartened if other staff members within their school are not yet aware of our trauma-informed, strengths-based concepts, language, and strategies. If you are on an individual journey, we invite you to consider that you are creating a lighthouse classroom of best practice at your school. We invite you to identify one or more colleagues who hold similar values to you and create a partnership or team approach, sharing resources, strategies, and peer support. We invite you to be part of systemic change through sharing this book with others in your community. We have seen many examples where a commitment

---

to change has started with one or two individual teachers and gained momentum as a whole-school approach when other staff members come to see the value in the developmental domains of Body, Relationship, Stamina, Engagement, and Character.

FUTURE DIRECTIONS FOR YOU

We invite you to consider, acknowledge, and explore who you are in the classroom. Teachers experience many times when their work fulfills their needs for a sense of accomplishment, engagement, self-efficacy, and wellbeing. But when working with students for educational equity in communities of great need, we also anticipate that most teachers experience times when the work is exhausting; times when their resources feel stretched, and when it all feels too much.

As we consider the impact of this work on you, we want to briefly explore the concept of *secondary traumatic stress* in the workplace. This is defined as the negative impacts on professionals of working with and caring for people who have complex unmet needs (Stamm 1995). When teachers work with vulnerable children and communities, they are exposed to the impacts of trauma every day (Alisic *et al.* 2012; Caringi *et al.* 2015). We are aware of the emotional toll on teachers when they wave goodbye to children and young people at the end of the school day, not always knowing they are going to be safe and secure after school. Teachers hear about children and young people's difficulties and struggles, and they bear witness to the adversity students experience through the art they create and in the stories they write. It is also important to acknowledge the impact of trauma in non-verbal domains. When teachers are exposed continuously to childhood trauma, they can begin to mirror the physical dysregulation of their students (Halevi and Idisis 2018).

In particular, we draw your attention to three important terms:

- *Vicarious traumatization:* the negative feelings and physical impacts associated with regular exposure to other people's trauma stories and trauma histories (Hopwood, Schutte, and Loi 2019).

- *Compassion fatigue:* the draining of resources of empathy and compassion when teachers do not feel reciprocation for their efforts to care (Figley 1995; Koenig, Rodger, and Specht 2018).

- *Burnout:* the prolonged exposure to negative workplace conditions, including unmanageable class sizes, too many demands, and insufficient resources (MacDonald, Kelly, and Christen 2019; Maslach, Schaufeli, and Leiter 2001).

With this in mind, we recommend that teachers make a priority investment in their own wellbeing strategies and take active steps to nurture their own self-care. Prioritizing care for oneself can feel like another task on one's to-do list already filled with the often-competing priorities of classroom, school, and home life. We strongly recommend that teachers see caring for their own wellbeing as an essential investment. The wellbeing of teachers is incredibly important: to bring their calmest and most-regulated selves to the classroom, they need to care for themselves.

We encourage you to create a personal self-care plan covering physical, emotional, spiritual, energetic, and cognitive needs. What simple strategies can you do after work to move your physical body? Who can you connect with to refuel your reserves of care and empathy? What non-work-related interests can you look into to give your brain a rest from problem-solving work concerns?

Proactively brainstorming these strategies and having personal routines in place can ensure that you will do them when you most need to do so. Importantly, if you are feeling overwhelmed or notice the physical and psychological impacts of stress persist, we encourage you to seek help from qualified health professionals. Asking for help is an act of great strength, courage, resilience, and self-compassion.

RETURNING TO VALUES

As we come to the end of this book, we would like to return to our values of social action. Knowing our values, and acting in alignment with those values, is a pathway to wellbeing and resilience (Harris 2007). Furthermore, sharing values with others creates feelings of belonging and provides members of the school community with a common direction and purpose (Allen *et al.* 2018). We would like our journey to be charted by the values that motivate and anchor us. Box 9.3 invites you to reflect on the values that guide and anchor you.

We value relationships. We want every student to feel that their teachers want them in the room and hold a positive vision for their futures. Students succeed when they can feel teachers believe in their potential for academic progress and their capacity for emotional and relational growth.

We value teachers. We believe in the everyday courage and grit teachers bring to their classrooms. We do not underestimate the role that nurturing student-teacher relationships play in healthy child development.

We believe that teachers must be supported to love what they do. It is our aspiration that teachers build on what already works for them. We know teachers require strategies they can embed and integrate into the existing rhythms of their classrooms and schools.

We value and recognize the emancipatory power of education. We believe that all students, including those with significant behavioral concerns and those who sit on the boundaries of the school community, have the right to enriching educational opportunities and pathways towards future learning.

We value all students. We remind ourselves that often students who appear the most defiant or resistant, those whom teachers may find the most difficult to connect with, are students who may most need our care, help, and support.

We value culturally responsive pedagogy. We are committed to learning about and connecting with culture, and ensuring that our school communities are culturally safe. We are dedicated to teaching in ways that empower students of all cultures through an emancipatory mindset.

BOX 9.3: Teacher reflection and discussion questions

We invite you to reflect on your values in your classroom. You can use these questions to help you write a vision statement for your classroom that you share publicly with your students.

- What kind of future community do you want to foster in your classroom today?

- Who are you in the classroom when you are at your best?

- What values underpin your work with students?

- What fills you with a sense of meaning and purpose in your work?

FINISHING WITH GRATITUDE

We started this journey by saying that this book is for teachers—we would like to end this journey by acknowledging and thanking our greatest teachers: the children and young people we have worked with over the years. We are deeply committed to creating classrooms and schools that help students heal, learn, and grow. We live for the conversations with teachers and principals that recognize student strengths, that report school feels safe and welcoming, that tell us reading and numeracy levels are increasing in incremental ways every day. Thank you to the students who have taken our strategies on board and who have amazed us all with their progress and growth—we are so proud of you.

We especially want to thank the students who have challenged us to do better. The students with significant behavioral, emotional, and physiological unmet needs are the ones who have taught us our greatest lessons. These students have made us dig deeper, work harder, read more widely, and think more creatively as we consider how to meet their needs within the classroom. We know that because many of these students have experienced adversity that is unacceptable beyond words, they hold special places in our hearts. To the students who have taught us our greatest lessons, please know that in our minds you have become beacons of resilience, determination, resourcefulness, humor, and courage. We dedicate to you our efforts to create schools that are places of healing, growth, and learning. We believe that one student falling through the gaps in the educational system is one too many. We believe that every single teacher who has a well-developed toolkit of strategies for trauma-informed, strengths-based classrooms is one step closer to our overarching vision: an educational system in which all children and young people have full access to the emancipatory power of education.

References

Abraham, D., Heffron, C., Braley, P., and Drobnjak, L. (2015) *Sensory Processing 101*. Bedford, OH: Lemon Lime Adventures and The Inspired Treehouse.

Ainsworth, M.D. (1964) 'Patterns of attachment behavior shown by the infant in interaction with his mother.' *Merrill-Palmer Quarterly of Behavior and Development, 10*, 51–58.

Ainsworth, M.D. (1968) 'Object relations, dependency, and attachment: A theoretical review of the infant-mother relationship.' *Child Development, 40*, 4, 969–1025.

Alisic, E., Bus, M., Dulack, W., Pennings, L., *et al.* (2012) 'Teachers' experiences supporting children after traumatic exposure.' *Journal of Traumatic Stress, 25*, 1, 98–101.

Allen, K., Kern, M.L., Vella-Brodrick, D., Hattie, J., *et al.* (2018) 'What schools need to know about fostering school belonging: A meta-analysis.' *Educational Psychology Review, 30*, 1, 1–34.

Anda, R.F., Felitti, V.J., Bremner, J.D., Walker, J.D., *et al.* (2006) 'The enduring effects of abuse and related adverse experiences in childhood: A convergence of evidence from neurobiology and epidemiology.' *European Archive of Psychiatry and Clinical Neuroscience, 256*, 3, 174–186.

Ashby, F.G., Isen, A.M., and Turken, A.U. (1999) 'A neuropsychological theory of positive affect and its influence on cognition.' *Psychological Review, 106*, 3, 529–550.

Atkinson, J., Nelson, J., and Atkinson, C. (2010) 'Trauma, Transgenerational Transfer and Effects on Community Wellbeing.' In N. Purdie, P. Dudgeon, and R. Walker (eds) *Working Together: Aboriginal and Torres Strait Islander Mental Health and Wellbeing Principles and Practice*. Canberra, Australia: Australian Institute of Health and Welfare.

Australian Childhood Foundation (2010) *Making Space for Learning: Trauma Informed Practice in Schools*. Melbourne, Australia: Australian Childhood Foundation.

Bath, H. (2008) 'The three pillars of trauma-informed care.' *Reclaiming Children and Youth, 17*, 3, 17–21.

Baumeister, R.F., Bratslavsky, E., Muraven, M., and Tice, D.M. (1998) 'Ego depletion: Is the active self a limited resource?' *Journal of Personality and Social Psychology, 74*, 5, 1252–1265.

Baumeister, R.F., Leith, K.P., Muraven, M., and Bratslavsky, E. (1998) 'Self-Regulation as a Key to Success in Life.' In D. Pushkar, W. Bukowski, A. Schwartzman, D.M. Stack, *et al.* (eds) *Improving Competence Across the Lifespan: Building Interventions Based on Theory and Research*. New York, NY: Plenum Press.

Baumeister, R.F. and Tierney, J. (2012) *Willpower: Re-Discovering the Greatest Human Strength*. New York, NY: Penguin Books.

Baumeister, R.F., Zell, A.L., and Tice, D.M. (2007) 'How Emotions Facilitate and Impair Self-Regulation.' In J.J. Gross (ed.) *Handbook of Emotion Regulation*. New York, NY: The Guilford Press.

Bermond, B., Clayton, K., Liberova, A., Luminet, O., *et al.* (2007) 'A cognitive and an affective dimension of alexithymia in six languages and seven populations.' *Cognition and Emotion, 21*, 5, 1125–1136.

Berry Street Victoria (2013) *Foundations for Practice: Trauma Module.* Melbourne, Australia: Berry Street Victoria.

Bethell, C., Gombojav, N., Solloway, M., and Wissow, L. (2016) 'Adverse childhood experience, resilience and mindfulness-based approaches: Common denominator issues for children with emotional, mental, or behavioral problems.' *Child and Adolescent Psychiatric Clinics of North America, 25*, 2, 139–156.

Bombèr, L.M. (2007) *Inside I'm Hurting: Practical Strategies for Supporting Children with Attachment Difficulties in Schools.* London, UK: Worth Publishing.

Bowlby, J. (1969) *Attachment and Loss, Vol 1: Attachment.* New York, NY: Basic Books.

Bremner, J.D. (2006) 'Traumatic stress: Effects on the brain.' *Dialogues in Clinical Neuroscience, 8*, 4, 445–461.

Bronfenbrenner, U. (1979) *The Ecology of Human Development.* Boston, MA: Harvard University Press.

Brumariu, L.E. (2015) 'Parent-child attachment and emotion regulation.' *New Directions in Child and Adolescent Development, 148*, 31–45.

Brunzell, T., Norrish, J., Ralston, S., Abbott, L., *et al.* (2015) *Berry Street Education Model: Curriculum and Classroom Strategies.* Melbourne, Australia: Berry Street Victoria.

Brunzell, T., Stokes, H., and Waters, L. (2016a) 'Trauma-informed positive education: Using positive psychology to strengthen vulnerable students.' *Contemporary School Psychology, 20*, 1, 63–83.

Brunzell, T., Stokes, H., and Waters, L. (2016b) 'Trauma-informed flexible learning: Classrooms that strengthen regulatory abilities.' *International Journal of Child, Youth and Family Studies, 7*, 2, 218–239.

Brunzell, T., Stokes, H., and Waters, L. (2018) 'Why do you work with struggling students? Teacher perceptions of meaningful work in trauma-impacted classrooms.' *Australian Journal of Teacher Education, 43*, 2, 116–142.

Bryant, F.B. and Veroff, J. (2007) *Savoring: A New Model of Positive Experiences.* Mahwah, NJ: Lawrence Erlbaum Associates.

Bunting, L., Davidson, G., McCartan, C., Hanratty, J., *et al.* (2018) 'The association between child maltreatment and adult poverty—A systematic review of longitudinal research.' *Child Abuse and Neglect, 77*, 121–133.

Burns, A.B., Brown, J.S., Sachs-Ericsson, N., Plant, E.A. *et al.* (2008) 'Upward spirals of positive emotion and coping: Replication, extension, and initial exploration of neurochemical substrates.' *Personality and Individual Differences, 44*, 2, 360–370.

Callina, K.S., Johnson, S.K., Tirrell, J.M., Batanova, M., *et al.* (2017) 'Modeling pathways of character development across the first three decades of life: An application of integrative data analysis techniques to understanding the development of hopeful future expectations.' *Journal of Youth and Adolescence, 46*, 6, 1216–1237.

Caringi, J.C., Stanick, C., Trautman, A., Crosby, L., *et al.* (2015) 'Secondary traumatic stress in public school teachers: Contributing and mitigating factors.' *Advances in School Mental Health Promotion, 8*, 4, 244–256.

Child Welfare Information Gateway (2015) *Understanding the Effects of Maltreatment on Brain Development.* Washington, DC: Children's Bureau. Accessed on 19/3/2020 at www.childwelfare.gov/pubPDFs/brain_development.pdf.

Cornelius-White, J. (2007) 'Learner-centered teacher-student relationships are effective: A meta-analysis.' *Review of Educational Research, 77,* 1, 114–143.

Cox, K.F. (2006) 'Investigating the impact of strengths-based assessment on youth with emotional or behavioural disorders.' *Journal of Child and Family Studies, 15,* 3, 287–301.

Csikszentmihalyi, M. (1990) *Flow: The Psychology of Optimal Experience.* New York, NY: Harper Row.

Csikszentmihalyi, M. (1997) *Finding Flow: The Psychology of Engagement with Everyday Life.* New York, NY: Basic Books.

Dahlsgaard, K., Peterson, C., and Seligman, M.E.P. (2005) 'Shared virtue: The convergence of valued human strengths across culture and history.' *Review of General Psychology, 9,* 3, 203–213.

Dalgleish, T., Moradi, A.R., Taghavi, M.R., Neshat-Doost, H.T., *et al.* (2001) 'An experimental investigation of hypervigilance for threat in children and adolescents with post-traumatic stress disorder.' *Psychological Medicine, 31,* 3, 541–547.

de Arellano, M.A. and Danielson, C.K. (2008) 'Assessment of trauma history and trauma-related problems in ethnic minority child populations: An INFORMED approach.' *Cognitive and Behavioral Practice, 15,* 1, 53–66.

de Arellano, M.A., Ko, S., Danielson, C.K., and Sprague, C. (2008) *Trauma-Informed Interventions: Clinical and Research Evidence and Cultured-Specific Information Project.* Los Angeles, CA and Durham, NC: National Center for Child Traumatic Stress.

De Bellis, M.D. and Zisk, A. (2014) 'The biological effects of childhood trauma.' *Child and Adolescent Psychiatric Clinics of North America, 23,* 2, 185–222.

Duckworth, A.L., Kirby, T.A., Gollwitzer, A., and Oettingen, G. (2013) 'From fantasy to action: Mental contrasting with implementation intentions (MCII) improves academic performance in children.' *Social Psychological and Personality Science, 4,* 6, 745–753.

Duckworth, A.L., Kirby, T.A., Tsukayama, E., Berstein, H., *et al.* (2011) 'Deliberate practice spells success: Why grittier competitors triumph at the National Spelling Bee.' *Social Psychological and Personality Science, 2,* 2, 174–181.

Duckworth, A.L., Peterson, C., Matthews, M.D., and Kelly, D.R. (2007) 'Grit: Perseverance and passion for long-term goals.' *Journal of Personality and Social Psychology, 92,* 6, 1087–1101.

Duckworth, A.L. and Seligman, M.E.P. (2005) 'Self-discipline outdoes IQ in predicting academic performance in adolescents.' *Psychological Science, 16,* 12, 939–944.

Durlak, J.A., Weissberg, R.P., Dymnicki, A.B., Taylor, R.D., *et al.* (2011) 'The impact of enhancing students' social and emotional learning: A meta-analysis of school-based universal interventions.' *Child Development, 82,* 1, 405–443.

Dweck, C.S. (2007) 'The perils and promises of praise.' *Educational Leadership, 65,* 2, 34–39.

Dweck, C.S. (2008) *Mindset: The New Psychology of Success.* New York, NY: Ballantine Books.

Dweck, C.S. (2015) 'Growth mindset, revisited.' *Education Week, 35,* 20–24.

Emmons, R.A. (2007) *Thanks! How the New Science of Gratitude Can Make You Happier.* New York, NY: Houghton Mifflin Harcourt.

Farrelly, A., Stokes, H., and Forster, R. (2019) *Evaluation of the Berry Street Education Model (BSEM): Darebin Schools Program Learning for All.* Melbourne, Australia: University of Melbourne Graduate School of Education, Youth Research Centre.

Felitti, V.J., Anda, R.F., Nordenberg, D., Williamson, D.F., *et al.* (1998) 'Relationship of childhood abuse and household dysfunction to many of the leading causes of death in adults: The Adverse Childhood Experiences (ACE) study.' *American Journal of Preventative Medicine, 14,* 4, 245–258.

Figley, C.R. (1995) 'Compassion Fatigue: Toward a New Understanding of the Costs of Caring.' In B.H. Stamm (ed.) *Secondary Traumatic Stress: Self-Care Issues for Clinicians, Researchers, and Educators.* Lutherville, MD: Sidran Press.

Fox Eades, J.M. (2008) *Celebrating Strengths: Building Strengths-Based Schools.* Coventry, UK: CAPP Press.

Fredrickson, B.L. (1998) 'What good are positive emotions?' *Review of General Psychology, 2,* 3, 300–319.

Fredrickson, B.L. (2001) 'The role of positive emotions in positive psychology: The broaden-and-build theory of positive emotions.' *American Psychologist, 56,* 3, 218–226.

Fredrickson, B.L. (2009) *Positivity.* New York, NY: Three Rivers Press.

Fredrickson, B.L. (2013) 'Positive emotions broaden and build.' *Advances in Experimental Social Psychology, 47,* 1–53.

Fredrickson, B.L. and Joiner, T. (2002) 'Positive emotions trigger upward spirals toward emotional well-being.' *Psychological Science, 13,* 2, 172–175.

Froh, J., Bono, G., and Emmons, R. (2010) 'Being grateful is beyond good manners: Gratitude and motivation to contribute to society among early adolescents.' *Motivation and Emotion, 34,* 2, 144–157.

Froh, J., Kashdan, T.B., Ozimkowski, K.M., and Miller, N. (2009) 'Who benefits the most from a gratitude intervention in children and adolescents? Examining positive affect as a moderator.' *Journal of Positive Psychology, 4,* 5, 408–422.

Fry, D., Fang, X., Elliott, S., Casey, T., *et al.* (2018) 'The relationships between violence in childhood and educational outcomes: A global systematic review and meta-analysis.' *Child Abuse and Neglect, 75,* 6–28.

Gable, S.L. and Haidt, J. (2005) 'What (and why) is positive psychology?' *Review of General Psychology, 9,* 2, 103–110.

Gailliot, M.T. and Baumeister, R.F. (2007) 'The physiology of willpower: Linking blood glucose to self-control.' *Personality and Social Psychology Review, 11,* 4, 303–327.

Gillham, J., Adams-Deutsch, Z., Werner, J., Reivich, K., *et al.* (2011) 'Character strengths predict subjective well-being during adolescence.' *Journal of Positive Psychology, 6,* 1, 31–44.

Goodall, E. (2016) *Interoception 101.* South Australia: Department for Education and Child Development.

Gunnar, M.R. (1998) 'Quality of early care and buffering of neuroendocrine stress reactions: Potential effects on the developing human brain.' *Preventive Medicine: An International Journal Devoted to Practice and Theory, 27,* 2, 208–211.

Halevi, E. and Idisis, Y. (2018) 'Who helps the helper? Differentiation of self as an indicator for resisting vicarious traumatization.' *Psychological Trauma: Theory, Research, Practice, and Policy, 10,* 6, 698–705.

Hamilton, J.L., Connolly, S.L., Liu, R.T., Stange, J.P., *et al.* (2015) 'It gets better: Future orientation buffers the development of hopelessness and depressive symptoms following emotional victimization during early adolescence.' *Journal of Abnormal Child Psychology, 43,* 3, 465–474.

Harris, R. (2007) *The Happiness Trap: Stop Struggling, Start Living.* Wollombi, NSW, Australia: Exisle.

Hassed, C. (2002) *Know Thyself: The Stress Release Programme*. Melbourne, Australia: Michelle Anderson Publishing.

Hassed, C. and Chambers, R. (2014) *Mindful Learning: Reduce Stress and Improve Brain Performance for Effective Learning*. Wollombi, Australia: Exisle Publishing.

Hattie, J. (1998) *Visible Learning: A Synthesis of Over 800 Meta-Analyses Relating to Achievement*. New York, NY: Routledge.

Hattie, J. (2012) *Visible Learning for Teachers: Maximizing Impact on Learning*. New York, NY: Routledge.

Hiebert, M., Platt, J., Schpok, K., and Whitesel, J. (2013) *Doodles, Dances and Ditties: A Trauma-Informed Somatosensory Handbook*. Denver, CO: Mount Saint Vincent Home.

Hoffman, K., Cooper, G., Powell, B., and Benton, C.M. (2017) *Raising a Secure Child: How Circle of Security Parenting Can Help You Nurture Your Child's Attachment, Emotional Resilience, and Freedom to Explore*. New York, NY: The Guilford Press.

Hopwood, T.L., Schutte, N.S., and Loi, N.M. (2019) 'Stress responses to secondary trauma: Compassion fatigue and anticipatory traumatic reaction among youth workers.' *The Social Science Journal, 56*, 3, 337–348.

Howell, R.T., Kern, M.L., and Lyubomirsky, S. (2007) 'Health benefits: Meta-analytically determining the impact of well-being on objective health outcomes.' *Health Psychology Review, 1*, 1, 83–136.

Howells, K. (2012) *Gratitude in Education: A Radical View*. Rotterdam: Sense Publishers.

Hughes, K., Bellis, M.A., Hardcastle, K.A., Sethi, D., *et al.* (2017) 'The effect of multiple adverse childhood experiences on health: A systematic review and meta-analysis.' *The Lancet Public Health, 2*, 8, e356–e366.

Jose, P.E., Lim, B.T., and Bryant, F.B. (2012) 'Does savoring increase happiness? A daily diary study.' *Journal of Positive Psychology, 7*, 3, 176–187.

Kabat-Zinn, J. (1990) *Full Catastrophe Living: Using the Wisdom of Your Body and Mind to Face Stress, Pain, and Illness*. New York, NY: Delacort Press.

Kavanaugh, B.C., Dupont-Frechette, J.A., Jerskey, B.A., and Holler, K.A. (2017) 'Neurocognitive deficits in children and adolescents following maltreatment: Neurodevelopmental consequences and neuropsychological implications of traumatic stress.' *Applied Neuropsychology: Child, 6*, 1, 64–78.

Kelly-Irving, M. and Delpierre, C. (2019) 'A critique of the adverse childhood experiences framework in epidemiology and public health: Uses and misuses.' *Social Policy and Society, 18*, 3, 445–456.

Keyes, C. (2002) 'The mental health continuum: From languishing to flourishing in life.' *Journal of Health and Social Behaviour, 43*, 2, 207–222.

Klem, A.M. and Connell, J.P. (2004) 'Relationships matter: Linking teacher support to student engagement and achievement.' *Journal of School Health, 74*, 7, 262–273.

Koenig, A., Rodger, S., and Specht, J. (2018) 'Educator burnout and compassion fatigue: A pilot study.' *Canadian Journal of School Psychology, 33*, 4, 259–278.

Langer, E.J. (2000) 'Mindful learning.' *Current Directions in Psychological Science, 9*, 6, 220–223.

Larsen, J.K., Brand, N., Bermond, B., and Hijman, R. (2003) 'Cognitive and emotional characteristics of alexithymia: A review of neurobiological studies.' *Journal of Psychosomatic Research, 54*, 6, 533–541.

Lavy, S. (2019) 'A review of character strengths interventions in twenty-first-century schools: Their importance and how they can be fostered.' *Applied Research in Quality of Life, 15*, 573–596.

Linley, A. (2008) *Average to A+: Realising Strengths in Yourself and Others*. Coventry, UK: CAPP Press.

Linley, A., Nielsen, K.M., Wood, A.M., Gillett, R., *et al.* (2010) 'Using signature strengths in pursuit of goals: Effects on goal progress, need satisfaction, and well-being, and implications for coaching psychologists.' *International Coaching Psychology Review, 5*, 1, 8–17.

Locke, E.A. and Latham, G.P. (2002) 'Building a practically useful theory of goal setting and task motivation: A 35-year odyssey.' *American Psychologist, 57*, 9, 705–717.

Lyubomirsky, S., King, L., and Diener, E. (2005) 'The benefits of frequent positive affect: Does happiness lead to success?' *Psychological Bulletin, 131*, 6, 803–835.

Ma, L.K., Tunney, R.J., and Ferguson, E. (2017) 'Does gratitude enhance prosociality? A meta-analytic review.' *Psychological Bulletin, 143*, 6, 601–635.

MacDonald, P., Kelly, S., and Christen, S. (2019) 'A path model of workplace solidarity, satisfaction, burnout, and motivation.' *International Journal of Business Communication, 56*, 1, 31–49.

MacLean, P.D. (1990) *The Triune Brain in Evolution: Role in Paleocerebral Functions.* New York, NY: Plenum Press.

Mahler, K. (2017) *Interoception: The Eighth Sensory System.* Lenexa, KS: AAPC Publishing.

Marques, S., Lopez, S., and Pais-Ribeiro, J. (2011) '"Building Hope for the Future": A program to foster strengths in middle-school students.' *Journal of Happiness Studies, 12*, 1, 139–152.

Maslach, C., Schaufeli, W.B., and Leiter, M.P. (2001) 'Job burnout.' *Annual Review of Psychology, 52*, 391–422.

Matulich, B. (2013) *How to do Motivational Interviewing: A Guidebook for Beginners* (second edition). San Diego, CA: Motivational Interviewing Online.

McCluskey, G., Lloyd, G., Kane, J., Riddell, S., *et al.* (2008) 'Can restorative practices in schools make a difference?' *Educational Review, 60*, 4, 405–417.

Miller, W.R. and Rollnick, S. (2012) *Motivational Interviewing: Helping People Change* (third edition). New York, NY: The Guilford Press.

Miller, W.R. and Rose, G.S. (2009) 'Towards a theory of motivational interviewing.' *American Psychologist, 64*, 6, 527–537.

Morrison, A., Rigney, L., Hattam, R., and Diplock, A. (2019) *Toward an Australian Culturally Responsive Pedagogy: A Narrative Review of the Literature.* Adelaide: University of South Australia.

Mueller, C.M. and Dweck, C.S. (1998) 'Praise for intelligence can undermine children's motivation and performance.' *Journal of Personality and Social Psychology, 75*, 1, 33–52.

Myers, D.G. (2000) 'The funds, friends, and faith of happy people.' *American Psychologist, 55*, 1, 56–67.

Nakamura, J. and Csikszentmihalyi, M. (2009) 'The Concept of Flow.' In S.J. Lopez and R. Snyder (eds) *Handbook of Positive Psychology* (second edition). New York, NY: Oxford University Press.

National Child Traumatic Stress Network (2020) *Understanding Child Trauma and the NCTSN.* Los Angeles, CA: National Child Traumatic Stress Network. Accessed on 31/8/2020 at www.nctsn.org/sites/default/files/resources/fact-sheet/understanding_child_trauma_and_the_nctsn_0.pdf.

National Scientific Council on the Developing Child (2014) *Excessive Stress Disrupts the Architecture of the Developing Brain, Working Paper 3.* Center on the Developing Child, Harvard University. Accessed on 26/2/2020 at https://developingchild.

harvard.edu/wp-content/uploads/2005/05/Stress_Disrupts_Architecture_Developing_Brain-1.pdf.

Niemiec, R. (2019) 'Finding the golden mean: The overuse, underuse, and optimal use of character strengths.' *Counselling Psychology Quarterly, 32*, 3–4, 453–471.

Niemiec, R. and McGrath, R. (2019) *The Power of Character Strengths: Appreciate and Ignite Your Positive Personality.* Cincinnati, OH: VIA Institute on Character.

Norrish, J. (2015) *Positive Education: The Geelong Grammar School Journey.* Oxford, UK: Oxford University Press.

Ogden, P., Minton, K., and Pain, C. (2006) *Trauma and the Body: A Sensorimotor Approach to Psychotherapy.* New York, NY: W.W. Norton & Company.

Ogden, P., Pain, C., and Fisher, J. (2006) 'A sensorimotor approach to the treatment of trauma and dissociation.' *Psychiatric Clinics of North America, 29*, 1, 263–279.

Ong, A.D., Mroczek, D.K., and Riffin, C. (2011) 'The health significance of positive emotions in adulthood and later life.' *Social and Personality Psychology Compass, 5*, 8, 538–551.

Ortiz, R. and Sibinga, E.M. (2017) 'The role of mindfulness in reducing the adverse effects of childhood stress and trauma.' *Children, 4*, 3, 16–34.

Orygen (2018) *Dissociation and Trauma in Young People.* Melbourne, Australia: Orygen: The National Centre for Excellence in Youth Mental Health. Accessed on 19/3/2020 at www.orygen.org.au/Training/Resources/Trauma/Fact-sheets/Dissociation-trauma.

Park, D., Tsukayama, E., Goodwin, G.P., Patrick, S., *et al.* (2017) 'A tripartite taxonomy of character: Evidence for intrapersonal, interpersonal, and intellectual competencies in children.' *Contemporary Educational Psychology, 48*, 16–27.

Park, N. and Peterson, C. (2006) 'Moral competence and character strengths among adolescents: The development and validation of the Values in Action Inventory of Strengths for Youth.' *Journal of Adolescence, 29*, 6, 891–905.

Park, N. and Peterson, C. (2009) 'Character strengths: Research and practice.' *Journal of College and Character, 10*, 4, 1–10.

Park, N., Peterson, C., and Seligman, M.E.P. (2004) 'Strengths of character and well-being.' *Journal of Social and Clinical Psychology, 23*, 5, 603–619.

Payton, J., Weissberg, R.P., Durlak, J.A., Dymnicki, A.B., *et al.* (2008) *The Positive Impact of Social and Emotional Learning for Kindergarten to Eighth-Grade Students: Findings from Three Scientific Reviews.* Chicago, IL: Collaborative for Academic, Social, and Emotional Learning.

Pearce, C. (2016) *A Short Introduction to Attachment and Attachment Disorder* (second edition). London, UK: Jessica Kingsley Publishers.

Penman, D. (2016) *The Art of Breathing: The Secret to Living Mindfully.* London, UK: HarperCollins.

Peterson, C. and Seligman, M.E.P. (2004) *Character Strengths and Virtues: A Handbook and Classification.* New York, NY: Oxford University Press & Washington, DC: American Psychological Association.

Porges, S.W. (2004) 'Neuroception: A subconscious system for detecting threats and safety.' *Zero to Three, 24*, 5, 19–24.

Porges, S.W. (2011) *The Polyvagal Theory: Neurophysiological Foundations of Emotions, Attachment, Communication, Self-Regulation.* New York, NY: W.W. Norton & Company.

Porges, S.W. (2015) 'Making the world safe for our children: Down-regulating defence and up-regulating social engagement to "optimise" the human experience.' *Children Australia, 40*, 2, 114–123.

Powell, B., Cooper, G., Hoffman, K., and Marvin, R.S. (2016) *The Circle of Security Intervention: Enhancing Attachment in Early Parent-Child Relationships*. New York, NY: The Guilford Press.

Pressman, S.D., Jenkins, B., and Moskowitz, J. (2019) 'Positive affect and health: What do we know and where next should we go?' *Annual Review of Psychology, 70*, 627–650.

Price, C.J. and Hooven, C. (2018) 'Interoceptive awareness skills for emotion regulation: Theory and approach of mindful awareness in body-oriented therapy (MABT).' *Frontiers in Psychology, 9*, 798, 1–12.

Proyer, R.T., Gander, F., Wellenzohn, S., and Ruch, W. (2015) 'Strengths-based positive psychology interventions: A randomized placebo-controlled online trial on long term effects for a signature strengths vs. a lesser strengths intervention.' *Frontiers in Psychology, 6*, 456, 1–14.

Quin, D. (2017) 'Longitudinal and contextual associations between teacher-student relationships and student engagement: A systematic review.' *Review of Educational Research, 87*, 2, 345–387.

Quinlan, D., Swain, N., Cameron, C., and Vella-Brodrick, D.A. (2014) 'How "other people matter" in a classroom-based strengths intervention: Exploring interpersonal strategies and classroom outcomes.' *Journal of Positive Psychology, 10*, 1, 77–89.

Quinlan, D., Vella-Brodrick, D.A., Gray, A., and Swain, N. (2018) 'Teachers matter: Student outcomes following a strengths intervention are mediated by teacher strengths spotting.' *Journal of Happiness Studies, 20*, 2507–2523.

Quoidbach, J., Berry, E.V., Hansenne, M., and Mikolajczak, M. (2010) 'Positive emotion regulation and well-being: Comparing the impact of eight savoring and dampening strategies.' *Personality and Individual Differences, 49*, 5, 368–373.

Rashid, T., Anjum, A., Lennox, C., Quinlan, D., *et al.* (2013) 'Assessment of Character Strengths in Children and Adolescents.' In C. Proctor and P.A. Linley (eds) *Research, Applications, and Interventions for Children and Adolescents: A Positive Psychology Perspective*. New York, NY: Springer.

Rath, T. and Clifton, D.O. (2004) *How Full is Your Bucket?* Omaha, NE: Gallup Press.

Reid, L.F. and Kawash, J. (2017) 'Let's talk about power: How teacher use of power shapes relationships and learning.' *Papers on Postsecondary Learning and Teaching: Proceedings of the University of Calgary Conference on Learning and Teaching, 2*, 34–41.

Reivich, K. and Shatté, A. (2002) *The Resilience Factor: 7 Keys to Finding Your Inner Strength and Overcoming Life's Hurdles*. New York, NY: Broadway Books.

Rizzolatti, G. and Craighero, L. (2004) 'The mirror-neuron system.' *Annual Review of Neuroscience, 27*, 169–192.

Roelofs, K. (2017) 'Freeze for action: Neurobiological mechanisms in animal and human freezing.' *Philosophical Transactions of the Royal Society B: Biological Sciences, 372*, 1718, 1–10.

Roffey, S. (2006) *Circle Time for Emotional Literacy*. London, UK: Sage Publications.

Rogers, C. (1961) *On Becoming a Person: A Therapist's View of Psychotherapy*. Boston, MA: Houghton Mifflin.

Rollnick, S., Kaplan, S.G., and Rutschman, R. (2016) *Motivational Interviewing in Schools: Conversations to Improve Behavior and Learning*. New York, NY: The Guilford Press.

Roorda, D., Koomen, H., Spilt, J., and Oort, F.J. (2011) 'The influence of affective teacher-student relationships on students' school engagement and achievement: A meta-analytic approach.' *Review of Educational Research, 81*, 4, 493–529.

Schore, A. (2003) *Affect Regulation and the Repair of the Self*. New York, NY: W.W. Norton & Co.

Schore, J. and Schore, A. (2007) 'Modern attachment theory: The central role of affect regulation in development and treatment.' *Clinical Social Work Journal, 36*, 1, 9–20.

Schutte, N.S. and Malouff, J.M. (2019) 'The impact of signature character strengths interventions: A meta-analysis.' *Journal of Happiness Studies, 20*, 4, 1179–1196.

Seligman, M.E.P. (1990) *Learned Optimism*. New York, NY: Knopf.

Seligman, M.E.P. (1995) *The Optimistic Child*. Boston, MA: Houghton Mifflin.

Seligman, M.E.P. and Csikszentmihalyi, M. (2000) 'Positive psychology: An introduction.' *American Psychologist, 55*, 1, 5–14.

Seligman, M.E.P., Railton, P., Baumeister, R., and Sripada, C. (2013) 'Navigating into the future or driven by the past: Prospection as an organizing theory of mind.' *Perspectives on Psychological Science, 8*, 2, 119–141.

Shernoff, D.J., Csikszentmihalyi, M., Schneider, B., and Shernoff, E.S. (2003) 'Student engagement in high school classrooms from the perspective of flow theory.' *School Psychology Quarterly, 18*, 2, 158–176.

Shonkoff, J.P. and Garner, A.S. (2012) 'The lifelong effects of early childhood adversity and toxic stress.' *Pediatrics, 129*, 1, e232–e246.

Shoshani, A. (2019) 'Young children's character strengths and emotional well-being: Development of the character strengths inventory for early childhood.' *Journal of Positive Psychology, 14*, 1, 86–102.

Shoshani, A. and Sloane, M. (2012) 'Middle school transition from the strengths perspective: Young adolescents' character strengths, subjective well-being, and school adjustment.' *Journal of Happiness Studies, 14*, 1163–1181.

Sibinga, E.M., Webb, L., Ghazarian, S.R., and Ellen, J.M. (2016) 'School-based mindfulness instruction: A RCT.' *Pediatrics, 137*, 1, 1–8.

Siegel, D. (2020) *The Developing Mind: How Relationships and the Brain Interact to Shape Who We Are* (third edition). New York, NY: The Guilford Press.

Siegel, D. and Payne Bryson, T. (2012) *The Whole-Brain Child: 12 Revolutionary Strategies to Nurture Your Child's Developing Mind*. New York, NY: Bantam Books.

Snyder, C. (2002) 'Hope theory: Rainbows in the mind.' *Psychological Inquiry, 13*, 4, 249–275.

Snyder, C., Hoza, B., Pelham, W., Rapoff, M., *et al.* (1997) 'The development and validation of the Children's Hope Scale.' *Journal of Pediatric Psychology, 22*, 3, 399–421.

Spilt, J.L., Koomen, H.M.Y., and Thijs, J.T. (2011) 'Teacher wellbeing: The importance of teacher-student relationships.' *Educational Psychology Review, 23*, 457–477.

Spratt, E.G., Friedenberg, S.L., Swenson, C.C., LaRosa, A., *et al.* (2012) 'The effects of early neglect on cognitive, language, and behavioral functioning in childhood.' *Psychology (Irvine), 3*, 2, 175–182.

Stamm, B.H. (ed.) (1995) *Secondary Traumatic Stress: Self-Care Issues for Clinicians, Researchers, and Educators*. Lutherville, MD: Sidran Press.

Standal, S. (1954) *The Need for Positive Regard: A Contribution to Client-Centered Theory* (PhD thesis). Chicago, IL: The University of Chicago.

Stokes, H., Kern, M.L., Turnbull, M., Farrelly, A., *et al.* (2019) *Trauma Informed Positive Education: Research and Evaluation of the Berry Street Education Model (BSEM) as a Whole-School Approach to Student Engagement and Wellbeing (2016–2018)*. Melbourne, Australia: University of Melbourne Graduate School of Education, Youth Research Centre.

Stokes, H. and Turnbull, M. (2016) *Evaluation of the Berry Street Education Model: Trauma Informed Positive Education Enacted in Mainstream Schools*. Melbourne, Australia: University of Melbourne Graduate School of Education, Youth Research Centre.

Stokes, H., Turnbull, M., Forster, R., and Farrelly, A. (2019) *Young People's Voices, Young People's Lives: A Berry Street Education Model (BSEM) Project*. Melbourne, Australia: University of Melbourne Graduate School of Education, Youth Research Centre.

Talge, N.M., Neal, C., and Glover, V. (2007) 'Antenatal maternal stress and long-term effects on child neurodevelopment: How and why?' *Journal of Child Psychology and Psychiatry, 48*, 3–4, 245–261.

Teicher, M.H., Andersen, S.L., Polcari, A., Anderson, C.M., *et al.* (2002) 'Developmental neurobiology of childhood stress and trauma.' *The Psychiatric Clinics of North America, 25*, 2, 397–426.

Uchino, B., Cacioppo, J., and Kiecolt-Glaser, J. (1996) 'The relationship between social support and physiological processes: A review with emphasis on underlying mechanisms and implications for health.' *Psychological Bulletin, 119*, 3, 488–531.

van der Kolk, B.A. (2003) 'The neurobiology of childhood trauma and abuse.' *Child and Adolescent Psychiatric Clinics of North America, 12*, 2, 293–317.

van der Kolk, B.A. (2005) 'Developmental trauma disorder: Toward a rational diagnosis for children with complex trauma histories.' *Psychiatric Annals, 35*, 5, 401–408.

van der Kolk, B.A. (2014) *The Body Keeps the Score: Brain, Mind, and Body in the Healing of Trauma*. New York, NY: Penguin Books.

van der Kolk, B.A., Pelcovitz, D., Roth, S., Mandel, F.S., *et al.* (1996) 'Dissociation, somatization, and affect dysregulation: The complexity of adaptation of trauma.' *American Journal of Psychiatry, 153* (7 Suppl), 83–93.

Victoria State Government Department of Education and Training (2020) *School-Wide Positive Behaviour Support (SWPBS)*. Melbourne, Australia: Victoria State Government Department of Education and Training. Accessed on 18/4/2020 at www.education.vic.gov.au/school/teachers/management/improvement/Pages/swpbs.aspx.

Vohs, K., Baumeister, R., Twenge, J., Schmeichel, B., *et al.* (2008) 'Making choices impairs subsequent self-control: A limited-resource account of decision making, self-regulation, and active initiative.' *Personality Processes and Individual Differences, 94*, 5, 883–898.

Wagner, L. (2018) 'Good character is what we look for in a friend: Character strengths are positively related to peer acceptance and friendship quality in early adolescents.' *Journal of Early Adolescence, 39*, 6, 864–903.

Walker, J. (2008) 'Looking at teacher practices through the lens of parenting style.' *Journal of Experimental Education, 76*, 2, 218–240.

Waters, L. (2017) *The Strengths Switch: How the New Science of Strengths-Based Parenting Can Help Your Child and Teen to Flourish*. Sydney, Australia: Penguin Random House.

Waters, L., Barsky, A., Ridd, A., and Allen, K. (2015) 'Contemplative education: A systemic evidence-based review of the effect of meditation interventions in schools.' *Education Psychology Review, 27*, 103–134.

Weber, M. and Ruch, W. (2012) 'The role of good character in 12-year-old school children: Do character strengths matter in the classroom?' *Child Indicators Research, 5*, 317–334.

Weber, M., Wagner, L., and Ruch, W. (2016) 'Positive feelings at school: On the relationships between students' character strengths, school-related affect, and school functioning.' *Journal of Happiness Studies, 17*, 341–355.

Wiliam, D. and Leahy, S. (2015) *Embedding Formative Assessment: Practical Techniques for K-12 Classrooms*. West Palm Beach, FL: Learning Sciences International.

Williams, K.E. and Sciberras, E. (2016) 'Sleep and self-regulation from birth to 7 years: A retrospective study of children with and without attention-deficit hyperactivity disorder at 8 to 9 years.' *Journal of Developmental and Behavioral Pediatrics, 37*, 5, 385–394.

Wilson, J.Q. and Kelling, G.L. (1982) 'Broken windows: The police and neighborhood safety.' *The Atlantic Monthly, 249*, 29–38.

Witter, M. (2013) *Reading Without Limits: Teaching Strategies to Build Independent Reading for Life*. San Francisco, CA: Jossey-Bass.

Wood, A., Froh, J., and Geraghty, A. (2010) 'Gratitude and well-being: A review and theoretical integration.' *Clinical Psychology Review, 30*, 7, 890–905.

Wood, A., Linley, P.A., Maltby, J., Kashdan, T.B., *et al.* (2011) 'Using personal and psychological strengths leads to increases in well-being over time: A longitudinal study and the development of the strengths use questionnaire.' *Personality and Individual Differences, 50*, 1, 15–19.

Zaccaro, A., Piarulli, A., Laurino, M., Garbella, E., *et al.* (2018) 'How breath-control can change your life: A systematic review on psycho-physiological correlates of slow breathing.' *Frontiers in Human Neuroscience, 12*, 353, 1–16.

Zenner, C., Herrnleben-Kurz, S., and Walach, H. (2014) 'Mindfulness-based interventions in schools—A systematic review and meta-analysis.' *Frontiers in Psychology, 5*, 603, 1–20.

Subject Index

Author Index